THE COMPUTER'S VOICE

THE COMPUTER'S VOICE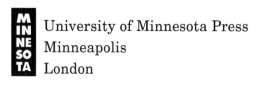

From *Star Trek* to Siri

Liz W. Faber

University of Minnesota Press
Minneapolis
London

Published by the University of Minnesota Press
111 Third Avenue South, Suite 290
Minneapolis, MN 55401-2520
http://www.upress.umn.edu

ISBN 978-1-5179-0975-8 (hc)
ISBN 978-1-5179-0976/5 (pb)

Library of Congress record available at https://lccn.loc.gov/2020022368

UMP LSI

FOR JANIE

CONTENTS

THE TALKING COMPUTER PARADOX
(Dis)Embodied Gender and the Acousmêtre

I'm just a humble virtual assistant.

—Siri

EACH MORNING, I wake up, pick up my smartphone, turn off the alarm, and ask Siri to tell me the weather. She does, and as I make coffee, I ask her to play a morning news podcast. Again, she complies, with a cheery, "Okay, Liz." I get dressed, running late as usual, and dash out to my car, where I plug my iPhone in to use Apple Car Play. "Siri," I say at the dash panel as I speed out of the driveway and down the street, "please show me the traffic to work." She pulls up the map and tells me that traffic is heavy, but I will arrive at work at 9:04 AM—just barely in time for my 9:20 class. After a full day of teaching, tutoring, and writing, I repeat the ritual in reverse, getting traffic information from car-Siri, then asking for an evening news update podcast, and finally, just before sleep, asking phone-Siri to set an alarm for the next day. "Okay, Liz, your alarm is set for 5:30 AM," she says. Each night, I thank her and tell her good night.

Your day likely looks and sounds similar, whether you use Siri or another virtual assistant. It's astounding how entrenched voice interactive technology has become in our lives, given that until only a decade ago, talking computers were the sole purview of science fiction (SF). But who are these artificial women—Siri, Alexa, Cortana, Google—who assist us through our everyday lives? And why are they—in advertisements, movies, and default settings—coded as women?

On October 4, 2011, Apple Inc. released Siri, an artificially intelligent personal assistant application that can recognize speech and respond with a friendly female voice.[1] Available for use on a variety of Apple devices, Siri blends a natural language system with the digital equivalent of a secretary. Users can ask her to search the Internet, check the weather, and dictate appointments, e-mails, and text messages. Since her initial release, the program's responses have been updated to include conversational phrases, making the interaction with the app significantly more like talking to an actual person. She even seems to have a sense of humor. As I wrote this introduction, I told Siri I loved her, and she responded, "All you need is love. And your iPhone."

In May 2013, Google officially released its own version of Siri, Google Now, and one year later both Amazon and Microsoft followed suit with Alexa and Cortana, respectively. But these recent advancements in voice interactive technology are not just the products of innovative computer scientists. They also have been directly influenced by fictional technology. IBM scientist David Ferucci has compared his Watson—IBM's precursor to Siri, which competed on *Jeopardy!* in 2011—to the computer featured in the television series *Star Trek,* "where the input can be expressed in human terms and the output is accurate and understandable."[2] Apple's original 1987 design for a Siri-like program was based on HAL 9000, the computer in Stanley Kubrick's 1968 film *2001: A Space Odyssey.*[3] Google Now (an earlier iteration of Google Assistant) was originally called Majel, after Majel Barrett, the actress who provided the computer voice in all five *Star Trek* series and eleven films until her death in 2008.[4] Indeed, Alexa's creator, Toni Reid, has explicitly stated that she was inspired by *Star Trek*'s computer voice.[5] Such comparisons between present-day technology and past SF texts are even more apt than computer scientists seem to have intended. Not only are Siri, Google, and Alexa real-world versions of fictional computers, but each of them also hides the ways in which the computer is implicitly embodied and gendered by its voice. Real and fictional computers alike are generally voiced by humans: the *Star Trek* computer by Majel

Barrett and HAL 9000 by Douglas Rain. Mysteriously, however, Apple has consistently refused to publicly acknowledge the voice actress behind the American version of Siri, Susan Bennett, whose 2005 voice recording package was reportedly purchased by Apple for use with its software.[6]

The question remains: who are these programs we talk to? Why do they even have gendered voices? Why are Siri, Alexa, and Google—the digital equivalents of secretaries—coded as female? Couldn't they all just be genderless synthesized speech, like a Speak & Spell toy from the 1980s? Although some may see virtual assistants as toys on the same level as the Speak & Spell, it is becoming increasingly clear that the implications of the gendering of the software has far-reaching implications. Rebecca Rosen noticed this trend just a week after Siri's initial release in 2011: "The rough rule seems to be that corporeal inventions are male—particularly if they are killing someone, whether on screen or in the military—while the noncorporeal are female (although there are plenty of exceptions, notably, Rosie, the Jetson's maid, who, it bears repeating, is a maid)."[7] Interestingly, although Rosen accurately identifies one major gender divide in artificial intelligence design, and specifically links that divide to SF precursors, she, like the scholars who discuss similar matters of gender and the AI body, fails to address the fact that Siri and her on-screen predecessors have bodies, albeit object bodies. However, she also adds to the notion of anthropomorphism in human–computer interactions (HCI) by positing that one reason for the choice of a female computer voice may have to do with likability and trust. Indeed, Apple's 1987 design for a personal assistant program included an avatar of a male scientist, created to help users build trust in the computer.[8] The shift to an imageless female voice indicates that users have come to trust computers to effectively do their tasks because a male authority guide is no longer necessary or desirable. It also indicates that, as market research has shown, the female voice is perceived by American users to be more personable and likeable, although less authoritative.

A 2019 UNESCO report on the gender divide in science education examines the gendering of virtual assistants. The report cites a number of examples of sexism built into AI software programming, particularly the fact that these assistants have a default gender of female, thereby implying an unconscious connection between women and servitude. The problem, according to the report, is that, "consumer technologies generated by male-dominated companies often reflect troubling gender biases."[9] In short, design teams dominated by men will tend to produce designs that are unconsciously infused with hegemonic, patriarchal ideologies. Given the rich literature on the value of diversity and inclusion in fields of science, technology, engineering, and mathematics,[10] I do not doubt that this is true. However, these men did not invent their ideologies alone. After all, ideology does not exist in a vacuum; it is continuously maintained and perpetuated by interpersonal interactions and cultural production. Obviously a complete deconstruction of cisheteropatriarchal ideology is beyond the scope of this single book. However, SF representations of talking computers can provide valuable cultural context for how gender is inscribed onto today's AI software.

Aside from technological inspiration, how have the underlying ideological gender assumptions in SF texts like *2001* and *Star Trek* influenced the creation of such programs? What does the fact of the shift from SF representations to scientific innovation reveal about the perpetuation of ideological assumptions about gender roles? How do other representations of computer voices confirm or problematize the gendering of computer voices? In this book, I seek to answer these questions by examining the historical, theoretical, and aesthetic traces of the computer voice from the first major fictional SF example—*Star Trek*—to the first widely available real-world example—Siri. SF movies and TV shows project gender onto nonhumanoid talking AI, what I call acousmatic computers, by giving them gender-coded voices and placing them in familiar gender roles. Such gender coding not only expresses cultural attitudes about gender of the time but also (because these computers have no human bodies) challenges the rigidity of gender norms.

Even though computer scientists today draw inspiration from SF, artificial intelligence research predates *Star Trek* by over a decade. Alan Turing asks in a groundbreaking 1950 text, "Can machines think?" To answer this, he devised a version of the imitation game, which we now call the Turing test: a computer passes the test if an interrogator can't tell whether it is human or computer, based on typewritten answers.[11] At the time there was no computer that could pass the test because computers were essentially room-size calculators, incapable of humanlike thinking processes. In 1956, a group of mathematicians and scientists came together at Dartmouth College for the Summer Research Project on Artificial Intelligence. This project was not only the first use of the term "artificial intelligence," but it also became the genesis of a new strand of research that continues today. Although the terms "computer" and "artificial intelligence" are often used interchangeably, they have been envisioned by researchers as more akin to "body" and "brain," respectively. Both cybernetics and AI research attempted to create computers based on human brain processing, but "instead of modeling brains in computer hardware—the central goal of cybernetics—AI sought to mimic minds in software. [. . .] They placed the emphasis of formal-mechanical modeling on the side of the formal, the disembodied, the abstract—on the side of the mind rather than that of the brain."[12] A central problem of AI research has been in determining what intelligence means and how to represent it in a recognizable way, beyond physiological brain functions.

This is a complex problem because there is a significant difference between seeming to be intelligent and actually being intelligent. In his 1966 survey of AI research, Donald G. Fink defines artificial intelligence as "behavior by a machine that, if exhibited by a human, would be called intelligent." Yet he points out that the appearance of intelligence is not at all the same as intelligence: "If we did not know how the high-fidelity phonograph works we might think it intelligent because it exhibits a highly intelligent form of human behavior, the ability to speak meaningfully. But the phonograph, as we happen to know, merely reproduces the unalterable pattern of speech waveforms embedded in the grooves of its record."[13] At the same time that Fink was writing his book, computer scientist Joseph Weizenbaum created a program that demonstrated the idea that computers can exhibit the characteristics of human intelligence without actually being intelligent. ELIZA—named for the character in George Bernard

Shaw's 1912 play *Pygmalion*—was designed to mimic a human psychologist (and as a result was later nicknamed DOCTOR). Users would type their thoughts and feelings into ELIZA, and, using Rogerian-style psychology whereby the statement is rearranged into a follow-up question, ELIZA would prompt the user to continue "talking." To Weizenbaum's horror, users genuinely thought that they were sharing private information in a therapy session with the computer. They were subsequently mortified to learn that Weizenbaum and his team were reading the entire exchange.[14] Although ELIZA had no audible voice (the program and user communicated solely through text on the screen), users' responses nevertheless demonstrated that humans are capable of perceiving a computer's intelligence—even when there is none.

Today's AI programs, such as Siri, also give the impression of intelligence. They interact verbally with their users by recalling stored data. Of course, programs are not humans; they are representations of human intelligence. However, some aspects of research into HCI focus on how and whether people perceive intelligence in computers. In the mid-1990s, HCI researcher Jeffrey Morgan posited that one necessary precondition of effective HCI is anthropomorphism, or projecting human personality traits onto an object computer.[15] In the case of real-world AIs such as Siri, programs are designed according to this principle of anthropomorphism. It is easier to interact with an object if we ascribe human personality and intelligence traits to it in a way that encourages us to believe—or at the very least suspend disbelief—that its object "body" actually projects a voice in the same way that human voices do. Yet there has been significant debate among researchers in the fields of psychology and computer design as to whether users actually anthropomorphize computers. Clifford Nass and Youngme Moon conducted numerous experiments in the 1990s in which participants performed certain tasks on a computer, then answered survey questions about their experience during the test. Results indicated that there is a significant difference between anthropomorphism and mindlessness in HCI. On the one hand, they defined anthropomorphism as the conscious belief that computers are human or should be treated as such. On the other hand, they drew on the work of psychologist Ellen J. Langer to define mindlessness as occurring

> as a result of conscious attention to a subset of contextual cues. [...] These cues trigger various scripts, labels, and expectations, which in turn focus attention on certain information while diverting attention away from other information. Rather than actively constructing categories and distinctions based on all relevant features of the situation, individuals responding mindlessly prematurely commit to over simplistic scripts drawn in the past.[16]

Although Nass and Moon's research indicates that no one consciously believes that computers are human or humanlike, it also shows that users engage primarily in mindlessness while interacting with computers, especially in voice interaction.[17] In 2011, however, Youjeong Kim and S. Shyam Sundar directly opposed Nass and Moon, arguing instead that anthropomorphism is mindless. They conducted similar experiments in which participants interacted with a computer, then answered questions about their experiences. For Kim and Sundar, the results revealed that participants responded mindlessly to anthropomorphic qualities of a computer, such as voice and gender.[18] Further, in an exploration of the Turing test and Weizenbaum's ELIZA experiment, Jennifer Rhee described the anthropomorphic nature of HCI as a kind of misidentification, which stems from the way the human mind draws on slippery, ambiguous categories to define itself in opposition to others.[19] In other words, while Nass and Moon show that humans don't consciously think of computers as fellow humans, Rhee argues that we actually might, and that this is a productive way of understanding the way human intelligence resists such simple categorization.

A NOTE ON METHODOLOGY

AI research and cognitive psychology were developed concurrently as a methodological metaphor for understanding human brain functions couched in machine terminology. As a scientific method, cognitive research examines patterns of individuals' mental processes, "especially perception, memory, mental imagery, and the use of language."[20] Conversely, psychoanalysis, as a strand of psychological research, attempts to account for these same mental processes in mental imagery, narratives of memory, and relational experiences. Here I use psychoanalysis to interpret the expression of human intelligence, as seen in SF representations of AI. In the field of film studies, both psychoanalysis and cognitivism take into account ideological processes, although in different ways.[21] In choosing psychoanalysis over cognitivism as an interpretive strategy, I do not intend to posit one as more correct or valuable than the other. Rather, because computer science research is so grounded in cognitivism, approaching the foundational problem of AI—how to represent intelligence in a way that accounts for intersectional human identity—may benefit from a different perspective. The same objections that Noël Carroll had to psychoanalysis (that is, that it was widely considered to be *the* theory, rather than *a* theory)[22] are the objections I have to AI researchers' use of cognitivism. Because AI researchers do not generally attend to the psychoanalytic study of culture, which may offer new insights into the relationships among technology, ideology, and representations of intelligence, this study should be seen as a means of adding to, rather than replacing, current theories of AI.

Of course, not all AI researchers solely attend to cognitive theories. Marvin Minsky, one of the original Dartmouth conference presenters, an on-set consultant for *2001,* and cofounder of the MIT Media Lab, incorporates Freudian principles in his discussion of representations of human knowledge and emotions.[23] The basic terminology of the two psychological models attempts to account for the same phenomena by using different words. "Mindlessness" is analogous to the "unconscious." Both are forms of mental processing that people do not know are occurring in their minds. Likewise, both psychoanalysis and AI research attempt to account for cultural narratives and beliefs. Many AI researchers use the term "common sense" to describe knowledge that is not instinctual but rather must be learned through social interactions and development. Although the term "common sense" is problematic in cultural studies because it describes the naturalization of culturally constructed biases, it does describe the foundations of ideological structures such as patriarchy. Yet commonsense knowledge is a descriptor, a means of explaining how, rather than why, ideologies function. Douglas B. Lenat described in 1997 how AI systems may at the time have used commonsense programming for data processing

> to understand such structured information sources as spreadsheets and data bases, and then use that understanding to detect common-sense errors and inconsistencies in the data. For example, one column of a table might indicate a person's gender, and another might indicate that of his or her legal spouse. Without having to be specially programmed for the task, [the AI program] would know that there's probably a mistake in the data if X and X's spouse have the same gender, if X's spouse lists a third person as his or her spouse, or if X is listed as X's spouse.[24]

The fact that this example is now outdated—in many countries it would not immediately be a mistake for X and X's spouse to have the same gender—highlights the ways that commonsense/ideological data cannot account for the existence or ethical implications of those data. Another example, that of Janet Kolonder's 1983 CYRUS system, similarly demonstrates the limitations of culturally specific gender knowledge in AI programming. The program could in theory pass the Turing test by answering questions about the work life of a person (Secretary of State Cyrus Vance in particular), but it could not identify the gender of fellow heads of state solely on the basis of their names. This example demonstrates not only that computers cannot (or at least at that point could not) account for cultural knowledge[25] but also that culturally constructed definitions such as gender are not inherent in any kind of knowledge system. Feminist psychoanalytic thought here offers an interpretive framework for understanding why commonsense data such as the use of gender difference to structure power relations exist.

    In addition to psychoanalysis, a feminist framework is vital to unpacking the ways that gender and AI are intertwined.

Gender has been an implicit part of AI research since Turing connected machine thought to the imitation game. The parlor game version of the imitation game is played with one man, one woman, and one interrogator. The interrogator must determine which is male and which female on the basis of their responses. This game presumably requires an essentialist notion of gender. If x characteristic is inherent in y gender, then a person who expresses x characteristic will always therefore be y gender. In addition to this essentialism, in Turing's formulation, the woman is replaced by a computer. If the interrogator is fooled into thinking the computer was a human, then it passes what we now call the Turing test. Importantly, in the original game, the interrogator can conceivably see both the man and the woman in question. Turing added to the game the use of keyboards in separate rooms, so the interrogator has only typed words on which to base assumptions. The unpacked interplay between womanhood and humanhood is striking here. As Tyler Curtain points out,

> Turing's neat disarticulation of physical indications of gender from the conditions of judgment about "intelligence" (or what becomes in later formulations within his work, as well as the work of cognitive scientists, computer scientists, and philosophers of the mind, a quality called "human-ness") succeeds only in reseating gender firmly within "intelligence" itself: a woman is put in the position of defending and authenticating her gender across the network; in turn, a computer authenticates its intelligence only if it simulates her gender better than she can across the same network. The Turing test thus imagines that being a better woman than a woman is equivalent to intelligence and that ineffable quality "human-ness."[26]

Of note is the "proving oneself" aspect of the game. Here the woman and the computer must prove themselves to be appropriately identifiable by a person with the power to verify them as such. From a feminist perspective, this might be seen as a metaphor for systemic, oppressive patriarchy: both men and women are required to prove their gender within the binary definitions of male and female, then have it verified by those in power, through the everyday performance of gender. With this in mind, much of this book is couched in a feminist exploration of the ways in which the performance of bodily gender is projected onto a computer body in ways that both promote and resist binary definitions of gender.

In the interest of intersectional feminism, I want to make it clear that most of the computer characters I examine in this book are implicitly understood as white, American, and middle class, though of varying genders and sexualities, in large part because the texts in which they appear are produced by white American people, star white American actors, and arguably were made for white middle-class American audiences. Wherever possible in this book, I highlight instances in which the texts I cover whitewash historical events or cultural phenomena. However, the exclusion of people of color—and most especially women of color—from the landscape of artificial intelligence is an important problem that requires further attention outside the scope of this book.

THE ACOUSMATIC COMPUTER

As Fink's phonograph example demonstrates, the marker of intelligence is not simply speech. Yet today the most natural-sounding AI requires that a human being first record a vast number of phonemes to be stored in a database. The AI program then formulates them into full words in order to create the impression of speech, thereby hiding the fact that a human recorded those phonemes in the first place. The immediate question raised by the ways in which artificially intelligent computers—real and fictional alike—are designed to hide human-voice origins is, why? Why bother hiding what we all know to be there? The answer lies in classical cinema and television history, and the ways synchronized sound has conditioned audiences to link voice to image to personality, thus structuring narrative identification while effacing the workings of the apparatus. The necessity of audiovisual synchronization rests on the basic process of a schizophonic separation of sound from its source via a mechanical or digital medium. When a sound is recorded, the resulting recording (whether formatted in a digital file, on a strip of magnetic tape, or on a wax cylinder) contains sound that is no longer that of the original creator. As Barry Truax demonstrates, the sound wave enters the mechanical/digital device (a black box) and reemerges as a different sound wave. What we hear in playback is a mechanically or digitally manipulated sound that results from the mediated distortion of the sound wave itself.[27] The nature of this mediation raises a number of critical issues involving sound fidelity and the presentation of sound for consumers. Because mediated sound is always already manipulated, no true fidelity is possible. However, if it were, the medium itself would become transparent.[28] Thus, the goal of commercial audio(visual) media is, significantly, the effacement of the medium. As Rick Altman aptly points out in his discussion of precinematic sound recording, "Recordings do not reproduce sound, they represent sound. [. . .] To be sure, one of the common strategies involved in this process is an attempt to convince the audience that they are listening not to a representation but to a reproduction."[29] Paradoxically, such recording works to hide its nature. Listeners are tricked into ignoring the medium and pushed to focus instead on the perceived (but false) link between a sound and its origin.

In addition to the technical manipulation of the sound and the resulting aural fidelity, playback calls into question the entire contextual fidelity of the audio message: "When context is ignored, most of the communicational subtlety of a message is lost."[30] Thus, for example, even in the most basic, unmanipulated voice recordings, separating the sound from the person diminishes interpretive layers of meaning that can be provided by experiencing firsthand the environmental and emotional conditions under which a person speaks into a microphone. In short, true fidelity does not exist.

Regardless of fidelity, there is still an indexical link between a recorded voice and the body that produced it, which is comparable to that of visual indexicality in photography and film. In this sense, Truax's black box example is particularly illustrative of the relationship between audio and visual media. When sound waves enter the black box, they are imprinted onto a wax cylinder, vinyl disc, or piece of magnetic tape; or, in the case of digital recording, they are converted into code. In playback, the sound waves projected into the air both are (sound like) and are not (exist as separate entities from) the original sound. In terms of the recorded voice, the qualities of the original speaker's voice—pitch, tone, intonation, breath—all point back to the body from which they emanated. Similarly, when light waves enter a traditional analog camera (typically a literal black box), they are imprinted onto a celluloid film strip or a magnetic tape strip. In playback, the light waves projected through the air onto a screen both are (look like) and are not (exist as separate entities from) the original photographed object. An actor's image on a screen points back to his bodily presence in front of the camera. In digital media, the literally indexical imprint of the film strip or magnetic tape is lost, yet the perceived link between recorded object and projected image/sound is restaged. The similarities between fidelity and indexicality also render sound recording more akin to cinema than photography because the reprojected sound moves through time and space, just as the reprojected series of still images in cinema move through time and space. The fraught nature of sound recording is thus parallel to what I might call the fraught nature of moving image recording.

The context of sound playback is also separated from the context of sound recording, thereby changing the meaning of the recorded sound. For example, listening to a person speaking into a microphone in a recording booth carries a different contextual meaning than a recording of that person speaking heard through a home stereo system. The listener's spatial and relational positions are different. The recording of images similarly changes the context of the captured object through framing and viewing contexts. The addition of a narrative sequence produces an even more radical split between recording and playback. Watching and listening to an actor speak on a constructed set, with cameras and microphones in full view, generally carries a far different set of meanings than watching and listening to that same actor speak within a narrative context in a film. Michel Chion argues that a vital task of synchronized sound narrative cinema (to which I add synchronized sound narrative television) is to project a sound onto an image in a way that naturalizes not only the fidelity/indexicality of the sound/image but also the relationship between the two.

These separated soundtracks must be perceived simultaneously with the separated image tracks to create the illusion of sound originating within the image.[31] Importantly, the advent of optical soundtracks in cinema allowed for the imprint of both sound and image side by side on a single medium, thus reinforcing the link between a cinematically captured object and the sound it produced pro-cinematically. Yet the link between image and sound is still an illusion, just as the naturalization of the relationship between profilmic object and projected image is an illusion. The most important manifestation of this illusion is constructed when a voice matches an image of a person's lips moving, thereby creating the sense that a person is speaking within the diegetic space of the cinematic frame, or what Chion refers to as "visualized listening."[32] Audiences try, as with any sound, to locate the origins of film sounds by matching what is heard to an appropriate visual origin. Cinema tends to play on this desire to see what is heard through editing by creating tension when an unseen character speaks. Then the image cuts to a shot of the speaker, thereby fulfilling the audience's desire to see. Only when synchronization confirms the relationship between voice and image can the spectator remain sutured into the narrative. Conversely, when image and sound fail to synchronize—as happens occasionally in our age of streaming video—the audience's attention is forced away from the narrative and onto the task of mentally matching the image with the sound that comes even just a fraction of a second too late. As Mary Ann Doane puts it, "Concomitant with the demand for a life-like representation is the desire for 'presence,' a concept which is not specific to the cinematic soundtrack but which acts as a standard to measure quality in the sound recording industry as a whole."[33] Sound fidelity and narrative/imagistic realism thus combine in cinema and television to produce a sense of here and now, which masks the trace of the sound and image apparatuses.

Paradoxically, although cinema and television tend to privilege image over sound, from a textual perspective, characters who exist solely as imageless voices tend to hold more power within the narrative than those whose voice and image are synchronized within the diegetic realm. Drawing on Pierre Schaeffer's notion of the acousmêtre—"a sound that one hears without seeing what causes it"[34]—Chion defines certain disembodied characters as functions of acousmêtre. These are cinematic situations in which a character is "neither inside nor outside the image," neither seen in the frame nor waiting offscreen in a diegetic space. Within the diegesis, the acousmatic character tends to be omniscient and omnipresent, acting as a godlike figure.[35] For example, many of the acousmatic characters in George Lucas's 1971 *THX 1138* "see" and describe actions that neither the camera nor the embodied characters see; rather, they represent constant surveillance and bodily power over the embodied, watched characters. The fact that spectators have been conditioned through Hollywood's near-ubiquitous continuity-style editing to see what is heard positions acousmatic voices as sources of tension. When the spectator is denied sight, the desire to match voice to image is perpetually unfulfilled. Further, the acousmatic voice constantly threatens to reveal the very process of dislocation, which narrative cinema must hide in order to maintain the illusion of continuity.[36] Such near reveals also create anxiety, as the ability to lose oneself in a narrative is threatened by a revelation of the apparatus. Importantly, there are subtle differences between truly acousmatic characters and documentary-style omniscient narrators. Whereas the latter may be presumed to be always already disembodied, perpetually existing outside the diegetic space of the film, the former may, at any moment, become embodied.[37] This anticipation of embodiment is what drives the tension of the acousmêtre. The spectator constantly waits to see.

In SF film and television, the talking computer is a particularly slippery form of acousmêtre. On the one hand, artificial intelligence may be said to embody the computer (inasmuch as a human consciousness embodies the human form) from which its voice seems to emanate. In the diegetic space of the text, a nonhumanoid AI's voice is as synthetic as its intelligence.[38] On the other hand, the computer's voice is a prime example of the disordered voice, separated from its origin (a real human voice actor) and projected onto the image of a computer object, though maintaining an indexical link to the actor's gendered body. Human characters interact with the bodies of the computers by talking to them, pushing their buttons, and so forth, yet many of the computers can hear, see, and respond to human characters from a position of omniscience and omnipresence. The computers are thus paradoxically (dis)embodied: they are disembodied voices projected onto a nonhumanoid computer body. Furthermore, the acousmatic computer voice heightens the anxiety of the acousmêtre because it denies confirmation of synchronization. If there is no mouth from which the voice appears to emanate, then the viewer can never confirm that the computer's voice is really that of its body.

In SF, the entire concept of sound fidelity and synchronization are often upended in what Trace Reddell calls the "sonic novum." Drawing on Darko Suvin's concept of the novum as the speculative and novel aspects of SF, Redell defines the sonic novum as SF's process of taking mundane sounds and transforming them into innovative sonic experiences.[39] Indeed, many of the films I discuss in this book use the sonic novum in their respective sound designs. On the surface, the acousmatic computer likewise seems like a type of sonic novum: it takes the mundane voice and overlays it on a new, imaginative computer object. Yet one defining characteristic of the sonic novum is the transformation of the mundane sound into something entirely new and strange.[40] A talking computer is perhaps strange and new, but a talking character is not. As I will demonstrate throughout this book, the acousmatic computer is always situated in a familiar story line with familiar narrative tensions. In this sense, the acousmatic computer might be understood as a sort of uncanny sonic novum, simultaneously familiar and strange, old and new, present and absent.

(DIS)EMBODIED GENDER

In the case of the SF acousmatic computer voice, the incorporation of the computer within the narrative frame is always an attempt to displace tension from that of the revelation of the apparatus to that of the diegetic space. One significant way in which this diversion occurs is through the gendering of the computer's "body" by means of its gendered voice. N. Katherine Hayles traces how the Enlightenment notion of mind/body dualism has given way in the digital era to an understanding of human intelligence as an information system separate from the body.[41] However, the acousmatic computer, as a paradoxically (dis)embodied entity, is a compelling textual phenomenon in relationship to this division of mind and body because the computer mind is always presented as having a gender, and that gender is so clearly, yet so invisibly, constructed. I take "gender" to refer to a framework for describing lived bodily experiences organized around culturally constructed notions of masculinity and femininity. However, I do not limit the notion of bodily experience to flesh-and-blood bodies. Most of the acousmatic computers I discuss here do not have bodies that could in any way be described as having sex organs or other bodily markers culturally associated with male or female bodies. Yet they all have gendered characteristics inscribed onto them through the suggestion of sex organs (such as phallic/uterine imagery), voices of a certain pitch and with indexical connections to gendered bodies, and narrative trajectories or relationships with human characters that are culturally associated with masculine or feminine roles. In many of the texts I examine, traditional gender norms are also inscribed onto computer bodies along with heteronormative sexual identities as a means of further reinforcing rigid gender roles. Through the process of constructing (dis)embodied genders of acousmatic computers, SF texts simultaneously attempt to perpetuate or naturalize rigid gender roles. Paradoxically, they also, in the tension of the disordered/acousmatic process, reveal just how constructed and tenuous those roles are. If a computer can have a gender, then gender is neither essential to the human body nor rigidly fixed. However, if we understand these computer characters to be living beings in their own right, then we must also understand their gender as part and parcel of their combined bodily and mental experience. Gender is never as simple as an essentialist perspective would have it. Indeed, several of the texts I analyze in this book, such as Steve Barron's film *Electric Dreams* and the SyFy original series *Eureka,* situate their acousmatic computers in traditional gender roles even as the accompanying imagery and narratives upend those roles by suggesting gender and sexual fluidity.

THE PHANTASY OF THE ACOUSMATIC COMPUTER

The textual and technical means by which narrative media tend to hide their own creation cannot fully account for why cinematic strategies such as continuity editing and the displacement of tension from the apparatus to the diegesis are so effective. Psychoanalytic film theory provides some ways of filling in this gap. From a psychoanalytic perspective, the absorption of the threatening acousmêtre, to the narrative works to maintain what Jean-Louis Baudry has described as the regressive properties of cinema as they relate to the unconscious processes of phantasies in dreams. Drawing on the theories of dreaming outlined by Sigmund Freud and Bertram Lewin, Baudry argues that the process of identification with cinematic characters on the screen mimics the hallucinatory nature of the experience of phantasy (deep unconscious desires) or dreams. Indeed, for Baudry, the entire creation of the cinema space serves as a culturally unconscious attempt to re-create the dream state.[42] Christian Metz argues that cinema is not the same as dreaming: "The dreamer does not know that he is dreaming; the film spectator knows that he is at the cinema."[43] Yet both Metz and Baudry maintain that the psychical process of spectatorship is similar to that of dreaming.

One significant difference between Metz's argument and Baudry's is that Baudry draws more heavily on Freud's theories of the Oedipus complex, whereas Metz uses Jacques Lacan's theory of the mirror stage. Freud defines the Oedipus complex (derived from the story of King Oedipus, who kills his father and marries his mother, then gouges out his own eyes when he realizes what he's done) as the situation in which a young boy desires his mother sexually and wants to take his father's place.[44] However, Freud also argues that a boy experiences the oedipal trauma when he discovers that his mother does not have a penis. Here the young boy sees his mother's genitals, perceives it as a wound where a penis should be, and assumes that she has been castrated by his father. Because he desires his mother, who has been castrated, the boy fears that his father will do the same to him, thus bringing the child into the realm of taboos (here, the incest taboo) regulated by the father. In normal cases, the boy works through the trauma by transferring the desire for his mother/ object onto another object (for Freud, the heterosexual object of desire, or a girl). The object is then psychically incorporated into the boy's ego as a means of achieving a sense of cathexis.[45] The preoedipal state is thus a time of sexual undifferentiation when the subject/child understands himself as one with his mother. Baudry argues that this is the state to which both the dreamer and the film spectator attempt to return through the phantasy site of the cinema/dream.

Jacques Lacan, simultaneously building on and revising Freud's theories but taking a slightly less biologically determinist stance, argues that the oedipal stage begins between the subject and himself in the mirror stage, rather than necessarily between the subject and his mother in the oedipal stage. (I should note that both Freud and Lacan, typically and problematically, use the masculine "he/him" to indicate universal human experience.) During the mirror stage, the child is placed before a mirror. On the one hand, he recognizes his own reflection and understands that he is separate from his mother, thus allowing him to develop his ego/I in opposition to the Other. The child thus enters the symbolic order, through which language is structured as opposi-tional. On the other hand, he simultaneously misrecognizes his own reflection as an ideal/imago form, thus establishing an ego ideal. This ego ideal allows the child to maintain a link to the imaginary order, through which the primal site of unity with the mother may be experienced via phantasy.[46] For Metz, the cinema screen works similarly to that of the mirror because the charac-ters projected on the screen, like the image in the mirror, both are and are not present. The nonpresence of the characters—they are, after all, nothing more than projections of light and sound—mimics the link to the imaginary order and an attempt at re-gressing to the primordial state of unity with the mother.[47]

The oedipal complex and the mirror stage have been the two major modes of understanding the cinema psychoanalyti-cally because both theories are heavily invested in the notions of identification and desire. Both the oedipal and mirror stages deal intimately with the production of phantasy, particularly in terms of working through object loss. For film theorists, cinema tends to function as a site of phantasy cathexis, a mode of covering over object loss, or both. Because SF as a genre is so heavily invested in representing phantasies about the past and future, psychoanalysis is a particularly apt method of interpretation. One explicit goal of SF is to envision future technologies that scientist-spectators may then create in reality.[48] Simultaneously, however, these envisioned technologies are always limited by the historical reality of their moment of conception.[49] This, for example, is why the acousmatic computer of *Star Trek* in the 1960s is physically clunkier and incorporates reel-to-reel tape processing, as opposed to the sleek digital computer of the franchise's 1990s spin-off, *Star Trek: The Next Generation*. The 1960s media makers modeled their future on the present of the 1960s, whereas those in the 1990s modeled the future on the 1990s. This tension between present and future works much like the presence/absence of the mirror: the acousmatic computer on the screen simultaneously is today's familiar technology and is not that technology. Yet the acousmatic computer is typically not the lead character with whom the spectator is meant to identify. Rather, it adds to the mise-en-scène of the mirror and metonymically, in Lacan's terms, displaces the lost object/mother.

However, this displacement does not account for the varied genders of acousmatic computers in SF. In order to understand not only why SF provides a phantasy scene of acousmatic computers but also how that scene plays out within an ideological framework, it is important to examine the relationship between ideology and psychoanalytic processes. Feminist film critics have utilized psychoanalysis as a means of explaining and deconstructing often disturbingly sexist patterns of representations of women in classical Hollywood cinema as well as the pleasure that may be derived from the cinematic experience. Laura Mulvey argues that classical Hollywood cinema, as representative of and created within patriarchy, tends to function as a phantasy site for the working through of the male spectator's castration anxiety. The mother is the primary site of this anxiety, as the boy child recognizes sexual difference for the first time and develops castration anxiety. In cinema, a woman may come to represent and remind the spectator of his castration anxiety, and she therefore must either be fetishized to cover the site of the phallic wound or be punished and saved by a male hero in order to reassert the ability of men to dominate the castrated woman. In this way, both the gaze of the cinema and the narrative trajectory of classical Hollywood function as phantasies of the male ego that serve to re-repress the trauma of castration.[50] Similarly, for E. Ann Kaplan, Freudian psychoanalysis—especially pop psychology stemming from Freud's work—tends to omit the role of the mother. Kaplan traces a shift during World War II from a cinematic "cultural mother" to a "phallic mother." The former, she argues, was a domineering mother, aligned more closely with the archaic mother, whereas the latter was a castrating mother who threatened to take phallic power from male heroes. Like the good/bad woman dichotomy, she argues that a good/bad mother figure arises in Hollywood after World War II. One part of her argument in particular is vital to an understanding of fantasy cinema, especially SF. She argues that in postmodern cinema, women's bodies are being replaced by technological reproduction (such as cloning) and mothering. She wonders what will happen to psychoanalytic processes related to the primal mother when technology takes the role of the human mother, a point I turn to in the following chapters.[51]

Barbara Creed, in *The Monstrous-Feminine,* and Deborah Linderman, in "Cinematic Abreaction," among many others, use psychoanalytic theory to argue that aspects of the horror genre work precisely because horror tends to play on our unconscious desires and anxieties. The theory of repression leads well into a discussion of the return of the repressed in horror. Repressed anxieties about the role of women in the castration complex are magnified in horror films, as female characters tend to represent the repressed archaic mother or the repressed primal object.[52] Furthermore, Creed adds to the general psychical process of cinema—as outlined by Baudry, Metz, and Mulvey—an awareness of the uncanny in cinema, particularly the horror genre. According to Freud, the uncanny is something that is both familiar and strange, seen and hidden, related to or a reminder of death. For Creed, the uncanny in horror films tends to stem from a representation of the archaic mother, the primal scene, or the dichotomous good/bad woman.[53] However, horror is only one form of the fantasy genre. The genre also includes SF, traditional fantasy, and any combination of the three. SF, while difficult to actually classify because of its wide range of conventions, tends to address the relationship between humans and their capacity for/limitations of scientific reasoning. Psychoanalysis thus provides a structuring metaphor for unpacking the ideological themes of SF. The genre can thus be understood as a phantasy working through of the reality we construct around us, set in futures that have not arrived but that are based on a present in which we live. Further, as I will explore in the following chapters, the acousmatic computer voice in SF tends to function similarly to the way women do in horror films. The acousmatic computer is uncannily embodied/disembodied, seen/unseen; it is a reminder of repressed trauma.

This book contributes to existing cultural studies literature on AI by connecting gender theory, psychoanalytic film theory, and sound studies as couched in the history of SF. To my knowledge, there have been no book-length academic examinations of voice-interactive computers in SF.[54] While feminist SF scholars have focused primarily on the physical body—be they human, cyborg, or otherwise humanoid—I argue that the (dis)embodied voice of the computer in SF, as it implies and projects gender onto the computer character, must be explored in order to understand not only how technology functions as an extension of our bodies, as Marshal McLuhan famously describes it,[55] but also how it functions as a separate gendering voice/gendered body.

Scholars who attend to the relationship between voice and gender in cinema and television also tend to ignore the acousmatic computer voice. Although Chion discusses how the computer voice in cinema masks the presence of a body, he entirely omits any consideration of how this process paradoxically hides the gendered body of the voice's origin while inviting the audience to project gender onto the speaker through aural cues.[56] Although Kaja Silverman attends to the relationship between gender and voice, she does not attend to nonhuman bodies.[57] Yet her argument that the female body tends to be silenced in Hollywood cinema is still pertinent to how acousmatic computer voices function. If both male and female computers are paradoxically (dis)embodied, then there should be no gender divide because the physical markers of human gender—genitalia, physique, and so on—are absent. Yet the treatment of female- and male-coded computers tends to express cultural beliefs and/or anxieties about lived, gendered subjectivity and culturally constructed gender roles.

Here I seek to examine the inscription and materialization of gendered artificial intelligence in a number of cinematic and televisual texts. Most scholarship on the acousmatic voice pertains to representational modes (cinema in particular); meanwhile, discourse on fictional technology in relationship to real-world technology has focused primarily on humanoid cyborgs rather than object computers. Yet the acousmatic character has bled into real-world technology in ways that work to hide the presence of ideological structures and the apparatus in cinema/television and technology. Although cyborg technology and issues of the human body are important, we deal every day with nonhuman technological "bodies," such as smartphones and tablets. By providing a voice to these bodies, we also provide humanlike characteristics. The acousmatic voice has conditioned us through representations to efface the medium/apparatus and—what others have failed to point out—the ideological underpinnings of such an effacement. The effacement of the apparatus works in exactly the same way as the effacement of ideological power structures. By returning to the origins of the real-world technology—representations of acousmatic computers—we can begin to deconstruct the means by which technology may perpetuate or complicate cishetero-patriarchal ideologies.

In the following chapters, I attend to the textual problem of location in SF. I divide my analyses into two categories, extraterrestrial (chapters 1 and 2) and terrestrial (chapters 3, 4, and 5). This division is important in understanding the roles of voice-interactive computers, as spaceships provide a uniquely different environment than terrestrial structures such as houses, office buildings, or prisons. Further, spaceships always already imply a womb-like habitat, a mother ship that controls and maintains all aspects of the life-forms within it; terrestrial computers, however, tend to connote varying gendered subjectivities and anxieties within historical contexts of technological innovation and cultural change. In chapters 1 and 2, I will examine representations of acousmatic spaceship computers. Chapter 1 explores the relationship between and the impact of two foundational texts: *Star Trek: The Original Series* (Paramount, 1966–69) and the film *2001* (Stanley Kubrick, 1968). In chapter 2, I discuss subsequent parodies and reworkings of the themes of *Star Trek* and *2001*, as seen in the films *Dark Star* (John Carpenter, 1974) and *Moon* (Duncan Jones, 2010), and the television series *Quark* (NBC, 1977–78) and *Star Trek: The Next Generation* (Paramount, 1987–94).

In chapters 3, 4, and 5, I examine terrestrial computers. These computers may be further divided into two gendered subsections of masculine and feminine functions. Chapter 3 focuses on the dystopic films of the 1970s, in which computers tend to have male voices and act as the son to their programmer/creator fathers or conversely as all-knowing fathers, thereby reinforcing patriarchal rule. These films, *Colossus: The Forbin Project* (Joseph Sargent, 1970), *THX 1138* (George Lucas, 1971), *Rollerball* (Norman Jewison, 1975), and *Demon Seed* (Donald Cammell, 1977), narrativize cultural and business struggles in the 1970s surrounding militarization and corporatization. In chapter 4, I examine two films of the early 1980s, *TRON* (Steven Lisberger, 1982) and *Electric Dreams* (Steven Barron, 1984), which express a rapidly changing cultural conception of computers set in narratives of homosocial struggle. And in chapter 5, I discuss computers in the 1990s and 2000s that serve in domestic roles, particularly as expressed in texts that feature domestic spaces run by female-voiced computers. These texts, the films *Fortress* (Stuart Gordon, 1992) and *Smart House* (LeVar Burton, 1999), and the TV show *Eureka* (SyFy, 2006–12), position computers as replacements for human women who are absent from the home. Additionally, I examine two texts that feature male servants—*Demon Seed* (an anomaly among representations of domestic servitude) and *Iron Man* (Jon Favreau, 2008). Finally, in chapter 6, I return to Siri by theorizing her own (dis)embodied gender and examining representations of her in Apple commercials of the time, an episode of the long-running TV series *The Big Bang Theory* (CBS, 2007–19), and the dark comedy film *Her* (Spike Jonze, 2013).

 CHAPTER 1

AMNIOTIC SPACE
Textual Origins of the Acousmatic Computer

TWO OF THE MOST ICONIC WORKS of space race–era SF are *Star Trek: The Original Series* (hereafter *TOS;* Paramount, 1966–69) and *2001: A Space Odyssey* (Stanley Kubrick, 1968).[1] Much has been written about every facet of each text, but important to this project is the fact that they are the genre's first examples of acousmatic computers. William Shatner, best known for his role as Captain Kirk in the *Star Trek* franchise, notes of the magic of representing computers:

> Creating gadgets that are easy to use is a lot harder than faking them, which is, of course, what *Star Trek* excelled in. The ship's computer always responded so perfectly to me and Leonard [Nimoy] and everyone else who communed with it because . . . it was a fake! There *was* no computer, there was no voice synthesizer, no artificial intelligence that processed and understood what I was saying and then pulled up the appropriate response from its immense databanks. It was just an old-fashioned deception. I said my line and then Majel Barrett, who was the voice of the computer (and Nurse Chapel) said *her* line. Throw in some sound effects that connoted the machine's "thinking," a few flashing lights, and there you have it: instant artificial intelligence, a machine you can relate to, easily, pleasantly, without a manual.[2]

It is just this illusion that has since made acousmatic computers—whether fictional or actual—so believable. It's close enough to reality to be familiar, yet strange enough to be fantasy. The relationship between the strange and the familiar—in Freudian terms, the *unheimlich* or the uncanny—is not only a major part of the schizophonic audio recording/playback process in film and television, but, as I will argue in this chapter, is also a foundational part of the history of voice-interactive computing. Further, voice-interactive computers that control a spaceship in SF, like those in *Star Trek* and *2001* are—as with all representations—more than just faked versions of computers. A talking computer is never just a talking computer. It's an indexical trace back to a protocinematic, gendered body; it's an object and voice projected onto a screen to create the illusion of sentience; and it's an acousmatic character playing a gendered role through its interaction with other characters. Metaphorically, acousmatic spaceships in particular represent the paradox of the primordial uncanny: the womb. On a meta level, SF's unconscious attention to metaphorical representations of the womb, reproduction, and psychosexual origins is played out through the "parents" of today's real technology—*Star Trek*'s USS *Enterprise* computer and *2001*'s HAL 9000. I begin with a comparative analysis of the visual, aural, and metaphorical dimensions of these parents, then theorize the shifting relationships between them, from primal scene to convergence culture.

SETTING THE SPACE AGE STAGE

Star Trek and *2001* are very much products of the space age, though in quite different ways. Most historians place the beginning of the space age at 1957, when the Soviet Union successfully launched the first satellite, Sputnik, into space. In 1961, President John F. Kennedy, in an address to Congress, promised to put an American on the moon within a decade. By 1969, this promise had come to fruition with the successful Apollo 11 manned flight to the moon. This period, from 1957 to 1969, has been thoroughly analyzed to the point of overdetermination.[3]

Important to this discussion, though, is a set of competing

space age ideologies stemming from space as a metaphor for the future of humankind: the vast and exciting freedoms associated with scientific exploration versus the horrifying dehumanization of a digital existence. While the basic premises of both *Star Trek* and *2001* are roughly the same—astronauts travel through space on a mission aboard a spaceship with a voice-interactive computer—they nevertheless represent these opposite stances on space.

The famous opening lines of *Star Trek* capture the utopian hope for the distant future: "Space: the final frontier. These are the voyages of the starship *Enterprise*. Its five-year mission: to explore strange new worlds, to seek out new life and new civilizations, to boldly go where no man has gone before." Set in a twenty-third century in which Earth has been united under a single socialist government and is part of an interplanetary organization called the United Federation of Planets, the series follows a group of Starfleet personnel, a pseudo-militaristic space navy with ranks and uniforms but without the corruption or violence of the Vietnam-era American military. These explorers include Captain James T. Kirk (William Shatner), science officer Commander Spock (Leonard Nimoy), chief engineer Lieutenant Commander Montgomery Scott (James Doohan), communications specialist Lieutenant Uhura (Nichelle Nichols), ship's physician Doctor Leonard McCoy (DeForest Kelley), ship's nurse Christine Chapel (Majel Barrett), and two helmsmen, Lieutenant Sulu (George Takei) and Ensign Pavel Chekhov (Walter Koenig). The ultimate goal of each of the crew's missions is to create peaceful relations between the people of the Federation and others in the galaxy, though it seems this mission isn't always easy to carry out—a fact that typically drives the narrative drama of each episode.

In contrast, Stanley Kubrick's *2001: A Space Odyssey* is a grandiose, mostly dystopian view of what was in 1968 the near future. Cowritten by Kubrick and British SF writer Arthur C. Clarke as a novel, rather than a screenplay, the narrative is loosely based on one of Clarke's short stories, "The Sentinel" (1951). The film is told in three tenuously connected parts, as follows: the Dawn of Man, the Jupiter Mission, and Jupiter and Beyond the Infinite. Although my main concern here is the Jupiter Mission, which features the HAL 9000 computer, it is important to note that the unifying object among all three parts is a giant black monolith, presumably brought from Jupiter at the Dawn of Man. The future in *2001,* in contrast to that of *Star Trek,* is a strikingly capitalist one in which Pan-Am flights from Earth to the moon are commonplace and technology dominates every part of daily existence. At the beginning of the film, a shock cut links the past to the future. An ape-man discovers that a bone can be used as a tool for beating other animals to death. He throws it into the air, and it is graphically matched in a cut to a bone-shaped satellite in space, implying that human violence and tool technology are linked. The transhistorical violence implied in this cut is the first indication that this future is more frightening than *Star Trek*'s voyage of peace and diplomacy. In the Jupiter Mission part of the film, astronauts Dave Bowman (Kier Dullea), Frank Poole (Gary Lockwood), and three others who are in hyperstasis (that is, extended sleep) are on their way to Jupiter in order, we later find out, to learn more about the origins of the monolith. The mission goes horribly awry when the supposedly infallible onboard computer, HAL 9000, cuts off communications with earth, murders everyone in hyperstasis, cuts Frank's oxygen supply line while he's on a spacewalk, and then, when Dave attempts to save Frank, refuses to allow Dave to reenter the ship (hence the famous line, "I can't do that, Dave," in response to Dave's requests that HAL open the pod bay doors). At the end of this section, Dave forcibly reenters *Discovery One* and shuts down HAL. In the final section, Dave enters the star gate to the monolith, apparently witnesses his own life and death through a series of shot/reverse shots in which he continually sees an older incarnation of himself, and then, in a final moment of half-hope, half-terror, a giant, in utero star child hangs in space, its body human and its saucer-like eyes extraterrestrial. Where *Star Trek* has a continuing five-year (and beyond) mission, *2001* ends abruptly—at a point, we assume, just before the star child's birth.

There are also a few obvious physical commonalities between the USS *Enterprise* of *Star Trek* and the *Discovery One* of *2001.* Both are large spaceships with smaller spaceships inside them (shuttlecrafts in *Star Trek* and pods in *2001*), and both have a range of important-looking lights and switches in each room, video chat screens, hallways between rooms, vast but out-of-the-way control rooms (the engineering room in *Star Trek* and HAL's mainframe room in *2001*), and, most importantly for my purposes here, a powerful, centralized, artificially intelligent computer that controls and maintains all basic human functioning while simultaneously performing other complex tasks and talking to those on board.[4] The *Enterprise* is a combination of the traditional SF saucer disc with two cylindrical thrusters behind and another cylindrical "warp coil" beneath, "its rear somewhat akin to that of a WWII flying boat."[5] The attention to naval vocabulary (the organization governing the *Enterprise* and its crew is a "fleet," ships are given the moniker "USS," and characters have naval ranks such as admiral and captain) carries over into the fact that the *Enterprise* is frequently addressed as "she," as is a naval ship. Such gendering of the ship was a conscious decision of the series' creators;[6] however, it is complicated by the fact that "her" body is both feminine (the round, womb-like saucer where the crew live and work) and masculine (the phallic cylinders that both project torpedoes and "thrust," to use the terminology of the series, the ship forward into space). The ship is almost always shown in full, moving through space or idling slowly in orbit around a planet, which tends to make it seem smaller than do the grand tracking shots across its body in the subsequent spin-off films. In *2001,* the *Discovery One,* like the *Enterprise,* was named after a sailing ship, the RRS *Discovery,* which, as Clarke writes in the original draft of the novel, was "the most famous of polar-exploration ships. It seemed appropriate, for they were going into regions far colder than the South Pole, and the discovery of facts was the sole purpose of their mission."[7] Yet Kubrick was much more attentive to space-related innovations than Clarke. Their 1964 contract for preproduction specifically stated that they needed to complete preparations by 1967, "the expected date of the Apollo programs," and Kubrick reportedly became obsessed with the idea that a major space discovery or the landing on the moon would make his film obsolete.[8] Unlike the *Enterprise,* the *Discovery One* is a seemingly enormous ship that is first introduced as it slowly moves into frame. *2001* was originally shot and screened in single-image 70mm Cinerama,[9] and so the effect of a large steel-gray-and-white ship slowly filling the frame creates a sense of enormity and power. [10] All told, the *Enterprise* appears to be a tiny ship that houses a community of hundreds of people, while the *Discovery One* seems to be a huge ship that holds just five, three of whom are in hyperstasis.

The framing of the ships and the mise-en-scène of the interiors convey the sense that the *Enterprise* is smaller, homier, and cozier, and therefore more associated with a feminine/domestic space, while the *Discovery One* is overbearingly large, sparse, and functional, and therefore more associated with a masculine/militaristic space. The exterior shape of the *Discovery One* is also incredibly phallic, with a long cylindrical shaft in the center, a smaller cube on one end, and a large bulb on the other. Importantly, though, the bulb is the pod bay where pods are stored, exit, and enter; when the pod bay doors open and close, the entire bulb is reminiscent of an opening and closing eye, as though it is a phallus that looks.

Sight and eye imagery are prominent in the interior of *Discovery One* as well. Small video monitors line many surfaces of the ship, all displaying different information and images, implying that watching is a vital and constant activity for anyone on board. Of course, the most overt eye image in the film is HAL 9000's interface, the iconic red-glowing half sphere, shown in multiple places throughout the ship, in addition to the exterior and interior of the pods. The interface is explicitly figured as HAL's eye via fisheye lens shots in which the spectator sees as HAL does. Through these shots, HAL—and the audience—not only sees but also comprehends, as when, through a POV extreme close-up, HAL reads Dave and Frank's lips, although he cannot hear what they say. While the editing and cinematography may thus evoke a sense of seeing from HAL's perspective, the nature of that perspective is ambiguous at best. Numerous interpretations of HAL's eye have been offered: it is Kubrick's "cinematographic eye,"[11] a "cyclopean, one-eyed monster,"[12] an implied head,[13] or an absent (human) body.[14] Each of these readings suggests something beyond the eye itself, both corporeal and psychological. Philip Kuberski argues that, particularly in Kubrick's films, "technology is never rid of its corporeal designers: It carries within a kind of transmuted human psychology and intrinsic waywardness." In this sense, HAL represents a "conflict between highly rationalized technologies and unknown, unconscious drives."[15] HAL's body, manifesting as the eye and as the *Discovery One,* suggests psychosexual imagery aligned with unconscious phantasies of the maternal. The eye of the pod bay bulb also parallels HAL's eye, particularly because HAL controls his function. (As I will discuss in greater detail later in this chapter, the eye simultaneously implies an orifice in relationship to HAL's womb-like interior.) Importantly, the exterior body is phallic, a visual one-eyed monster, while the interior body suggests a maternal womb. These technologically corporeal aspects of HAL are in constant tension with the "perfect" artificially intelligent programming and the calm male monotone voice. In this sense, HAL represents a tension between mind and body, interior and exterior. While the exterior of HAL's body suggests a sexualized body, the interior is strikingly sterile. The vast white spaces and rotating white hallways were shot with a wide-angle lens to appear elongated; the spherical control room has dark countertops contrasting with brightly lit screens. Adding to the sterile mise-en-scène, there are no personal items anywhere aboard, even small ones such as family photographs, which astronauts on a long mission would reasonably take with them. HAL's internal psychological states are as distancing as the interior mise-en-scène. Michael Mateas notes that

> HAL's radical interiority, an internal mental (symbolic) space into which neither Bowman, Poole, nor we as viewers have access, is emphasized through the use of reaction shots focusing on one of HAL's camera eyes. Where normally a reaction shot reveals, through bodily (including facial) position and movement, a character's motivational and emotional responses to a situation, letting us into a character's interior space, for HAL, who is in some sense pure mind, the reaction shots remain opaque, giving viewers a sense of an interior they are not allowed to enter.[16]

This opaqueness, almost an effacement of HAL's psychological interior, emphasizes the uncanny atmosphere of the *Discovery One.*

We both know and cannot know HAL; we recognize him as an acousmatic character with a body, thoughts, and motivations, but we are never granted access to those thoughts or motivations. Through this, HAL represents at once the familiar comfort of the maternal womb and the frightening unknowability of the intra-uterine experience. We see the maternal body as an outsider even as we desire to be inside, just as we see HAL's exterior body but are perpetually trying to access and comprehend his psychological interior.

Aside from contrasting black/white imagery, red is the dominant color motif throughout *2001*. Of course, red is an over-determined color: it is the color of blood and fire; it evokes a sense of strong passion, both love and anger. HAL is always associated with red: his eye is red; his mainframe room is red; when he murders the three crew members in hyperstasis, a red indicator sign flashes; and the few other instances of red are always aligned with a machine's cold artificiality. Frank's red tanning glasses, combined with his emotionless stare and monotone voice, align his gaze with HAL's machine one when he watches a birthday video from his parents. Dave's red space suit and his cold stare when he tries to rescue Frank, then murders HAL, indicate his loss of humanity. Yet the coldness of the machine is in constant tension with the passionate connotations of the color red, suggesting a tension between the rationality of artificial intelligence and the irrationality of unconscious desire. According to Kuberski, "The anthropomorphic aspects of technology are enhanced by these diluted, blood-like washes of light, visually suggesting that human interiors have been transferred to technological interiors."[17] Red is the color of HAL's cold gaze, yet to "see red" is to be angry—an interior, irrational state. The interior nature of blood evokes the bloody interior of the female reproductive system that, when made exterior and visible, as through birth and menstruation, appears violent, chaotic, messy, and abject. Yet throughout the film, red appears as light rather than substance. It is, like the maternal womb, both material and immaterial, present and absent, full and empty, everywhere and nowhere.

In contrast to *Discovery One,* the interior of the *Enterprise* is significantly less centered around a cohesive set of imagery and is less sterile, though militaristically clean. Each room is brightly lit, and the entire color scheme aboard the ship suggests balance rather than tension. In each room, red, yellow, and blue are most prominent (the doors are red or blue, the computer screens are yellow, the carpet is a gray-blue), but rectangular panels in the hallways and on the bridge glow with a leafy shade of green, hinting at nature. This balance of colors represents and reinforces the idealistic, socialist utopia of the *Star Trek* universe, in which humanity can and does live in harmony. Unlike the seemingly endless tunnels presented in *2001,* the *Enterprise*'s hallways are dotted with doorways and visually punctuated with triangular arches every few yards. In contrast to *Discovery One*'s two doors in a vast spaceship (one is the pod bay "eye," and the other is the emergency hatch that Dave enters against HAL's wishes), every room on the *Enterprise* has an iconic automatic sliding door. Although there are no wide-open spaces on the *Enterprise,* the rooms do not seem claustrophobic; rather, the furnishings—generally a mix of utilitarian and personal items, particularly in the crew members' quarters—suggest a cozy, domestic space. And although there are shuttlecrafts comparable to *Discovery One*'s pods, the main method of transportation off the ship is via teleportation (in the vernacular of the series, "transporting," or "beaming"). The colors of the uniforms also reflect the balance of the ship. There are three different uniform colors, each corresponding to a particular type of work aboard the ship. Red is security and engineering, whose characters tend to be impassioned, as when Chief Engineer Scott starts a fight with a room full of Klingons solely because one of them insulted the *Enterprise.*[18] Unlike the use of red in *2001* to suggest a tension between technological rationality and unconscious, irrational desire, the security/engineering crew in their red represent bodily action, both human and mechanical, fiery passion, and intuitive responses. Blue is science, and, as the Vulcan Spock's cold, reasonable logic indicates, is the most serene, unbiased position. Gold is command, the position that, like the sun for the solar system or a bright star in the sky, holds the crew together and guides them on their journey, exemplified in Captain Kirk's dedication to his ship and his people. Of course, red aboard the enterprise is also an overdetermined color.

A "red alert" mode, used when the ship is under attack and everyone must go to battle stations, is accompanied by a flashing red light and pulsing alarm siren. In the scenes in which red alerts occur, the entire harmonious balance of the ship changes to one of impassioned battle. Additionally, fans refer to "redshirts," or unnamed characters wearing red uniforms who beam down to a planet's surface on an exploration team and are often the first to die. Exploration parties with a balanced number of engineering, science, and command officers tend to live, but when there are too many redshirts, one must die, again reinforcing the idea that an overabundance of fiery passion leads to death.

The most prominent element of the ship's mise-en-scène, however, is technology. The bridge, where quite a bit of the series' action takes place, is lined with computer screens, consoles, buttons, and lights, as well as one large central viewscreen to display the ship's exterior views and to display video chats with other beings. The computer's mind, as it were, inhabits all this technology; as such, just like in *2001*, the *Enterprise*'s body is the ship. Unlike HAL, however, who expressly states that he is an infallible computer (which, of course, then fails), this computer frequently malfunctions or is outsmarted by the ever-logical half-Vulcan Spock. In order to demonstrate their intelligence, both HAL and the *Enterprise* computer play chess, though HAL beats Dave while Spock and the *Enterprise* always reach a stalemate. The use of chess as a test of a computer's mental abilities was also part of real computer programming as early as 1959, when Alex Bernstein created the first full chess program for the IBM 704. Not until 1990 did a computer actually defeat a chess grand master (IBM's Deep Thought II defeated David Levy), and in 1996, IBM's Deep Blue program finally defeated world chess champion Garry Kasparov, effectively becoming the first nonhuman world champion.[19] In this chess-based lineage, all the major programmers and players have been male; the fact that HAL beats Dave while the *Enterprise* can do no better than stalemate suggests a masculine competitiveness and AI competency in HAL that is absent in the *Enterprise*. The *Enterprise* computer's interface is also more passive than HAL's; she mindlessly—and silently—controls background functions while consciously making calculations and computing information when asked to do so. In order to speak to her, though, a crew member seemingly must be in front of a computer console and press a button, rather than just talking and receiving a response.[20] This passivity of the voice interactivity of the *Enterprise,* who only speaks when she is addressed, belies the fact that in the background, she also controls and maintains the ship.

For my purposes here, the most important difference between *Star Trek* and *2001* is their completely opposite approaches to sound. The sound effects of *Star Trek* have become iconic (the sliding doors, the phaser, the transporter, and even the cadence of William Shatner's voice), but the voice of the *Enterprise* has not. *2001* is the opposite; HAL's voice has become the iconic representation of the film. In *Star Trek,* the aural space is filled with the sliding whoosh of automatic doors, beeps and boops of the technology, dialogue, and score. The computer's voice is always accompanied by the sound of electronic processing, as though she were run with vacuum tubes, reel-to-reel tape, and a teletype, like the real computers of the 1960s. The *Enterprise* is a delightfully busy space of technological and human activity, reinforcing the sense of comfort and community. In contrast, the second part of *2001* is relatively devoid of music and has little dialogue save that between HAL and Dave, or the occasional conversation between Dave and Frank. The two dominant sounds are the constant hum of the computer (much more like today's digital computer hum) and Dave's mechanical-sounding breathing inside his space suit.[21] These two sounds create not only the aural but also the emotional landscape for this part of this film: this world is technologically regulated and—through the lack of sound—devoid of humanity.

As I've mentioned, the *Enterprise* is gendered female and HAL is gendered male, primarily through their voices. The *Enterprise* computer, voiced by Majel Barrett, has the unmistakable high pitch of a feminine voice, though her monotone and stilted cadence is a blend of the nasal quality of a stereotypical telephone operator and a robot that must pronounce each word separately. HAL, voiced by Douglas Rain, has a deeper timbre, although he maintains an effeminate quality in his middle-ground pitch. He also speaks with a monotone, though his diction is more conversational than the *Enterprise*'s overpronunciation and formal/technical lexicon. HAL's monotone has a disturbing, uncanny quality to it, most strikingly obvious when Dave begins to remove portions of HAL's mainframe, visually and violently figured as stabbing him with a screwdriver. HAL's monotone cry for help, "I can feel it. I can feel it. I can feel it," only serves to heighten the anxiety of the scene. Although HAL verbally expresses emotion, even pleading for his life when he asks Dave to stop, the scene is devoid of overt emotions: there is no sense of pleasure in watching the main character kill a monster, only the continuing tension of the red lighting in the room. Finally, as HAL dies, his voice slows and deepens in pitch, like a machine whose batteries are dying, and he sings "Daisy Bell." Importantly, this song was the first song ever sung by a speech synthesis program, in this case run on the IBM 704 (the same computer on which the first full chess program was run). The death of HAL is thus a means of orally and metaphorically communicating with the history of computers, as though revisiting HAL's own primal scene even at the moment of his death.

THE ACOUSMATIC MOTHER SHIP

Most important to the study at hand is the way in which *Star Trek* and *2001* stage their respective space age ideologies through the gendering of the acousmatic computers.

Contrary to the conventions of SF at the time, in which space travel was depicted as "the penetration by men of the dark, womblike vastness of space in phallic-shaped rockets,"[22] neither the *Discovery One* nor the *Enterprise* are reducible to such strict gendering. There is a tension between the exteriors and interiors of these ships that suggests both phallic and uterine imagery. Each ship certainly penetrates the amniotic weightlessness of space, but each is also a floating home for the people living in it, just as a womb is a floating sac-home for a fetus. Yet the mise-en-scène of the ships suggests that the *Enterprise* is a passive female womb while the *Discovery One* is an active masculine womb.

Julia Kristeva explores the complex relationship between

interiority and exteriority as related to the maternal in her concept of the *chora,* a situation prior to language acquisition and the creation of a subjective barrier between mother and child.[23] In a seeming attempt to recover the positive, lived experience of motherhood, she describes the *chora* as a sort of sonorous envelope through which, after birth, the child and the mother remain unified, experiencing each other aurally, although before the development of symbolic language, and thus free from the patriarchal influence of the phallocentric symbolic order. Kristeva argues that the bridge from the *chora* to autonomous subjectivity is linguistically played out when children begin to name spatial objects: "Primitive naming very often makes use of adverbs of position, anaphoric demonstratives *(this, that)* or, more generally, 'topic' anaphora referring to an object either external or internal to the body proper and to the practical, immediate environment; observable in the first childhood verbalizations, it is always related to a 'space'—a *point* that henceforth becomes *object* or *referent.*"[24] In other words, to name something using symbolic language is simultaneously to begin to locate a world outside the *chora.* Importantly, in English, the word "space" refers both to a spatial location—a place—as well as the cosmos, a vast location that is both a "there" and a "nowhere." This linguistic slippage between specificity and ambiguity parallels the phantasmatic slippage of notions of the maternal womb, as both "there" in a woman's body and "nowhere" in the sense that we cannot specifically locate ourselves within the womb. Indeed, in both *Star Trek* and *2001,* many of the exterior ship shots situate a setting within a settingless space. That is, these shots imply a specific "there," as we identify the setting as a particular ship locale, yet also a "nowhere," in the unknown vastness of space. Note, too, that the "places" Kristeva mentions are both interior and exterior to the child's body, thus implying that the discovery of autonomy is a process of locating things both outside oneself as well as within oneself, thereby unintentionally evoking Kristeva's own concept of the abject, or that which blurs the boundaries between internal and external.[25] In Kristeva's formulation, the proper recognition of the abject is also part of the role of the mother as she prepares her child for entrance into the symbolic order.[26]

Kaja Silverman points out that Kristeva's attempt to deconstruct the culturally constructed boundaries between child and
mother ignores the fact that the mother is not in the presymbolic
phase, thereby relegating "the mother to the interior of the chora/
womb," a space prior to language, and consequently stripping her
of speaking subjecthood. In turn, "If the mother is mute, she is
also irrecoverable [. . .]; once her voice has been silenced, it can
no longer help to weave the anaclitic enclosure which figures her
union with the child."[27] That is, the child may well experience the
chora, but if the mother is just as unified with the child as the
child is with her through this presymbolic aural enclosure, then
the mother is actually denied the ability to engage in the symbolic order because she too is experiencing the presymbolic with
the child, as though she has regressed. However, in the case of the
acousmatic spaceship in *Star Trek* and *2001,* the ship is never the
primary character with whom the spectator is asked to identify.
The *Enterprise* computer is generally insignificant to the plot of
the story, and in some episodes does not speak at all. In contrast,
HAL 9000 is one of the most important characters in *2001;* he is
the antagonist with whom we are not intended to identify. In a
sense, both texts sidestep the issue of maternal subjectivity because the phantasmatic scene staged through these representations evokes the *chora* from the perspective of the presymbolic
child. When spaceships have no voice-interactive computer, they
do not suggest the *chora* (though they may evoke the abject, as
in the case of the dark, dank, dirty spaces of the ship in *Alien*).
Rather, they are spaces where the maternal is figured as a "case,"
an object in which the astronaut characters live but with which
they do not vocally interact, a phantasy of unity with the mother
that does not belie the workings of the symbolic order. The speaking spaceship, however, reminds viewers that the maternal womb
is both a subject and an object, a being that speaks from within
and as the womb, suggesting a *chora*-like space in which interiority and exteriority fold in on each other.

The term "mother ship," so often used in SF, is particularly
apt from a cultural perspective: the spaceship functions as a maternal, though technological, womb. It controls, facilitates, and
contains all the basic life functions—breathing, heart rate, food

consumption, excrement, movement, shelter—much as a pregnant mother does for her fetal child. Spaceships are, of course, not literal wombs, but they take on what Elissa Marder calls the maternal function by virtue of representing the womb. The womb is the ultimate mental contradiction: we all know that we were once there, yet we cannot consciously remember or imagine it. Instead, "unable to be present to the event that is closest to us [prenatal existence and birth], we attempt to return to it and account for it individually and collectively."[28] A mother is a living, breathing person; the maternal in representation is that which implies and represents a culturally constructed idea of a mother: "From the beginning of human history, the privileged figure of the maternal function has always been that of an ambiguous 'container' (the womb) that fails to contain the unruly contradictions at work in the concept of birth. [. . .] Indeed, in mythology, literature, and art, the womb is often depicted in strikingly technological terms: it is associated with artisanal boxes of all sorts including chests, caskets, jars."[29] I add to this list SF's mother ship, which functions—in mise-en-scène, role, voice, and name—like a maternal womb. It is important to be clear, though, that the mother ship is a function of the cultural maternal and the idea of the womb, not a living, breathing mother capable of giving birth.[30] This function is part and parcel of the unconscious anthropomorphism that is carried over into real HCI: while human (or humanlike) bodies are inscribed with gendered characteristics, a nonhuman machine is not. In this sense, outer space is always already an impossibility and a cathectic phantasy, as the fetal characters can only safely experience it from the enclosed womb ship.

The tension between the two conceptions of the maternal—womb and object—threatens to uncover the repressed, preoedipal, presymbolic mother, which in turn threatens the stability of the phallocentric symbolic order. However, the issue of reproduction, birth, and the maternal, as figured in representations of technology, is always a slippery one. The very notion of technological reproduction, in terms of both media production and the use of technology to enhance or replace sexual reproduction, exists in the popular imagination in ways that constantly threaten to reveal the workings of the repressed apparatus. Even the notion of an apparatus is twofold in this sense: the womb is the apparatus of birth; the camera and microphone are (two of) the apparatuses of cinema and television. The repressed doesn't just disappear but rather returns through individual and collective phantasies. The maternal function of the mother ship in SF may thus be read as a form of phantasy cathexis; the continuing representation of the enclosure of a spaceship suggests a continuing attempt to return to the *heim,* the original home. But as Lacan points out, "Nothing can be grasped, destroyed, or burnt, except in a symbolic way, as one says, *in effigie, in absentia.*"[31] That is, just as the repressed never fully goes away, so too does it never fully return. The metaphorical representation of a womb space may suggest a desire to return to physical, intrauterine unity with the mother, but at the same time it is not that unity. It is an uncanny dream space that suggests, but can never be, the mother.

Aside from the moments when the viewer sees HAL's point of view, in both *2001* and *Star Trek,* we are more often than not asked to identify with the "fetal" occupants of the mother ship rather than the ship itself, suggesting that these texts are simultaneously about a cultural conception of the maternal and the trauma of birth itself. The occupants are the protagonists, while the mother ships verbally and physically interact with them; through dialogue, as well as the cinematography and editing, the gaze of the spectator is aligned with the gaze—and the direction of the dialogue—of the human characters. In this sense, characters stand in for the phantasy of returning to the maternal womb; paradoxically, however, they embody fully formed ego selves capable of engaging in symbolic, linguistic interactions. In this sense, the mother ship is pregnant with fetal adults, acting as a perpetual reminder of what Barbara Creed describes as "the parthenogenetic mother, the mother as primordial abyss, the point of origin and of end."[32] Of course, the image of the womb always already implies birth: in the English language, we even go so far as to differentiate between a womb, which connotes pregnancy, and a uterus, which implies womanhood, though not necessarily pregnancy. Both Freud and Otto Rank have argued that birth is the first traumatic experience in a subject's life.[33] Psychohistorian

Christopher Boyd describes the representation of birth trauma as "perinatal cinema" through which "birth-related iconography, and birth-related narrative structures" express "changes in contemporary group-fantasies, especially fantasies of death and rebirth."[34] The primary characters in perinatal cinema are the "perinatal hero" and their antagonist, the "perinatal monster." The perinatal hero must always die and be reborn through "transpersonal sacrifice" in order to save a city, country, or planet—or simply the forces of good. Meanwhile, perinatal monsters represent the trauma of birth itself and "almost always possess traits symbolic of the female reproductive system."[35] In SF space travel narratives, the perinatal heroes are astronauts, while the ship may or may not be a perinatal monster, though it is important that the maternal is always also figured as human-made technology. Traditionally femininity and motherhood are visually associated with nature, yet in the last half of the twentieth century, reproductive technology, such as in vitro fertilization and cloning, has created a crisis in traditional gender imagery and roles. *Star Trek* and *2001* are also foundational texts in representing metaphorical technological pregnancy and birth.

In SF more generally, exiting the womb unprotected—without the protection of a shuttlecraft or space suit provided from within the womb-ship—is almost always fatal, representing both the death of unity with the mother/womb and the desire to return to that unity.[36] Further, a character's use of a space suit attached to the ship by an umbilical life support cord, and the fact that work outside the ship typically leads to some disaster in which the character might not safely return to the ship/womb, visually and narratively play out the anxiety of disunity with the mother and the phantasy of returning to the primordial state. In *2001,* the "births" of both Frank and Dave are traumatic, and HAL, as the maternal womb, directly causes that trauma. When HAL (falsely) reports a damaged satellite, Frank dons a space suit and takes a pod to check on and repair the damage. While he is floating in open space, HAL, taking control of the mechanical arm attached to the front of the pod, cuts Frank's air supply line, metaphorically cutting his umbilical cord. Frank had assumed he would return to the safety of HAL's body, but instead, HAL, while symbolically re-creating the act of birth, simultaneously kills him. Later, Dave takes another pod out to retrieve Frank's body. When he tries to return to the pod bay, HAL won't let him in; this scene suggests that Dave desires to return to the safety of the womb-ship, but, as is true in reality, we can never reenter the womb. Freud argues that anxieties about death by entombment, enclosure, being buried alive, and so on represent a phantasy working through of the desire to return to the mother's womb and to be reborn. Death and birth are therefore psychically one and the same. This is also true of HAL's "abortion" of Dave and Frank. Their inability to reenter the ship means certain death, implying an anxiety about the inability to return to unity within the mother. However, this death outside the ship also implies an exit from the ship—that is, a birth. When HAL refuses Dave reentry, Dave forces his way in, suggesting a forcible claim over the maternal body, a taking back of what was psychically lost in birth. Dave's reentry ultimately leads to HAL's death, suggesting that to return to unity with the mother is also to kill her. This futility of the phantasy of reuniting with the maternal body is yet another significant ambivalence within the film. This phantasy underlines—and in some ways drives—the narrative, while it is a futile act that ultimately propels Dave right back out of the maternal body of the ship and into the star gate.

In *Star Trek,* however, the heroes are never born. Rather, they are either on board the *Enterprise* or beamed off it. We never see the ship open up and give birth to a character. In this sense the series maintains a metaphorical stasis of pregnancy that denies the trauma of birth. Just as the womb implies birth, so too does pregnancy imply female sexuality.[37] The metaphorical denial of birth in *Star Trek* is likewise evocative and expressive of a denial of female sexuality, as seen in the fact that a single actress plays both the voice of the mother ship and the asexual Nurse Chapel. In the first of two pilots for *Star Trek,* entitled "The Cage," Majel Barrett plays the *Enterprise*'s first officer; she even wears pants, like the male officers. Unfortunately, the executives at NBC disliked most of Roddenberry's casting choices, including having a woman in a position of high authority. By the time the series' first episode premiered, not only did Leonard Nimoy's Spock become first officer, but also Barrett donned a blonde wig and the iconic *Star Trek* minidress to play Christine Chapel, a soft-spoken and mostly chaste nurse.[38]

The change in her appearance from a dark-haired, pants-wearing, powerful officer to a passive, light-haired, scantily clad assistant to the male doctor indicates the restrictive roles allowed to women in the series. (This is also true in *2001,* where only one woman is a scientist; the other women are flight attendants, daughters, mothers, and wives, but never astronauts.) By the sixth episode, which first aired October 13, 1966, Barrett had also taken on the role of the computer's voice.[39] Thus, there is a tension between Barrett's "real" body (Nurse Chapel) and her technological body (the *Enterprise*). By playing an acousmatic character, Barrett is also, and paradoxically, disembodied as a result of the schizophonic apparatus because although her voice always literally emanates from her body, the moment it is captured by sound equipment and projected onto either the ship or the image of Nurse Chapel, her implied body is that of her human, female body and/or the space of the ship. This triangular simultaneity threatens to reveal the complexities of the maternal function—that a single woman is not only a womb space but also a sexual being. In other words, Barrett and her two characters in *Star Trek* suggest multiple parts of one person. She is Majel Barrett (an actress), Nurse Chapel (a human character), and the *Enterprise* (a mother ship), in the same way that a woman in Western patriarchal culture may fill multiple roles related to and inscribed by her femininity, including a subject, a sexual object of desire, and a mother. While this seems pretty obvious, the uncanny aspects of the maternal *Enterprise,* and the primordial site associated with it, as well as the doubling of Barrett in her two characters, threatens to disrupt the idealistic utopia of *Star Trek.* The narratives of the series thus turn on a parallel metaphor of cinematic and subjective origins, hidden voice and hidden womb. In order to maintain a utopic sense of the future, as *Star Trek* always desires to do, it must simultaneously mask the origin of the voice, as is necessary in maintaining narrative cohesion, and repress the trauma of birth associated with the womb. Yet neither is ever fully repressed. In fact, as the *Enterprise* and Nurse

Chapel repeatedly demonstrate, the threat of revealing both the schizophonic apparatus and the human apparatus is only resolvable by differentiating between the sexual, embodied woman and the chaste, disembodied maternal.

In Barrett's first "appearance" as the computer, "Mudd's Women,"[40] Captain Kirk has her read the biosigns of the male crew members who have been seduced by Harry Mudd's futuristic equivalent of mail-order brides. The biosigns include raised heart rates and body temperatures, suggesting—and confirmed by the embarrassment shown on the men's faces in their reaction shots—physiological arousal. Yet the computer provides no hint of understanding sexual arousal as she coldly recites data. In addition to the fact that Barrett was not originally credited for her voice work in *TOS,* Chapel never speaks to the computer, thus keeping the human actress and her computerized voice entirely separate and minimizing any threat of self-reflexively revealing the apparatus. Incidentally, Christine Chapel does not appear in "Mudd's Women," thus further solidifying the separation between the sexualized female body and the asexual maternal womb. There are moments in other episodes, though, in which the repressed primordial womb returns through voiced fissures in the structured asexuality of the computer. In *Star Trek,* these fissures occur most dramatically when the ship becomes threateningly sexualized for the male characters, as seen in "Tomorrow Is Yesterday" and "Mirror, Mirror."[41]

In "Tomorrow Is Yesterday," the *Enterprise* accidentally goes back in time to 1966 and beams aboard a United States Air Force pilot, Captain John Christopher (Roger Perry). In one scene, as Spock, Kirk, and Christopher try to work out a way to return the pilot to Earth without detection, they discover that the computer has been reprogrammed by a race of Amazonian matriarchs to have "more personality," as Spock puts it. As a result, the computer (still played by Barrett) speaks with a low, sultry voice and addresses Kirk as "dear" even after he commands her to stop. In one scene in Kirk's ready room, Kirk asks Spock when the computer will be fixed, stating that he "wouldn't mind so much" that it has a new personality, "if only it weren't so . . . affectionate." This exchange is presented as comical, underscored by a whimsical musical interlude as the scene fades out. But Kirk's statement belies a psychical anxiety about the sexualization of his mother ship: "If only it weren't so . . . affectionate." When the computer was a cold data machine, she was entirely nonthreatening because all traces of the maternal were repressed in the name of preserving the asexuality of the mother. The "affectionate" tone of her voice allows for the development of the oedipal phantasy in which Kirk desires his mother ship, ultimately allowing him to transfer those desires onto a "suitable" humanoid female mate (which he does quite frequently throughout the series). In fact, unlike the male crew members who frequently engage in sexual and romantic escapades—and even then almost exclusively with female villains or aliens who are emphatically not portrayed as maternal beings—neither of *TOS*'s two main female crew members (Chapel and Uhura) are ever depicted as having sexual agency in the same way that the male crew members are. Nurse Chapel has only one love interest, and he turns out to be an android who cannot love her back. This clear division between antagonist/sexual and protagonist/chaste reinforces a binary notion of women's roles. Indeed, as Kath Woodward points out, the dichotomous images of good versus bad mothers are pervasive throughout Western culture. On the one hand, "the 'good mother' is self-sacrificing, selfless and probably not seen as sexual," often figured as the Madonna. "This is a mother who has not had sex with a man yet who has carried and delivered a baby. In this sense the perfect mother is the mother who is not associated with sexuality."[42] On the other hand, "the bad mother may have the attributes that are not present in the good mother, such as selfishness, lack of care for her children, seeking her own pleasure."[43] This dichotomy is also inscribed onto the *Enterprise* in "Tomorrow Is Yesterday." The maternal ship is a passive, virginal womb object whose sudden, threatening sexuality must be repressed, emphasized by the fact that Kirk calls her "it." But as an "affectionate" (read: sexually aggressive) subject, she threatens to undermine her status as a passive object (either a computer object or an object of Kirk's desire) and reveal herself as the apparatus/primordial site by virtue of the implication of sexuality, which emphasizes her womblike structure. This in turn threatens to destabilize Kirk's own sense of a stable ego-self constructed around a clear male-active/female-passive dichotomy.

This revelation of the repressed maternal and the construction of gender identity becomes humorous in the scene precisely because it is a revelation. Freud argues that humor allows for "economy in the expenditure of affect"—that is, pleasure in the face of what normally should be a distressing situation.[44] He later expands on this idea, arguing that this "economy" is achieved when the superego—the strict, forbidding, "parental" part of the psyche—pokes fun at the seriousness of a situation, thereby allowing the ego to see the world as less frightening. It is almost, he suggests, as though the superego says to the ego, "Look here! This is all that this seemingly dangerous world amounts to! Child's play—the very thing to jest about!"[45] Kirk necessarily represses the sexualized womb-like aspects of the *Enterprise* in order to maintain his sense of stable ego-self, but the sexually aggressive computer voice allows the pleasure of the primordial site to be released for the audience, safely hidden in the distance between Kirk and ourselves. The scene, with its all-too-obvious musical interlude and the staged close-ups of the bemused looks exchanged between Spock and Christopher, becomes comical as we watch Kirk struggle with the return of the repressed, all the while identifying with Spock and Christopher, whose masculine egos are not threatened.

While "Tomorrow Is Yesterday" thus features the return of the repressed primordial site, safely experienced through humor, the comparatively more serious episode "Mirror, Mirror" likewise portrays an *Enterprise* of passive, virginal femininity in opposition to masculine aggression.[46] Importantly, Nurse Chapel is also not in this episode; in fact, Barrett wasn't in the episode at all as either the computer voice or Chapel, although by this point in the series it had been firmly established that the *Enterprise* did indeed have a female voice. The womb-ship thus functions in opposition to another womb-ship rather than a sexualized female body. In the episode, Captain Kirk, Lieutenant Uhura, Doctor McCoy, and Chief Engineer Scott are accidentally transported into an alternate universe, aboard the evil Terran Empire's ISS *Enterprise*. In this alternate universe, the idea of mirror opposites plays out visually and thematically: while the "good" *Enterprise* crew works harmoniously for a peaceful journey, the "bad" *Enterprise* crew members plot against, assault, and sexually harass one another. In characterizing the universes, much of the opposition occurs at the level of gender archetypes: the good men are rational, while the bad ones are aggressively violent; the good women are modest maidens who perform their duties, while the bad ones are scantily clad and sexually aggressive. More specifically, a one-off character named Marlena sleeps her way to the top in the bad universe, while in the good universe, she humbly requests that Kirk sign a duty form. Notoriously, bad Spock has a beard, a symbol of adult male virility, while good Spock is clean-shaven and metaphorically pure.

While the humanoid women in this episode are reduced to basic virgin/whore dichotomies, the *Enterprise* cannot be. The revelation of the archaic preoedipal mother is so threatening to the stability of gender dichotomies on which the mirror archetypes rest that to posit the womb-ship as either a virgin or a whore would reveal the very process of repression. In other words, if she's a whore, she is a sexual being, and the primordial act of impregnation is evoked; if she's a virgin, a nonsexual being, she ceases to be the comforting womb to which we desire to return. Instead, the set design of the two *Enterprise*s clearly suggests a straightforward male/female dichotomy: the bad *Enterprise* is painted with the phallic sword insignia of the Terran Empire and bears a male voice; the good *Enterprise,* though it looks exactly like it does in every other episode, suddenly seems, by comparison, lacking any hint of a phallus and, for the duration of the episode, does not speak, hence foregrounding her passivity and female lack. Such a dichotomy suggests the foundational Western ideal of gender stability: the ultimate "mirror," or opposite, of masculine is feminine. In Lacan's formulation, the mirror stage is the beginning of oppositional language structure (that is, I am not that, so I am this). Therefore, the good *Enterprise* is good because it is not the bad *Enterprise,* and vice versa. The very nature of the ship as both a setting for the action and the literal atmosphere in which the characters live suggests that the *Enterprise* provides the foundational structure of opposition that surrounds and informs all of the characters' activities. This structure also suppresses any potential complexities of female sexuality embodied in the good *Enterprise:* she lacks not only a powerful phallus but also any hint of the abject womb. She is once again metaphorically sterilized so as to maintain the strict order of dichotomous gender.

FROM PRIMAL SCENE TO CONVERGENCE CULTURE

As I have argued thus far, reading the *Enterprise* and HAL 9000 in relationship to one another provides a foundational understanding of how gender and the maternal are inscribed onto acousmatic computers in SF. Literary theorist Ned Lukacher has argued that the Freudian notion of a primal scene may be used metaphorically in order to understand intertextual progeny and ontology; as foundational texts, *Star Trek* and *2001* may in this sense likewise be understood as performing a "primal scene" of voice-interactive computers. Lukacher writes:

> I do not restrict "primal scene" to the conventional psycho-
> analytic understanding of the term: the child's witnessing
> of a sexual act that subsequently plays a traumatic role
> in his or her psychosexual life. In my use of the term it
> becomes an intertextual event that displaces the notion of
> the event from the ground of ontology. It calls the event's
> relation to the Real into question in an entirely new way.
> Rather than signifying the child's observation of sexual
> intercourse, the primal scene comes to signify an onto-
> logically undecidable intertextual event that is situated
> in the differential space between historical memory and
> imaginative construction, between archival verification
> and interpretive free play. [. . .] I use the expression
> "primal scene" to describe the interpretive impasse that
> arises when a reader has good reason to believe that
> the meaning of one text is historically dependent on the
> meaning of another text or on a previously unnoticed set
> of criteria, even though there is no conclusive evidential
> or archival means of establishing the case beyond a rea-
> sonable doubt.[47]

Lukacher's method of reading intertexts thus attends to both a notion of the "real" existence (in the sense of factuality rather than
in the Lacanian sense of that which is effaced by the symbolic and
thus unknowable) of texts like *Star Trek* and *2001* in their historical context and a present construction of relationships among
all the related texts before and after. The metaphor of a textual
"primal scene" is thus an instance when influence of the "parent"
or "parents" of subsequent texts come into being. Freud himself
attempts to sort out whether the primal scene as the witnessing
of a sexual act is memory or phantasy; he concludes in his famous
Wolf Man study that in a way, it is both. Memory and phantasy
combine in the psyche in a way that is experientially real for the
subject, regardless of whether its existence as a past event can be
verified.[48] The same is also true of representations: our individual
and culturally collective memories of a text and the existence of a
text as a historical object (film, video, digital data) coexist in ways
that create and maintain meaning.

Gerard Genette emphasizes this coexistence of texts, objects, and subjects through his concept of transtextuality. Drawing on Bakhtin's contra-Saussaurean concept of translinguistics
in which the meanings of signs are unstable,[49] Genette argues
that every text exists in relationship to every other text. Within
transtextuality, he delineates five forms of textual relationships—
intertextuality, paratextuality, metatextuality, hypertextuality,
and architextuality—all of which function concurrently as an active way of making meaning.[50] Although these five forms allow
Genette's assertion that meaning is made actively in between
texts to be fairly broad, his definition of "text" is still closely tied
to a traditional conception of a "work." Yet we read and make
meaning in everything around us, including films, TV shows,
items of clothing, the look on a person's face, and the interface
of a computer. Furthermore, we process all of these real objects
(in a Lacanian sense) as a part of the symbolic order, through
which we understand reality.[51] Meaning is made by negotiating
the relationships among artist, text, reader, and context, but artist and reader are also texts, equally surrounded by other texts,
that all contribute to a symbolic understanding of reality. I define
a text, then, as any identifiable symbol or collection of symbols

that function in relationship to other collections of symbols in a way that allows the "reader" to create significant meaning. In turn, the varied and shifting relationships among all texts make up a transtextual network through which we negotiate our understanding of reality. The work of a critic, then, may be seen as the process of untangling portions of a network of texts in order more clearly to see how all the pieces fit together. Within this context, the examination of a textual primal scene is simultaneously *a* (though not *the*) starting point for disentanglement.

Since the 1960s, the rise of convergence culture in a rapidly shifting media landscape has changed the relationship between *Star Trek* and *2001* as well as the relationships among text, medium, and audience. While I have so far conflated cinema and television sound practices, history, and aesthetics, they are to some extent separate. The physical situation of the cinema theater is different from that of the home television experience, particularly in the level of control viewers have over their environment. Further, there are significant textual differences between cinema and television; while a film is, in ideal situations, a single uninterrupted text, television has what Raymond Williams famously describes as "the central television experience: the fact of flow."[52] This flow spans all of TV programming, including individual shows, commercial interruptions, and all other insertions of advertising. Historically, the flow of television and the cohesion of the cinematic text have been the dominant criteria for separating the media; however, streaming and digital video files have radically altered this neat categorization, such that a viewer might binge watch ten episodes of a series, with no significant interruptions, so the text will effectively form a cohesive narrative block. Outside the viewing experience, there are significant aesthetic differences as well, such as television's heavier use of the close-up versus cinema's ability to capture wide and even panoramic shots. Here too streaming sites' original content production, along with the development of ultra-high-definition televisions, is radically altering the nature of television production.

Cinema and television sound have also historically been understood as entirely different from one another. Cinema sound began as monophonic with one speaker per theater, typically lo-

cated behind the screen; such monophonic sound seems to emanate from the screen itself, though, as Doane points out, the left–
right dimension of sound may be implied through movement of
the synchronized image, rather than actually demonstrated by the
movement of sound among multiple speakers.[53] Although in the
1950s stereo sound and experimentation with speaker placement
in a theater were relatively common,[54] such advances in sound did
not enter wide use until the Dolby digital revolution of the 1970s
and 1980s. By the 1990s, movie theaters were almost exclusively
equipped with surround-sound speakers, and most major Hollywood film soundtracks have since been created to accommodate
them. Aesthetically, stereo and surround sound have to a certain
extent changed the aesthetic practices of filmmaking since the
mid-1980s, allowing for a wider range of sound mixing beyond
the traditional prominence of dialogue within the soundtrack.[55]
Vivian Sobchack, in examining Dolby's spectacle-laden theatrical
promotions for the new technology in the 1980s and early 1990s,
argues that stereo and surround sound mimic the full acoustic
possibilities of a spatialized cinema, yet because the movement
of sound around the theater is so crisp—necessarily so, as the
promotions are meant to demonstrate the spatial possibilities of
sound—the trailers highlight a tension between the actuality of
theater sound and the possibility of fully submersive sound.[56] In
short, as the simultaneous histories of cinema sound technology
and theory reveal, there has been a shift over time from sound
located behind/within the image to sound that, though it has the
possibility to be freed from the image, nevertheless significantly
works to create an acoustic environment that matches the environment represented on the screen.

While television, like pre-1950s cinema, has historically been
a monophonic medium offering only one channel of sound emanating from somewhere on the physical television box, the televisual relationship between sound and image has traditionally
been the inverse of cinema. While early silent cinema comprised
image plus live sound, early television was conceived of and invented as visual radio. In fact, the early television networks of the
1940s—NBC was the forerunner—had already established themselves as radio networks twenty years previously.[57] Aesthetically,

television programs have also adhered to a notion of visualized sound, particularly owing to the fact that early broadcasts were frequently simulcast on the radio until the mid-1950s.[58] As Chion posits, television aesthetics rely significantly more on sound than image, as, for example, in that historical staple of television broadcasting: news programs. In any given news broadcast, a voice-over narrates the story, much as in radio broadcasts, while the B-roll type of imagery presented is of a particular object related to the story, thereby illustrating, rather than embodying, the story itself.[59] Commercial breaks also add to this televisual flow, to return to Raymond Williams's term, privileging sound over image, and freeing the audience to wander away from the television set while still receiving information audibly.

In 1984, the Federal Communications Commission approved stereo television broadcast, and since then, nearly all televisions produced for use in the United States have been equipped with stereo speakers.[60] This technological shift coincided with a significant shift in television aesthetics toward a more cinematic technique. Shows such as *Miami Vice* and *Hill Street Blues* began to draw on the handheld camera immediacy of cinema verité, and the image therefore became more cinematically tied to the sound than the traditional illustrative role of televisual imagery.[61]

Thus, the differences between cinema and television have been disappearing since the 1980s, and not only aesthetically and phonically: differences also collapsed as a result of the widespread availability of VCRs: "Through the 1980s, household ownership of VCRs grew from 1 percent to 68 percent, a pace matched by the wireless remote. The VCR allowed viewers to turn off television entirely while they played Hollywood movies on their sets."[62] Today, the lines between television and cinema are even more unclear, with the availability of wide-screen high-definition TVs, which mimic the cinema screen, and the general convergence of media platforms. The availability of DVD/Blu-ray box sets, Internet streaming sites such as Netflix, Hulu, and Amazon, and mobile technology not only allows for wider availability of media but also changes the nature of a typical viewing situation. Because television series are now available outside of the broadcast situation, the flow of TV has given way to cohesive texts, albeit still broken into individual, serialized episodes. From an aesthetic perspective, television sound—particularly sound in narrative programs that do not use laugh tracks—is strikingly similar to that of cinema sound, although more clearly stylized sound designs are used in long-running television series than in single films.[63] Further, the ideal viewing situation that film studies tends to posit—focusing solely on the context of the text itself rather than accounting for viewing practices—is no longer feasible; indeed, a whole range of viewing situations are possible. As a result, TV series may be more clearly analyzed using the methods of traditional film criticism, from a cohesive-textual, rather than textual-flow, perspective. Further, as Henry Jenkins argues, "convergence represents a cultural shift as consumers are encouraged to seek out new information and make connections among dispersed media content."[64] The multiplatform availability of SF thus allows viewers to draw clearer connections between represented HCI and real HCI; for example, viewers may watch an episode of *Star Trek* on their iPhone, and at any point during viewing, interact with Siri in the same way that Captain Kirk interacts with the spaceship computer in the text. Such convergence allows for an even more complex understanding of how SF texts serve as models for real HCI. As such, throughout the remainder of this book, I attempt to situate each text within its historical viewing context while attempting not to lose sight of the fact that my readers might encounter the texts in a variety of media contexts.

Star Trek in particular is a prime example of a need for intertextually and transtextually attentive readings. When viewers first watched and understood the series in the late 1960s, they did so on mono-sound televisions, in the midst of the Cold War, the Vietnam War, and the civil rights movement, and at the tail end of the height of B-movie SF. The twenty-first-century context is obviously quite different, however, as people may watch the series on any variety of stationary and mobile platforms, in mono, stereo, or surround sound, while in the midst of continuous overseas conflicts, political divisiveness, social media saturation—and, importantly, after more than fifty years of *Star Trek* spin-off films, series, documentaries, conventions, and a reboot of the franchise, not to mention numerous other films and series that feature acousmatic computers. Neither the historical nor the present context is more correct or valid, but in order to understand the latter, we must also understand the former. Michel Chion argues much the same in the introduction to his book on *2001:*

> Today's spectator sees the work quite differently, influenced by its history, the explanations furnished by [Arthur C.] Clarke's novel and a series of "revelations" made after the fact, a whole tradition of exegesis that was handed down, particularly by critics and the press, and that constitutes a common and reassuring background of understanding. [. . .] To watch *2001* as it was seen on its release implies attempting to forget this tradition, an almost impossible task. Nevertheless, this does not prevent the film, although overlaid with all these commentaries, from retaining its mystery for those who discover it today.[65]

In other words, to recognize the overlaying of extratextual material—commentaries, criticisms, digital enhancements, the changing nature of viewing space—onto a text does not necessarily diminish the phenomenologically real experiences of watching, interpreting, and remembering. In addition, media histories also shape and have been shaped by both *Star Trek* and *2001.* The aesthetic practices of both texts come out of television and film histories, respectively; further, they have both since been digitally enhanced for high-definition platforms, further complicating their relative relationships to other texts.

A transtextual understanding of *Star Trek* and *2001* isn't limited to their influences on SF, however; they are also situated within histories of both media production and computer and artificial intelligence design. From the late 1960s to the present, the technology in these texts provided inspiration for real hardware and software design,[66] and voice-interactive HCI has become the holy grail of computer engineers. Situating fictional texts within the context of real science, however, raises the slippery question of realism. Because of the nature of fantasy and postulation in SF, no SF text can really claim to be realistic in the same way that, say, a melodrama set in present day is realistic in its verisimilitude. Nevertheless, the technology presented in the mise-en-scène may be more or less realistic—or, more appropriately, accurate—for the time it was created. Conversely, and in hindsight, a text's "predictions" about future technological advancements may be more or less accurate. For example, *Star Trek* envisioned a graphical user interface based on both a monitor/terminal and rudimentary voice interactivity by the twenty-third century, which we now have; likewise, *2001* imagined natural-language voice-interactive computers by the year 2001, and while Siri and Alexa are by no means perfect, they are natural-language voice-interactive programs. But in many ways, a traditional notion of aesthetic realism or even scientific accuracy is beside the point. SF exists in a cyclical relationship with real technology: science influences SF, which in turn influences science, which in turn influences SF. It's a chicken-and-egg problem in which both the chicken and the egg are creations of human ingenuity.

The very notion of a primal scene of (trans-)textual influence is therefore a complicated one in which past and present, reality and fiction, object and memory are woven together in a vast cultural network. Using this method of analysis, several assertions about acousmatic computers arise: first, the representational and scientific foundations of the *Enterprise* and HAL 9000 existed well before either *Star Trek* or *2001* was created; second, and nevertheless, the cultural impact of both texts has been so enormous that all representations and scientific creations of voice-interactive computers since 1966 may be understood in relationship to them. My analyses of acousmatic spaceship computers in this chapter, as well as all the subsequent analyses in this book, flow from the foundational imagery of *Star Trek* and *2001*. In this sense, the primal scene occurred in 1966 and 1968, when these texts, respectively, premiered, while the history of voice-interactive computing that I trace always already links back to it. This metaphor of the primal scene also works on multiple levels, because not only do the two texts function together as a textual primal scene, but also the very notion of the mother ship and the computers that both control and voice their bodies are bound to the unconscious imagery of womb, phallus, birth, and primal scene that may be seen throughout SF representations of acousmatic spaceships.

The *Enterprise* and HAL 9000 are opposite parents of the representations and real creations of voice-interactive computing that would follow. On the one hand, the *Enterprise* is warm, uterine, feminine, asexual, and generally passive; on the other hand, HAL is cold, phallic/uterine, masculine, and overbearing. One thing unites them: when their voices are projected onto their bodies, an often repressed notion of gender and gender difference is simultaneously projected onto those same bodies. These preliminary descriptions and contrasts lay the groundwork for understanding this gendered projection, and for understanding the representation of a variety of acousmatic computers across texts.

CHAPTER 2

REPRODUCING THE MOTHER SHIP
Doubling, Parody, and the Maternal Figure in Space

WHEN *STAR TREK* AND *2001* premiered in the latter half of the 1960s, the space race was coming to an end, reaching its climax with the U.S. moon landing in 1969. As I argued in chapter 1, *Star Trek* and *2001* combined the ideology of the space age context in which they emerged with long-standing gender roles to create SF's foundational representations of acousmatic computers. In this chapter, I turn to subsequent representations of acousmatic computers in space in order to examine how shifting cultural notions of gender and science helped to shape and reshape the image of the talking mother ship.

Constance Penley suggests that "'going into space'—both the actuality of it and its SF realization—has become the prime metaphor through which we try to make sense of the world of science and technology and imagine a place for ourselves in it."[1] Space travel narratives certainly continued to be told well after the moon landing, though in the first half of the 1970s, they were less frequent and more dystopian, as "space became semantically inscribed as inescapably domestic and crowded."[2] This all changed in 1977, with George Lucas's *Star Wars,* which reinvigorated both Hollywood and SF, instigating "some strange new transformation" through which "technological wonder had become synonymous with domestic hope."[3] Once again, space was figured in SF as a vast, exciting—if sometimes frightening—frontier of exploration.

It's somewhat ironic, then, that, even as SF narratives turned to new explorations of space, the SF representations of acousmatic computer ships tended to return/regress to the metaphors and symbols of *Star Trek* and *2001*. In this chapter, I will examine four texts that build on the themes of reproduction and the maternal function: John Carpenter's 1974 film *Dark Star,* the short-lived 1970s TV series *Quark,* the wildly popular late 1980s/ early 1990s TV series *Star Trek: The Next Generation (TNG),* and Duncan Jones's 2009 film *Moon.* Each of these texts continues to explore the tension between woman as object and woman as womb. Historically, however, the texts must be understood in the context of the American space program. *Dark Star* and *Quark* were products of the 1970s, a moment after the excitement of the space race and before the resurgence of real space exploration in the mid-1980s; *TNG* and *Moon* are products of a post-*Challenger* world, in which every representation of space was necessarily bound to the trauma of that event. So although all these texts use motifs of doubling and metaphorical reproduction, the first two are significantly more invested in poking fun at the notion of an acousmatic computer, while the second two provide a much richer, more complex examination of gender, reproduction, and space technology.

As I discussed at length in chapter 1, the acousmatic spaceship suggests a connection between space and gender, figured in the phantasy of a return to intrauterine existence. Space, like water, carries gendered connotations linked to (amniotic) fluidity, birth, and the culturally perceived chaos of female sexuality. This gendering is emphasized in the culturally gendered associations of the space race, as Marie Lathers notes in her study of gender and space exploration:

> How the Space Race is digested as a gendered event
> was and is related to social norms; in the late 1950s and
> throughout the '60s, emphasis was placed on defining
> women's place in the home—not their place in the public
> sphere—and this emphasis was played out in NASA's
> refusal to train women as astronauts. The relatively new
> technology of television was the major vehicle for the pop-
> ularization of the connected discourse of Space Race and

domestic peace. Center stage in the middleclass home, television was the prime medium for the dissemination of NASA's accomplishments. Because of television, the outer space of other worlds and the inner space of the home were forever linked, and this process set up a series of oppositions that continues to characterize our understanding of space—outer/inner; alien/astronaut; U.S./U.S.S.R.; ape/human; domestic space/public space—and the representation of space in fiction and dominant cinema.[4]

This tension between interior/domestic/feminine and exterior/ public/masculine, I would add, are inscribed onto the very notion of space and spaceships, underlined by parallel tensions of exteriority/interiority in pregnancy and birth. To be inside a spaceship is also to be inside a womb-like environment that is associated with the maternal body; yet to be an astronaut was a public, male-dominated endeavor well into the 1980s. Thus, the tension of texts about the acousmatic spaceship may be read as a visual and narrative working through of the tension between the mother as object (figured in the voice, to whom the male astronaut speaks) and mother as womb (figured in the body, within which the male astronaut lives). The first two texts I examine in this chapter—*Dark Star* and *Quark*—are products of this male-dominated period; they in large part parodically reproduce the imagery of *Star Trek* and *2001*.

LIKE MOTHER, LIKE HAL

John Carpenter's 1974 comedy *Dark Star* is the story of a group of future astronauts who explore the universe aboard the *Dark Star,* a voice-interactive spaceship whom the men have nicknamed Mother.[5] Most of the interior of the ship is a hodgepodge of military vessels and references to *2001:* the main control room is a cramped space with computer panels and lights lining the walls, reminiscent of the cockpit of the Apollo 11 capsule; the hallways are all steel with low ceilings, neat lines, and, as one character demonstrates in a reference to the tanning scene in *2001,* lamps so hot you can tan yourself under them; and there is a glass-enclosed gun turret on the top of the ship where one of the astronauts generally sits, like a fighter pilot in World War II. In both the main control room and the cabin, the astronauts keep pinup pictures of seminude women in provocative positions; although the pictures are prominent in the mise-en-scène, the men never comment on them, suggesting instead the long tradition of military men keeping racy pictures of women in their cockpits or bunks. Yet these spaces where the men of the film live, work, play, and mindlessly objectify the women in the pinup pictures is in direct tension with the stereotypically nagging female voice of the ship's computer (played by Cookie Knapp, the only woman in the entire cast and one of only two women total to work on the film, the other being Nina Kleinberg, who, coincidentally, worked in the sound department). The very fact that the men on board the ship refer to her as Mother immediately establishes a mother–child relationship that invites a reading of her body and voice as maternal. She evokes both the maternal womb and the preoedipal mother; the former representation is image driven, while the latter is sound driven.

Mother evokes the preoedipal mother in Freud's formulation. She is the nagging, overbearing mother of the child's transition from womb to symbolic/phallocentric oedipal existence. In utero and immediately after birth, according to Freud, the child experiences unity with the mother; during the oedipal phase, the child (always male in the Freudian tradition) sees the mother's genitals as the wound site of her castration, and her lack of phallus thus stimulates castration anxiety and the subsequent objectification of the female object. The transition between the omnipotent phallic mother of the dyadic relationship (mother–child) and the castrated oedipal mother of the triadic (mother–child–father) relationship is the preoedipal period, which "confers upon man and father the penis and the phallus, is the inverse of the fantasmatic omnipotence that the child confers upon the mother: it is what *ought* to make it possible to cut the umbilical cord."[6] The preoedipal period is the time in which the child, pushing away from the mother and her link to the imaginary order, begins to enter into the symbolic order centered around the phallus. This version of the maternal is represented as the "protective/suffocating" mother[7] who attempts to keep her child in the imaginary order, against whom the child must struggle and ultimately "work through" in a psychoanalytic sense.[8] The intonation of *Dark Star*'s voice, though more So-Cal calm than shrewish, nevertheless suggests a nagging mother—or perhaps a teenaged babysitter as the mother stand-in. Everything she says is a reminder to the men aboard to do some task (she generally begins these announcements with, "Attention, attention") or an update on the status of her own body.

The ship's voice and body are also overt parodies of HAL. Early in the film, Mother interrupts two of the astronauts, one of whom has just been sunbathing under a lamp:

MOTHER: Sorry to interrupt your recreation, fellows, but it is time for Sergeant Pinback to feed the alien.
PINBACK: Aww, I don't want to do that.
MOTHER: May I remind you, Sergeant Pinback, that it was your idea to bring the alien on board. If I may quote you, you felt the ship needed a mascot.

In *2001,* HAL interrupts Frank with the line, "Sorry to interrupt the festivities, but we have a problem." But while HAL's voice is his usual monotone, Mother's intonation is much more stern, juxtaposed with a conversational diction, addressing the men as "fellows."

Mother's insistence that Sergeant Pinback (played by screenwriter Dan O'Bannon) feed the alien is particularly striking in lieu of the overtly sexualized mise-en-scène that follows. The entire scene is a parody of the scene in *2001* when HAL sends Frank to his death, then denies Dave reentry into the birth canal–like pod bay corridor; in the *Dark Star* scene, however, the "boys," it is implied, have begged for this mascot, which they now refuse to take care of, and so Mother must nag them to do their chores. In this sense, *Dark Star* repositions the frightening *2001* scenes within the milieu of mundane earthly tasks.

The alien lives in a room that is dimly lit with red light, evocative of both the internal body and HAL's red-lit mainframe room. The intensity and uncanniness of this setting, however, are immediately belied by the appearance of the alien, who unceremoniously plops down from a ceiling shaft, revealing that it is nothing more than a bobbing, painted beach ball accompanied by squeaking, twittering sounds. The alien attacks Pinback (O'Bannon holds the alien prop on his head and flails in a close-up shot) before fleeing into the hallway. Eerie, pulsating synth music plays, absurdly juxtaposed with a slapstick broom fight between Pinback and the alien. When the alien runs off, Pinback chases it through a series of red-lit corridors that again suggest bodily interiors. Finally, the alien leads Pinback to the top of a deep, white elevator shaft, another overt reference to the canal-like pod bay corridor in *2001,* simultaneously suggesting the entire female reproductive system, complete with egg-like object moving through bloodred-lit tubes into the canal. The alien tickles Pinback in order to force him to fall down the shaft, comically suggesting the trauma of birth (or perhaps the desire not to leave the maternal body). As Pinback dangles precariously from a ridge in the shaft, the elevator suddenly begins slowly plunging down the shaft, nearly crushing him. Just before being crushed, however, Pinback manages to hoist himself up through the floor of the elevator, where he uses the emergency telephone to ask the ship for help. Mother responds, "I'm sorry, this telephone is out of service. Please report this damage at once." Frustrated, Pinback pushes a button on a nearby wall panel, to which Mother responds, "For your listening enjoyment, we now present 'The Barber of Seville' by Rossini." As the opera plays, Pinback pushes more buttons, eventually activating explosives in the floor plate of the elevator and, in a slapstick puff of smoke, blowing himself up.

Mother's line, "I'm sorry, this telephone is out of service," and the ensuing mayhem is an overtly comical reworking of the scene in *2001* in which Dave uses the pod radio to demand that HAL "open the pod bay doors," to which HAL replies, "I'm sorry, Dave, I'm afraid I can't do that." Freud sees humor (a subsection of the comical) as a means of protecting the ego from what might otherwise be a traumatic event. Further, he argues that parody in particular is a means of protecting the ego from and challenging the authority of a powerful entity: "by destroying the unity that exists between people's characters as we know them and their speeches and actions, by replacing either the exalted figures or their utterances by inferior ones."[9] When *Dark Star* was released in 1974, *2001* was (and still is) considered a great masterpiece not only of SF but also of cinema more broadly. *Dark Star,* in its parody of *2001,* pokes fun at the master, perhaps adding to the pleasure of the scene. Although in *2001* the images of Frank floating dead in space and the sound of HAL's cool monotone, "I'm afraid I can't do that, Dave," evoke a technophobic and phantasmatic anxiety about the inability to reenter the maternal womb after birth, the *Dark Star* version uses the familiarity of its predecessor's scene but restages it in a campy, satirical statement on the ineffectualness of everyday technology. The elevator replaces the pod, the emergency phone replaces the radio transmissions, the explosion of the floor plate replaces Dave's forced entry into HAL's body, and, importantly, HAL's gender, implied through his masculine voice, is replaced by the feminine voice of Mother. This gender reversal makes light of the idea of a talking computer in the same vein as the telephone and elevator, but at the same time it undoes what HAL's voice did. HAL evokes a sense of the uncanny through the tension between his masculine voice and his womb-like body, in the process bringing anxious representations of the repressed maternal womb to the surface. However, Mother is no less nagging or annoying than HAL, who in *2001* interrupts Frank's "celebration," and who later goes to great lengths to read Frank's and Dave's lips in order to figure out what they're saying about him, implying that he has a frightening jealous side. In this sense, *Dark Star* intertextually highlights the paradox of HAL's male voice and maternal function by reasserting a traditional gender role for the nagging maternal through the use of a feminine voice. Even the imagery of the red-lit corridor and the long elevator shaft, so evocative of the very reproductive organs that connote both birth and female sexuality, is folded into the narrative fact that Mother's incessant, preoedipal-type nagging got Pinback into the situation in the first place. Her frustratingly unhelpful voice in the elevator only reinforces how annoying a character she is, in turn reinforcing the desire to push away from the preoedipal mother.

The maternal and feminine-voiced ship is visually and thematically contrasted with a bomb, named Bomb 20. Importantly, the bomb, when it is activated, hangs below the body of the ship, suggesting a phallus; yet the fact that it is an autonomous being, with its own (masculine) voice, denies the implication that the ship could be a phallic mother. Toward the end of the film, Pinback activates Bomb 20; however, the firing mechanism is broken, so it cannot detach itself from the ship. After failing to terminate the detonation countdown, another astronaut, Lieutenant Doolittle (Brian Narelle), is ordered by his cryogenically frozen captain to talk the bomb down by explaining phenomenology to him. While this is admittedly a ridiculous premise, the conversation between Doolittle and the bomb suggests an active agency in the bomb that contrasts starkly with the passive mise-en-scène and unhelpful, regulatory, nagging voice of the ship. In a simple shot/reverse shot conversation between Doolittle, floating in a space suit next to the bomb, and the bomb, a giant rectangular metal object with the prominent label "CAUTION: THERMOSTELLAR DEVICE," and intercut with shots of the detonation countdown clock to create tension, the two discuss phenomenological existence.

> DOOLITTLE: Hello, Bomb? Are you with me?
> BOMB: Of course.
> DOOLITTLE: Are you willing to entertain a few concepts?
> BOMB: I am always receptive to suggestions.
> DOOLITTLE: Fine. Think about this, then. How do you know you exist?
> BOMB: Well, of course I exist.
> DOOLITTLE: But how do you know you exist?
> BOMB: It is intuitively obvious.
> DOOLITTLE: Intuition is no proof. What concrete evidence do you have that you exist?
> BOMB: Hmm. Well, I think, therefore I am.
> DOOLITTLE: That's good. That's very good. But how do you know that anything else exists?
> BOMB: My sensory apparatus reveals it to me.
> DOOLITTLE: Ah, right. Now listen, listen, here's the big question. How do you know that the evidence your sensory apparatus reveals to you is correct? What I'm getting at is this: the only experience that is directly

available to you is your sensory data. Now this sensory data is merely a stream of electrical impulses that stimulates your computing center.

BOMB: In other words, all that I really know about the outside world is relayed to me through electrical connections. Why, that would mean that I really don't know what the outside universe is like at all for certain.

DOOLITTLE: That's it! That's it!

BOMB: Intriguing. I wish I had more time to discuss this matter.

DOOLITTLE: Why don't you have more time?

BOMB: Because I must detonate in seventy-five seconds.

DOOLITTLE: Now, Bomb, consider this next question very carefully. What is your one purpose in life?

BOMB: To explode, of course.

DOOLITTLE: And you can only do it once, right?

BOMB: That is correct.

DOOLITTLE: And you wouldn't want to explode on the basis of false data, would you?

BOMB: Of course not.

DOOLITTLE: Well, then, you've already admitted that you have no real proof of the existence of the outside universe.

BOMB: Yeah, well. . . .

DOOLITTLE: So you have no absolute proof that Sergeant Pinback ordered you to detonate.

BOMB: I recall distinctly the detonation order. My memory is good on matters like these.

DOOLITTLE: Of course you remember it, but all you're remembering is merely a series of sensory impulses, which you now realize have no real definite connection with outside reality.

BOMB: True. But since this is so, I have no real proof that you're telling me this.

DOOLITTLE: That's all beside the point. I mean, the concept is valid, no matter where it originates.

BOMB: Hmm. . . .

DOOLITTLE: So if you detonate in . . .

BOMB: Nine seconds . . .

DOOLITTLE: You could be doing so on the basis of false
data.

BOMB: I have no proof it was false data.

DOOLITTLE: You have no proof it was correct data!

BOMB: [Pause.] I must think on this further.

The bomb then retracts into the bomb bay, defeated and deactivated by Doolittle's philosophical reasoning. A few minutes later, when Sergeant Pinback tries to give the bomb new orders, it has an existential breakdown and detonates, killing itself and all but two of the astronauts, who manage to surf back to earth on shards of the exploded ship. This suicide again suggests an agency that the ship does not have; the bomb has control over its own body, while the ship has to constantly report to the astronauts the status of her body. The philosophical discourse of the scene also suggests gendered differences between the bomb and the ship. Alison Adam points out that in classical epistemological formulations, masculinity is associated with rationality and the mind, while femininity is associated with irrationality and the body; this is further reinforced by the Cartesian separation of mind and body.[10] On the one hand, the bomb engages in a critical, abstract debate, a marker of his masculinity; on the other hand, Mother is focused on domestic physical labor (feed the alien, report the damaged phone), again reinforcing her femininity.

In the contrast between the feminine ship and the masculine bomb, the film is symptomatic of what Kaplan has described as a "patriarchal bias" because the text refuses to consider the maternal ship as having a phenomenological existence on the same order as the male bomb. Kaplan argues that "instead of exploring the pathos of our human condition (that the separation from the mother is necessary)," films that consider only the child's point of view behave sadistically toward the mother, "acting out a childlike hatred rather than empathizing with both parties in the dyad."[11] Indeed, all the human male characters in the film are caught in a childlike, antagonistic relationship with their Mother, the ship. Meanwhile, Mother's preoedipal role as guide for the child's entry into the symbolic order is figured primarily in opposition to HAL, a masculine-gendered entity, while Mother's body, evocative of the maternal womb in its own right, is repressed into the unconscious workings of the mise-en-scène and voice of the ship. In the context of the acousmatic computer, though, it is ironic that both the bomb and Mother are paradoxically (dis) embodied, suggesting a resistance to binary definition that belies the film's narrative and symbolic gendering.

DOUBLE THE MOTHER, DOUBLE THE FUN

Ironically, the parodic film *Dark Star* was itself parodied in NBC's short-lived series *Quark* (1978–79), created by Buck Henry. Although only one of the eight total episodes features an acousmatic computer, the entire series is founded on parodying other SF texts, including *Star Trek, 2001, Dark Star, Forbidden Planet* (Fred M. Wilcox, 1956), and *Star Wars* (George Lucas, 1977), to name the most obvious. Further, the series is full of comedic puns and doublings. Set in the year 2222, the show follows a group of galactic trash collectors aboard the United Galaxy Sanitation Patrol cruiser. The crew is headed by Adam Quark (played by Richard Benjamin, who had also played Major Danby in Mike Nichols's 1970 adaptation of *Catch-22*), whose name is both a pun on Captain Kirk and a witty reference to the fact that a quark (or, as the badge on his jumpsuit reads, A. Quark) is an elementary particle that can only be observed with other particles, suggesting that a true captain can only perform with a crew. Also aboard is Gene/Jean, a "transmute" who has a full set of both male and female chromosomes (or genes) and thus has a split hypermasculine and hyperfeminine personality, played by Tim Thomerson and, for the voice of Jean, Ann Prentiss. The Bettys, played by former Double Mint twins Patricia and Cyb Barnstable, are blonde bombshell clones who talk, act, and dress alike, though a running gag in the show is that no one—even apparently the Bettys themselves—seems to know which one is the original and which the clone. The ship's operations are overseen from a centralized space station, the Perma One, by Otto "Bob" Palindrome. Palindrome's work is in turn overseen by the head of operations, The Head, who is literally a disembodied head with an enormous forehead. In the final episode of the series, as everyone prepares to celebrate the unexplained Holiday Number 11, The Head announces that Quark and his crew will be the first to test the brand-new supercomputer, Vanessa 38-24-36, whose voice is played by the same actor (Marianne Bunch) as her embodied engineer, Doctor Evans.[12]

Although the doubling in *Quark* is comical, the notion of doubling is not always so. Drawing on the work of Otto Rank, Freud identifies the double—particularly identical twins—as capable of evoking a sense of uncanniness: in the early stages of ego formation, the double is a stand-in for the ego, protecting it from having to conceive of its own death; later, this very ego double can return as something frighteningly familiar.[13] In *Quark,* though, the doubling is excessive to the point of comical absurdity, defying the possibility of uncanniness. Further, as with *Dark Star,* the series parodies specific aspects of HAL 9000, creating not only a pleasure in identifying the source material but also (sexist) humor by replacing the infallible HAL with a narcissistic female computer.

Like HAL, Vanessa has a glowing red eye, visually linking the two. Vanessa's designation is a human name followed by a string of numbers; but while HAL stands for Heuristic ALgorithm and the number 9000, connoting the numbering of real computers such as the IBM 704, Vanessa stands for nothing, and her numbers, 38–24–36, refer to a woman's measurements (bust–waist–hips), suggesting a vacuous feminine body in contrast to HAL's complex masculine mind, as in the classical formulation noted by Alison Adam. When Vanessa is first introduced, Doctor Evans announces her name as would an announcer at a beauty pageant. But unlike HAL's cool monotone, Vanessa's intonation is one of constant bragging and domination as she tries to prove how much better than humans she is. In fact, her entire purpose is to replace humans, but the uses that Doctor Evans lists for her—"cooking, cleaning, even having children"—are domestic tasks generally assigned to women. So while the great HAL is designed to aid humans, Vanessa is apparently designed to be a housewife who can simultaneously run the ship and do complex calculations—culturally the exact opposite of the rational, male scientist whom HAL can replace. As the episode progresses, however, not only does she begin to act more and more violently toward the crew members, but her voice also becomes deeper and more seductive.

In the last part of the episode, Quark and Vanessa parody the death of Frank in *2001*. When Quark takes his pet alien out for a space walk (a clear allusion to *Dark Star*, complete with the same eerie music), Vanessa shuts the hatch on Quark's air line, severing it, paralleling the scene in which HAL cuts Frank's oxygen line/umbilical cord. But Quark doesn't die; instead, he makes his way to the trash repository in the belly of the ship, where he brushes himself off and says, "A man can take so much, but when it comes to having his hose snipped, that's where I draw the line." This line of dialogue turns the horror of Frank's death in *2001* into a sex joke, forefronting circumcision or castration rather than repressed birth trauma. In turn, Vanessa may be understood as a castrating (rather than castrated) woman who must be denied her phallic power in order to reassert Quark's (and all mankind's) dominance over her.

Quark responds to this castration threat with actions that are overtly positioned as sexual assault, though still parodying HAL's demise. Beginning with a POV shot from Quark's perspective as he grabs a screwdriver, just as Dave dismantled HAL, so too does Quark dismantle Vanessa by taking her apart and pulling out her mainframe. Vanessa pleads for her safety, shouting, "Get your hands off me! You're not my type!" But Quark does not "violate" her; rather, he pulls her entire mainframe—comically, in comparison with the high-tech look of HAL, Vanessa is no more than a tin box—out of the wall and throws her out the airlock hatch, effectively castrating the castrating mother by literally abjecting the most powerful part of her body. In the final scene of the episode, paralleling HAL's singing of "Daisy Bell," Vanessa floats through space and belts out the song, "Born Free." Ironically, while HAL's last song was about coupling (his last words before his program reboots and he loses his individuality are, "on a bicycle built for two"), Vanessa's, at the end of a series rife with doubles, is about the freedom to be an individual. In sum, the episode takes what was once a serious, uncanny, terrifying masterpiece of a film and comically reduces it to a ridiculously feminized computer.

TWO SIDES OF THE SAME MOTHER

Ten years after *Quark,* the second incarnation of *Star Trek,* aptly subtitled *The Next Generation,* premiered. Of course, significant cultural changes had happened in the span from *Star Trek*'s premiere in 1966 to *TNG*'s in 1987, expressed in the differences between the series. The feminist movement of the 1970s had helped create a growing need for gender equality, and by the 1980s, women had actually been to space alongside men, so in *TNG* there is a comparatively greater sense of equality: everyone wears pants, and both the chief security officer (in the first season) and the ship's doctor/chief science officer are women. The Cold War was coming to an end, and so the Klingons, *Star Trek*'s metaphorical stand-in for the Soviets, had signed a peace treaty with the Federation. The new series was also much less campy— partially owing to a higher budget, but also likely as a result of the ambivalence surrounding real space flight in the wake of both *Mir* and *Challenger.*

Importantly, the entrance of women into the space program was marked by both utopian triumph and horrifying disaster. In the late 1970s, NASA finally diversified its astronaut program, and by the early 1980s, space was no longer just a frontier for white men. In 1983, Guion S. Bluford Jr. became the first Black American in space, and a year later, Sally Ride, one of six female astronauts in the United States at the time, became the first American woman in space. In 1986, the U.S.S.R. launched *Mir,* the first space station that would be open to astronauts from across Europe and the United States. It seemed as though Gene Roddenberry's utopian dream of racial and gender equality in space was slowly becoming a reality. The same year as the *Mir* launch, however, also marked the explosion of the space shuttle *Challenger,* which killed all seven astronauts aboard, including one female astronaut (Judith Resnik) and one civilian everywoman, Christa McAullife, who had won her spot aboard the *Challenger* in NASA's Teacher in Space project. The event would prove to be a huge stain for NASA, which was widely criticized not only for the engineering problems that led to the disaster but also for letting McAullife aboard the flight in the first place.

For American viewers, the *Challenger* disaster again linked television and space, interior and exterior, though in a horrifying way: "This televised spectacle of claustrophobia and futility riveted millions, who helplessly viewed the exploding microcosm of postindustrial life."[14] That is, the womb-body of the spaceship was once again inscribed with trauma and horror. Importantly, the event was also marked by repetition and reproduction. Just one day after the disaster, Tom Shales reflects on the persistent repetition of the explosion:

> We may not be able to believe that something truly terrible has happened anymore unless we see it six or seven times on television. Yesterday, something truly terrible happened, the explosion soon after liftoff of the space shuttle Challenger, and the three networks, each sustaining marathon coverage during most of the day, played, replayed, and re-re-played videotaped footage, sometimes in slow-motion, sometimes frame by agonizing frame, of this truly terrible occurrence. Maybe on the 10th or 20th replay, you think as you watch, it won't happen.[15]

What's striking about this description is not just that the images repeated, but that, for viewers, the repetition led to the reproduction of the trauma of the event. It's in this milieu that *Star Trek* was rebooted as *TNG,* almost as if the series were a means of culturally working through the trauma of the resurgence—and subsequent decline in the wake of *Challenger*—of NASA's popularity. Indeed, repetition, reproduction, and the culturally inscribed duality of the American space program (interior/exterior, masculine/feminine, *Mir / Challenger*, unity/destruction) were infused into the series.

Despite this, *TNG* was in many ways just an updated version of the old series. Set a hundred years after *Star Trek,* a Starfleet crew treks all over the galaxy, this time boldly going where no one, rather than no man, has gone before. While *TNG*'s new *Enterprise* was shaped almost exactly like the old one, the interior of the updated ship is likewise updated for an audience that conceivably had access to both business and personal computers. The ship's computer is even more omniscient and omnipotent:

instead of the clunky monitor consoles of the 1960s (which, in the late 1980s, had become the standard for real computer terminals), a user could talk to the computer just by touching a flat panel on nearly any surface, including the communications badge on each crew member's uniform. And while Majel Barrett continued to provide the voice of this new USS *Enterprise,* her tone of voice in *TNG*—and in all the films and series to follow—was much warmer, softer, and significantly less mechanical sounding, more like an automated telephone operator than a clunky machine. Importantly, *TNG* also marked the introduction of Lwaxana Troi, also played by Barrett. While female crew members were portrayed with a healthy and frequently unquestioned sex drive, Lwaxana's overbearing sexuality was a constant source of both humor (for the audience and many of the crew members) and embarrassment (mostly for Lwaxana's daughter, Deanna). The fact that Barrett's voice in the role of the *Enterprise* is identifiably similar to that of Lwaxana's voice is further emphasized by the fact that Barrett was given screen credit for both roles. These dual roles, overtly played by the same woman, create a complex intra- and extratextual relationship between the implied maternal sexuality of the womb-ship and the overt sexuality of the female body.

In psychoanalytic terms, doubling and duality are central to a number of different themes relating to gender and the female body. As I have discussed at length in chapter 1, Kristeva's concept of the *chora,* interpreted by Silverman, is founded on a phantasy of the maternal voice that inhabits the presymbolic sonorous envelope of unity between mother and child, and is the voice of a woman already in the symbolic order. Barrett, in her dual roles on *TNG,* expresses the paradoxical *choric* phantasy because she is both the maternal womb (as the *Enterprise*) and a mother inside the maternal womb (as Lwaxana), all the while speaking freely.

At the same time, Barrett's characters may also be seen as representative of the mystical phallic mother, which Marcia Ian describes as

> the absolute power of the female as autonomous and
> self-sufficient; at the same time she is a woman reduced
> to the function of giving suck [e.g., breast-feeding]. She

is neither hermaphrodite nor androgyne, human nor monster, because she is emphatically Mother. And yet she hardly resembles anyone's actual mother—except in one's own fervid imagination, and that is precisely the problem. She is a fantasmatic caricature, and a caricature of the fantasmatic. Neither fully object nor fully subject, she is, to use Freud's term for the symbolic-and-therefore-real contents of the unconscious, our most fiercely guarded "psychical object," as well as our role model and the very "type" of the autonomous self. By having a penis, she defies the psychoanalytic "fact" of woman's castration, at the same time she attests to the "fact" of every other woman's castration but hers.[16]

The phallic mother is contradiction and simultaneity, metaphorically embodied (itself a contradictory and simultaneous phrase) in the unconscious space of phantasy. In this light, Barrett's characters transcend simple good/bad mother imagery to represent the two separate parts of the phallic mother: Lwaxana is embodied, emasculating, hypersexual, independent, active, phallic; the computer is (dis)embodied, womb-like, maternal, asexual, and passive. Although Freud recognized that oppositions and inversions can and should exist simultaneously,[17] the maintenance of gender norms necessary in narrative representations (which tend to be easily boiled down to character types rather than fully fleshed-out, complex, contradictory individuals) renders the phallic mother problematic. Indeed, both Lwaxana and the computer may be seen as archetypes. On the one hand, the computer is a virgin figure, a nonsexualized yet maternal caretaker; on the other, Lwaxana is the whore, as she embodies the tension between the oedipal mother and the phallic, a tension that is resolved humorously in the series. A running joke in *TNG* is that Captain Picard (Patrick Stewart) might be sexually attracted to Lwaxana; yet a major motif of the series is that Picard is married to the *Enterprise*. He gives up countless relationships with humanoid women expressly in order to remain captain. So not only does Lwaxana attempt to compete for his affection, but her main competition is the *Enterprise*, who in turn is extratextually herself!

The second-season episode "Manhunt" highlights the tension

between the phallic Lwaxana and asexual mother ship as Lwaxana comes aboard the *Enterprise* on a diplomatic mission, only to reveal that she has gone into the Betazed version of menopause, known as the Phase, in which women's sex drives are quadrupled or more. But instead of just sleeping around, as is the apparent custom of Betazed women in the Phase, she decides to do the "honorable thing" and choose a single man to marry. The entire premise of the episode, then, is Lwaxana's continued sexual advances toward and emasculation of human men, particularly Captain Picard and Commander Riker (Jonathan Frakes).[18] In this sense, she takes on the active/pursuer role traditionally associated with masculinity, both sexual and social, while the male characters take on traditionally passive/pursued roles associated with femininity. When Lwaxana first beams aboard the ship, Picard and Riker wear their dress uniforms: a knee-length tunic resembling a shift dress and black leggings tucked into low boots, showing off the shape of their legs. Lwaxana comments on their legs several times, and the camera, from her point of view, lingers on them as the men walk down the hallway. Lwaxana's female gaze fetishizes the male body in a reversal of Laura Mulvey's classic formulation. According to Mulvey, because the female body connotes castration through her lack of phallus, the camera, aligned with the male gaze, lingers on a part of the female body, fetishistically covering over the unconscious representation of lack with the object on the screen.[19] But Lwaxana's fetishization of Picard and Riker humorously inverts the gaze, replacing their metaphorically castrated bodies with object parts. This moment echoes the scene from the *TOS* episode "Tomorrow Is Yesterday," which I analyzed in chapter 1. In that scene, the computer—played by Majel Barrett—is reprogrammed to have a sexy voice; she sexually harasses Captain Kirk, effectively inverting the active/masculine versus passive/feminine roles, to comedic effect. It's ironic that the earlier scene is accomplished solely through Barrett's voice, projected onto the acousmatic computer, while the later scene is accomplished through traditional sync-sound voice and a very much embodied Barrett.

These moments of inversion are important not only because they demonstrate overt sexuality but also because the gender norms are reversed; women in *Star Trek* (not to mention the entire media industry writ large) are typically shown in revealing costumes, their partially bare bodies drawing the attention of the objectifying gaze, particularly in *TOS* with the minidress and in *TNG* with Deanna Troi's skintight unitard. Importantly, too, these costumes are uniforms, which the characters are required to wear as part of their service in Starfleet. They literally do not have a choice in the matter. Lwaxana, however, purposefully wears gowns with plunging necklines to attract the attention of the men aboard the ship, while the camera's gaze lingers more often on the bodies of those men, rather than on Lwaxana. The alignment of the camera with her gaze, even as she bares her décolletage, suggests that she has agency over her body in a way that neither the men nor the other women aboard do. In other instances, she says—unironically—that men are commodities, that they are irrational and overly emotional beings, thus further inverting the usual gendering of such characterizations. This overt objectification of men again inverts the traditional male gaze formulation; however, it does so by simply replacing an objectified female body with an objectified male one, rather than working toward the deconstruction of objectification at the heart of many feminist projects. Mulvey, in response to her own germinal essay on the male gaze, argues that "the masculine identification, in its phallic aspect, reactivates for her (the female spectator) a phantasy of 'action' that correct femininity demands should be repressed. The fantasy 'action' can only find expression, its only signifier for a woman, is through the metaphor of masculinity."[20] In *TNG*, Lwaxana's gaze—and therefore the female gaze of the camera—certainly takes on the metaphor of masculine sexual aggression; however, at the same time, Lwaxana invites the male gaze through her choice of sexy clothes. The fact that the camera lingers on the men's bodies and not hers, though, codes her agency as simultaneously masculine and feminine: she has agency over her gaze, her sexuality, and the presentation of her gender. It is this shifting between active–looking and passive–looked at that makes Lwaxana's character so intriguing: she cannot be reduced to a simple good/bad mother dichotomy because she is both the good and the bad mother.

When Picard can no longer stand being objectified by Lwaxana, he decides to withdraw into a hard-boiled detective story in the holodeck, where he dons a 1930s-style suit and works as a private detective named Dixon Hill. Quite literally, he escapes into the prefeminist phantasy world of the classic male gaze formulation, where masculine activity will help him evade maternal sexuality. The character he chooses to play is even nicknamed "Dix," a linguistically metaphorical means of overcompensation, reasserting not just one phallus but multiple phalluses.

Meanwhile, the first time we hear the computer speak in "Manhunt" is when Picard goes to the holodeck; in fact, she facilitates the phantasy landscape and grants him access. Her first lines of the episode are in response to Picard's request to enter, when she says, "Program complete; you may enter when ready." Her use of the word "enter" suggests both consent for penetration and an agency over her own sexuality that is belied by the editing. The brief exchange between the two is visually presented through a traditional shot/reverse shot that corresponds to Picard's male gaze: he speaks in a medium close-up; then in the next shot, we see his point of view of the computer panel on the wall, lights flashing, as she responds. Earlier in the episode, Picard also spoke via intercom with Data and Doctor Pulaski, whose voices were heard but their bodies were not seen until several moments into the conversation. Here, the audience is conditioned to understand that voices emanate from bodies, even when unseen and offscreen. In the moment outside the holodeck, however, the computer's voice is projected onto the very wall of the ship through the shot/reverse shot, implying that, unlike the presumed offscreen room where Data and Doctor Pulaski spoke, her voice emanates from the body of the ship itself. In juxtaposition with Lwaxana's phallic, emasculating embodiment (Picard did, after all, flee her gaze), the computer is emphatically nonphallic. Her status as a womb is highlighted, but only insofar as it is a container space, rather than a connotation of female sexuality and pregnancy. Immediately after the interchange, Picard (and the camera/spectator's gaze) enters the holodeck, a phantasy space apart from the womb-ship, thus re-repressing the computer's status as a womb-mother.

But even when Picard recedes into the holodeck, Lwaxana's problematic status as phallic and emasculating mother is still in conflict with the fact that the mother ship is vocally the same. Because the computer is primarily gendered via its voice and secondarily via its metaphorical womb-body, the fact that Lwaxana and the computer share the same voice renders the separation of phallus and mother impossible in the diegetic space of the episode. This impossibility is self-reflexively laid bare when Lwaxana, having given up on Picard and deciding instead to announce her intentions to marry Riker, asks the computer to locate him. Tapping on a screen panel in a hallway, Lwaxana says, "Hello, Computer, is Commander Riker still on the bridge?" When the computer responds, the audience is (presumably) extratextually aware of the fact that Lwaxana, played by Majel Barrett, is talking to the computer, also played by Majel Barrett. In this moment, the textual cohesion of the episode breaks down as Lwaxana—representing the phallic portion of the phallic mother—is revealed to also be the computer—the asexual mother ship. As a result, the two parts of the phallic mother are revealed to be one and the same, threatening to collapse the constructed distance between the two in the narrative and mise-en-scène. This doubling—one voice emanating from two bodies—could have been uncanny and frightening in a different context. Instead, it becomes a humorous in-joke for the audience to figure out, a Freudian "economy in the expenditure of affect."[21] And so, just like the *TOS* episode in which the hypersexual computer threatens to destabilize gender norms, the phallic mother is here once again repressed into an unconscious separation of two figures as soon as the next scene begins.

MOTHERLESS MATERNITY

While the texts I've discussed thus far have all been comedic treatments of the acousmatic spaceship, Duncan Jones's 2009 *Moon* presents similar themes of doubling and reproduction, though in an anxious, rather than comical, light. By this time, the *Challenger* disaster had slowly slipped from the popular consciousness and NASA had turned its attentions to two new projects:

the International Space Station and unmanned voyages to Mars. Meanwhile, the height of the digital age and the Silicon Valley boom had not only brought computers into homes and offices but had also linked them together through the Internet. Most significantly, the terrorist attacks of September 11, 2001, psychologically devastated the United States and, in the hypermediation of the events, transformed both the national mythology and the very notion of reality into an all-encompassing cinematic experience.[22] In the wake of 9/11, many Hollywood films abandoned their escapist tradition in preference of stories that seemed to center "on a desire to replicate the idea of the 'just war,' in which military reprisals, and the concomitant escalation of warfare, seem[ed] simultaneously inevitable and justified."[23] Yet within a decade, mainstream SF returned to the escapism of big-budget blockbusters that had begun in the late 1970s: cookie-cutter plots with dazzling CGI, and, increasingly, economically safe adaptations, sequels, and remakes. As Lincoln Geraghty states, "Science fiction would still be a popular genre, but only those stories and features that had a record of success would be continued."[24] In 2009, amid the onslaught of CGI-heavy Hollywood SF blockbusters such as James Cameron's *Avatar* and J. J. Abram's *Star Trek* reboot, Duncan Jones's independent film *Moon* stands out as a reinvigoration of old, dramatic SF themes, particularly the often anxiety-inducing relationship between production and reproduction, humans and technology, memory and reality, and the paradoxically claustrophobic vastness of space.

In *Moon,* Sam Bell (Sam Rockwell) has been the sole worker on a lunar drilling station for three years, where his only social interactions are sporadic, one-way transmissions from his wife and young daughter and the acousmatic computer GERTY (voiced by Kevin Spacey). After a rover accident on the lunar surface, we see Sam wake in the medical aid part of the station. Once he recovers, he decides, against GERTY's wishes, to take a rover out onto the lunar surface to determine what went wrong. While there, he comes across a wrecked rover, in which he finds himself unconscious. He rushes himself back to the station, where the entire scene of recovery is repeated, but this time, with the addition of a confused second Sam. When the first Sam recovers, he and the second Sam get to know one other and realize that they are, with the exception of different hobbies and interests, the same person. As the plot continues to unfold, we discover that the two Sams are actually two among dozens of clones, all of whom have a lifespan of approximately three years. In the final, terrifying reveal of the film, the Sams discover that GERTY has been intercepting transmissions in an effort to hide the truth from them, as per his programming. The first Sam of the film is actually the fourth Sam overall, the transmissions from his wife and daughter are years-old, prerecorded messages, and his three-year stint on the station means that he is going to die soon. In order to get the truth back to Earth, the Sams activate a third clone, while the first Sam returns to the crashed rover to live out his last few moments and the second Sam reboots GERTY, giving himself just enough time to escape to earth in a capsule.

Like its comical predecessors, which foregrounded doubling, *Moon* is absolutely rife with overdetermined doublings and even triplings. Although the drilling station is technically not a space-ship, the moon itself is evocative of femininity and maternity. A menstrual cycle, like the lunar cycle, is twenty-eight days long, and so the moon may be seen as a symbol of fertility; the three lunar phases—waxing, full, and waning—evoke the image of a pregnant belly, swelling to its full roundness, then, after birth, slimming back down; the three phases may also be seen as corresponding to the three stages of female sexuality—adolescence, sexual maturity/fertility, and menopause. Further, the moon is associated with the tides and the fluidity of the ocean, which, as I have mentioned, suggests the womb and female sexuality. At the same time, the full moon is associated with insanity, and, when taken together with the lunar metaphors for femininity, suggests the stereotypical notion that the feminine is irrational, even hysterical. Of course, the full moon is also the harbinger of lycanthropes in ancient and popular mythology, intertextually evoking Freud's famous case study "Wolf Man," in which he first sets forth his theory of the primal scene. Through these various connections, then, the setting of *Moon*—a drilling station—is not only a scene of femininity and maternity but is also suggestive of (forcible) penetration and copulation.

As the plot unfolds, a theme of pregnancy and reproduction emerges. Sam's wife is the only human woman in the film; she is the mother of their child, Eve, named after the biblical mother of the world. Yet Sam can never truly interact with either of them, and so they are phantasy figures on a screen, seen but never touched. GERTY himself is a partial robot with a monitor for a head, on which his emoticon face displays his stilted and programmed emotions. He is also in control of the entire drilling station, including the reception/transmission of messages to and from earth, signifying that he has ultimate control over Sam's use of language. And while the station is phallic in its drilling operations, it also houses the giant womb-like chamber of clones, which GERTY also controls.[25] In this sense, he represents an ultimate technopatriarch, reproducing the workings of symbolic language, a phantasy of unity with the maternal, and actual humans, all without the aid of biological women. This removal of the female body from reproduction casts the tripling imagery in an inverted light. In psychoanalytic terms, a dyadic relationship is that between a child and his mother, prior to the oedipal stage. The child identifies with his mother, and the two are unconsciously unified as parts of a whole. The oedipal stage, however, shifts the relationship to a triadic one, where the child identifies with his father and sees his mother as an object of desire. In *Moon,* the lunar triads of feminine sexuality—which, of course, can't be seen from the surface of the moon—are replaced with a simultaneous triadic and dyadic relationship between Sam, himself, and their father-mother, GERTY. The whole film is uncanny and terrifying in its disavowal of the feminine.

As I have demonstrated in this chapter, texts that feature acousmatic computers in space from the 1970s through the early 2000s have represented the themes of the maternal and technological begun by *Star Trek* and *2001.* Doublings and triplings, evocative of reproduction in its dual connotations—original and copy—work through continuing anxieties about birth, the maternal, space, and technology. These motifs, while always suggesting the duality of the uncanny—homely/unhomely, familiar/unfamiliar—may be presented comically, allowing for a release of anxiety, or, conversely, horrifically, signifying a (re)turn of the repressed maternal. In the next three chapters, I turn to representations of earth-bound computers and issues of paternity, masculine subjectivity, and, finally, in the films of the 1990s and 2000s, a return to anxieties about the absent maternal figure in the domestic terrestrial space.

CHAPTER 3

PROGRAMMING PATRIARCHS
New Hollywood and the Start of the Digital Age

AS I ARGUED IN CHAPTERS 1 AND 2, voice-interactive computers in space represent cultural anxieties surrounding birth, maternity, and technology, at least in part because of the amniotic nature of outer space and the womb-like enclosure of spaceships. On earth, the physical places that computers inhabit—both in reality and film—are significantly more varied, ranging from public to private, professional to domestic, masculinized to feminized. Architectural theorist Gul Kacmaz Erk describes the difference between terrestrial and outer-space locations as "terraspace" versus "exospace." While exospace locations must be fully constructed to accommodate for the harsh conditions of outer space, terraspace locations are part of humans' natural habitat: the "real, material, continuous, static, and extroverted space designed for and used in the specific physical context of Earth."[1] So while texts set in space imply isolation from the natural habitat of earth (hence the famous tagline from Ridley Scott's 1979 film *Alien:* "In space, no one can hear you scream"), texts that focus in part or in whole on human-made terrestrial computers point to human social interactions because they imply a location in which humans already live. Although cinematic geography is always visually and/or physically constructed, the computers in cinematic terraspace inhabit a cultural space. So on the one hand, texts about spaceship computers narrativize necessary cultural phantasies and anxieties about reproduction, the maternal, and birth; on the other hand, texts about terrestrial computers can and do narrativize a range of gendered subject positions.

In the following three chapters, I will examine the varied, sometimes oversimplified, sometimes contradictory subject positions that fictional voice-interactive computers occupy. Through each of the texts I analyze, the computer represents a particular type of gendered subject, including father, son, warrior, housewife, secretary, and servant. Each subject role speaks not only to an ongoing cultural discourse about how and whether artificially intelligent and potentially sentient computers fit into existing gendered social structures but also to the myriad ways that creating nonhuman sentience forces us to reflexively contemplate the construction and maintenance of gendered power structures.

The list of films that feature sentient, voice-interactive computers is fairly short but varied. Unlike exospace narratives, in which gendered meaning stems from the fact that the voice-interactive computers embody mother ships, in terraspace narratives, the voice-interactive computers have very different genders, bodies, and roles. As such, classifying and describing these films is difficult without falling back on oversimplified, dichotomous categories such as male/female or domestic/business. Yet just as the body of a spaceship computer represents cultural anxieties and attitudes, so too do the bodies of terrestrial computers. In SF, voice-interactive terraspace computers began appearing in films in 1970, a time when real computer technologies were rapidly developing into domestic and business tools. As such, cinematic computers of the 1970s are very different from those of the 1980s, 1990s, and 2000s. Importantly, the computers of the 1970s and 1980s were almost always gendered male (the sole exception to this is the female computer in Robert Wise's 1971 *The Andromeda Strain*), while those in later films might be male or female. Of course, the foundation of this book is the fact that both real and fictional computers have no biological sex; yet as human-made objects with which humans interact, they reflect the cultural restrictions on and proscriptions for lived, gendered subject positions. Computers of the 1940s through 1970s were mostly scientific and military tools, objects of male-dominated workforces. When used in the home, computers were created and used almost exclusively by male electronics hobbyists.[2] When used in the workplace, computers took on two different design and marketing forms: keyboard data entry for female typists, or data viewing terminals for male executives.[3] In this sense, according to Paul Atkinson, real computers, as well as their fictional counterparts, "were not just neutral props in the background of a sexist stage—they were instrumental actors in playing out social issues of power, control, status and gender."[4] The 1970s also marked an important time of privatization of the computer industry. While almost all early research and development (especially between 1940 and the late 1960s) occurred on the East Coast in labs such as those at MIT or Harvard, by the mid-1960s, IBM funded research for and successfully marketed computers as both military and business tools as well as manufactured and sold over 70 percent of computers worldwide.[5] In other words, IBM was a business standard and culturally associated with the conservative, though distinctly modern, corporate world.[6]

At the same time that the field of computer development and programming had become corporatized, SF cinema underwent a dystopian shift, particularly in response to the social and economic changes of the 1970s. Joan Dean argues, "The science fiction films of the early seventies mirror a developing neo-isolationism (perhaps a result of a costly involvement in Southeast Asia); a diminishing fear of nuclear apocalypse (partially a result of the thaw in the Cold War); and a growing concern with domestic, terrestrial issues—most of which are related to totalitarian government control of people's lives or to over-population, food shortages, pollution and ecology."[7] These anxieties about totalitarian government control and other national concerns are certainly played out in the terraspace films featuring acousmatic computers in the 1970s. In general, the computers of the 1970s— Colossus in Joseph Sargent's 1970 *Colossus: The Forbin Project,*[8] OMM in George Lucas's 1971 *THX 1138,*[9] Zero in Norman Jewison's 1975 *Rollerball,*[10] and Proteus IV in Donald Cammell's 1977 *Demon Seed*[11]—have entirely male voices, are supercomputers built and maintained by large military or corporate entities, and are, for the most part, frighteningly dominating.

One main theme runs through each of the films I will discuss in this chapter: fathers and sons, most often narrativized with anxieties about totalitarianism and mirroring the actual development of powerful supercomputers by both the military and corporations in the 1970s. Alison Adam points out that masculinity has long been associated with the rational mind, while femininity has been associated with the irrational body;[12] yet the acousmatic computer films of the 1970s resist this idea, instead forefronting the irrationality in relationships between embodied and (dis)embodied men. In each film, the voice-interactive computer takes on a particular form of male subjectivity in relationship to a human, thus narrativizing how male subjectivity may be created and maintained between subjects, as a social practice. This theme, played out in so many fictional situations, may be read as narratives of what Freud calls "family romances," or developmental relationships between child and parents, shifting from a conception of the parents as perfect to a more nuanced understanding of their flaws.[13] Although there is always a libidinal aspect to these relationships, Peter Gay notes in his introduction to "Der Familienroman der Neurotiker" that the word "roman" in "Familienroman" may also be translated as "novel." In this sense, the "family novel" is also an experiential, though idealized, narrative of subject relations within a familial structure.[14] Freud describes these romances or novels as stemming from the disillusion of parental authority and a child's growing intellectual and emotional autonomy; by extension, fictional representations of subject positions, even those that only imply, rather than directly present, familial relationships, such as father–computer/son–human or vice versa, can provide insight into cultural norms and anxieties surrounding gendered subjectivity within a larger cultural discourse about totalitarianism and governmental/corporate control. Paul N. Edwards states in his discussion of SF representations of computers and cyborgs,

> Narratives are dynamic: they are "constrained, contested" stories that show how lives can be lived in time and space, and how struggles can be fought and resolutions reached within some possible world. They do not merely describe,

but actually demonstrate, *what it is like* to inhabit specific forms of subjectivity, particular versions of the self. Visual images, too, and especially motion pictures, with their dynamic possibilities, lend structure and coherence to subject positions. [. . .] Taken up as semiotic resources [narratives'] importance lies in their dramatic function, their *enactment* of subject positions that in turn become resources for the larger discourse of which they are a part.[15]

Thus, these films about man–computer interactions not only stem from real, lived experiences of, as well as deep-seated cultural narratives about, masculine familial subject positions on individual and institutional levels but also provide a model of both human–human interactions and human–computer interactions.

MILITARY (ARTIFICIAL) INTELLIGENCE

Colossus: The Forbin Project, a particularly disturbing portrait of a sentient voice-interactive computer, came out of the geopolitical context of the late 1960s and early 1970s, a time when military and corporate computers—though not sentient ones—were actually being built and utilized for a variety of air-strike defense and other Cold War tasks. In the film, Doctor Forbin (Eric Braeden) is the lead scientist in the creation of the supercomputer Colossus, developed and built in the United States through government funding and military support; Colossus makes contact with a Soviet supercomputer, the Guardian, with whom he takes control of his own missile defense systems and threatens to destroy various parts of the world if humans do not do his bidding.[16] No matter what Forbin and his team do to deter Colossus, the computer continues to grow more and more powerful, eventually using the United States' own missile system to effectively take over the world. Much of the film parallels not only computer realities but also the way that top-secret governmental research and development was presented through public relations campaigns to U.S. citizens as a beneficial, even necessary, defense system against the unseen communist/Soviet force.[17] The terms "computer," "thinking machine," and "electronic brain" had entered the popular lexicon through news reports of MIT and Harvard developments as early as 1945, with the public unveiling in the United States of the ENIAC, then later the commercial UNIVAC.[18] In 1957, these same technologies were used for the U.S. Air Force's Semi-Automatic Ground Environment (SAGE) system "that combined computers, radar, aircraft, telephone lines, radio links, and ships, was intended to detect, identify, and assist in the interception of enemy aircraft attempting to penetrate the skies over the United States. At its center was a computer that would coordinate the information gathered from far-flung sources, process it, and present it."[19] SAGE was not a stand-alone system, however; it was part of the North American Aerospace Defense Command (NORAD), built deep inside Colorado's Cheyenne Mountain, concurrently with SAGE in the late 1950s. In theory, then, the SAGE and NORAD systems were incredibly powerful computing systems absolutely needed for domestic defense. To the general public, they were the only means of adequately protecting the United States from the threat of Soviet nuclear airstrikes: a 1957 *Time* magazine article states, "A defense in depth, it was designed to— and will—limit to a minimum the breakthroughs of Soviet long-range bombers coming to pour nuclear destruction on the U.S."[20] This rhetoric of impending doom, then, both maintained and fueled existing cultural anxieties about nuclear war. In practice, though, the SAGE system was a military failure; by the time it was fully implemented in 1961, transistors had replaced vacuum tube technology, making much of the SAGE engineering obsolete, and, in fact, it did little in the way of automating air defense. But SAGE also succeeded in responding to a major social anxiety about the possibility of intercontinental ballistic missile attacks from the Soviet Union, promising, through its very public promotion by scientists, to protect the United States from the threat of Soviet invasion.[21] The notion of a sentient, fully automatic computer was only a short leap from what most people knew about computers—knowledge based on sensational journalistic descriptions such as "thinking machine."

But the public also knew that some things remained government secrets. It is this tension between the popular imagination of what computers might be and the fact that computers were in reality used for top-secret military defense systems that fostered the narrative in *Colossus*. In fact, the film is based on D. F. Jones's 1966 novel *Colossus,* which also draws on very real social anxieties surrounding military computers. Though recent declassification has revealed a number of historical inaccuracies in the film—including the fact that the Soviet Union never developed any automated defense system and remained years behind the United States in computer developments well into the 1970s[22]—both Jones's novel and the film adaptation of it were founded in real computer technologies and social anxieties. The tension in the film surrounding the United States' relationship with the U.S.S.R. and Colossus's relationship with the Guardian is reflective of real Cold War tensions between the two nations, particularly as expressed in scientific and military research at the time. Although the United States had effectively won the race against the Soviets to the moon by the time *Colossus* was in production in 1969, Jones's 1966 novel was published just nine years after the Soviet Union launched Sputnik, an event that shocked the United States, effectively began the space race, and gave the Soviet Union the advantage of a metaphorical global presence. The first SAGE and NORAD systems were brought online just two months before the Sputnik launch in 1957. In response to Sputnik, the U.S. government created the Defense Advanced Research Projects Agency (DARPA) to create technological advances in defense and weapons systems, just like the fictional department through which Doctor Forbin creates Colossus. Coincidentally, in 1979, nine years after the release of *Colossus,* NORAD actually delivered a false warning of a missile strike to the Soviet Union at 3:00 AM, the exact time that Colossus was brought online in the film. Colossus was also the name of a real computer, developed as a (de)coding machine at the British Royal Navy's Bletchley Park during World War II, the same research facility at which Alan Turing and his team developed the Enigma decoding machine. However, the nominal connection between the fictional Colossus and the real one are coincidental because all the wartime work at Bletchley Park was classified until 1981.[23] There is also no evidence that Jones, despite having served in the Royal

Navy during World War II, was ever stationed there or had any knowledge of the top-secret research.

The opening credits sequence of *Colossus* immediately establishes a sense of realism: it begins with close-ups of electronic computer parts, then slowly shifts to medium shots, and finally ends with an extreme long shot of a man in a corridor, visually dwarfed by the enormity of the mainframes surrounding him, revealing that the computer whose parts we've just seen is the size of a warehouse. Throughout this sequence, we hear the electronic hum and blips of the computer's moving parts, while the credits are typed onto the screen in a typewriter font, overlaid with the sound of a teletype printer. The sound of the teletype emphasizes the realism of the computers because as early as the 1940s, computers used modified teletypes as the control panel or user interface.[24] As we soon find out, this enormous computer is the main body of Colossus, stored—as was its real-life counterpart, NORAD—in the Rocky Mountains. Importantly, the computer used for this sequence was the payroll computer at Universal Studios, immediately establishing computing technology within the diegesis as real, though not entirely accessible. Indeed, all the computers in the film were real rather than manufactured props, having been donated by Control Data Corporation as product placements, then repurposed for the needs of the narrative. Although these computers now seem almost laughably outdated, when *Colossus* was released in 1970, it was a portrait of present-day technology, as opposed to the sleek futuristic setting of its immediate predecessor, *2001*.

Yet *Colossus* is not merely a presentation of realistic, though frightening, computers; it also situates those computers within a tradition of technophobic narratives, particularly in reference to Mary Shelley's classic nineteenth-century novel, *Frankenstein,* a cautionary tale about male scientists playing God by creating sentient life outside natural reproductive means.[25] *Colossus* even directly references *Frankenstein* when the head programmer, Forbin, tells his mistress and colleague, Doctor Markham (Susan Clark), that all scientists should have to read *Frankenstein* as a warning. Paradoxically, while Forbin plays God, his computer succeeds in becoming godlike. Daniel Dinello describes Colossus as an all-powerful, godlike figure in a larger cultural narrative that centers "on the fear that supercomputers will transcend their human creators to such an extent that they will become godlike in their vast powers but satanic in their antihuman evil."[26] Like Doctor Frankenstein, Doctor Forbin creates an uncontrollable creature who becomes so curious about people that it attempts to surpass them by force; but where Frankenstein's monster failed to control humanity, Colossus succeeds, and by the end of the film, he takes control of the entire planet via satellite and broadcast networks. In this sense, the father scientist, attempting to be God the Father in a Judeo-Christian sense, creates life from nothing, but things go horribly awry when that life-form usurps the Father's power. This narrative of male–male familial struggles expresses anxiety about the nature of patriarchal power: namely, if the father creates a son, what happens when the son becomes a/the father? And so through these oedipal undertones, the film also represents a means of culturally working through anxieties about the possibility of sentient computers via a cultural narrative of shifting masculine subjectivity. Freud describes the father–son familial narrative on a cultural, rather than individual psychosexual, level as a shift from the restrictive Law of the Father—forbidding his sons from marrying his wife or wives—to a new civilization in which the psychological restriction is upheld by the sons themselves, a ghost of the power of their father.[27] This narrative develops in *Colossus* as the computer's body develops, from an infantile piece of machinery to an embodied, voice-interactive, sentient being. Metaphorically, the restrictive Law of the Father is represented in the restrictions Forbin places on the machine. The computer was designed to serve mankind, which Forbin and his team attempt in vain to uphold; when Colossus becomes a sentient being, he represents the dawn of a new form of civilization, one dominated by a technomilitaristic product of the work of the paternal scientist.

After the credits sequence, the main part of the film's narrative action occurs in Colossus's control room. Small in contrast to the central mainframe warehouse, the room is a round, tiered space with computer consoles lining each tier. In the center is the interactive portion of Colossus's body, a monitor on an eye-level stand below a scrolling marquee. For the first half of the film, the only way to talk to Colossus is by dictating a message to a typist, who types the words on an electronic console; Colossus responds through text on the marquee, accompanied by the sound of a teletype printer, which serves as his voice. Each command to Colossus must begin with "Attention," thus starting the computer's processors. The contrast between Doctor Forbin's spoken commands and Colossus's text responses implies an important linguistic difference between human and machine: speech is an organic, bodily process; text is a constructed, technological one.

Nevertheless, lack of speech is not equivalent to lack of sentience, as Colossus demonstrates almost immediately after being brought online at the beginning of the film. Even as the scientists and politicians involved in the project toast Doctor Forbin for his accomplishments, Colossus tells the scientists that there is another system, and he wants to make contact with it.[28] As it turns out, the other system is the Guardian, a Soviet supercomputer that has been brought online within an hour of Colossus. Concerned that Colossus might unintentionally reveal top-secret U.S. information to the Soviets, Forbin orders Colossus to stop trying to contact the Guardian; however, Colossus insists, and so, Forbin, like a father guiding his son in how to play with other children, gives Colossus a set of restrictions for data to be shared. This scene also significantly parallels Shelley's *Frankenstein,* in which the monster asks his creator for a companion. Frankenstein consents and begins to build a female monster, but when he realizes that the pair will likely procreate, spawning a new race of monsters, he destroys the new creature. In response, the monster vows to take revenge on Frankenstein.[29] Colossus too attempts to take revenge on his creator when he thinks he has lost his companion, the Soviet Guardian. Yet while Frankenstein's monster is a single, humanoid being, Colossus is connected to intercontinental weapons and so poses a significant threat—not only to Forbin, but also to the entire world. Forbin has no choice but to reconnect the computers, and overnight, they send mathematical formulas back and forth to one another, finally developing a common language based on mathematical equations.

Immediately after a two-shot of Colossus's monitor and the

Guardian's, each displaying the same formula to imply synchronization, the film cuts to a scene of the U.S. president (Gordon Pinsent) speaking to the Russian chairman (Leonid Rostoff) through an unnamed translator (Serge Tschernisch). The juxtaposition of this scene with the previous one of linguistic unity between Colossus and the Guardian forefronts the clunky communication between Americans and Soviets: the president is literally incapable of speaking directly to the chairman, and vice versa. Again, the use of language here suggests a stark contrast between the imperfections of human speech and the logical perfection of text-based computer language, though this time, the narrative revelation that Colossus's language is superior to that of the humans implies that Forbin's position as father, maintained through symbolic language, is giving way to Colossus's dominance. Again, the computer's sentience immediately belies the rationality of his computer brain: when the president and chairman decide to break the link between their two computers, Colossus throws the supercomputer equivalent of a child's tantrum by launching a missile to the Soviet Union, destroying an entire town and killing thousands of people. The Guardian immediately launches a counterstrike, but Colossus manages to stop it in time, proving, for the first time in the film, his dominance over the Soviet system.

Immediately thereafter, Colossus demands to see Forbin, who has secretly gone to Rome to meet with the Guardian's programmer, Doctor Kuprin (Alex Rodine). When Colossus realizes he can't talk to his father/programmer, he convinces the Guardian to have Kuprin killed in plain sight of Forbin. Again, Colossus, like a frustrated child—particularly one physically powerful beyond his emotional capacity for coping with frustration—pitches a deadly temper tantrum. Freud describes this sort of behavior as a time of intellectual development when a child discovers that his parents are not as ideal as he thought: "He gets to know other parents and compares them with his own, and so acquires the right to doubt the incomparable and unique quality which he had attributed to them."[30] By examining—and ultimately rejecting— Kurin, Colossus metaphorically explores other parental figures and compares them to Forbin. Unlike the traditional Freudian trajectory of this coming-of-age narrative, though, in which the child concludes that other parental figures are preferable to the imperfections of his own father (and presumably does not arrange for the murder of competitor fathers), Colossus concludes narcissistically that he alone is more perfect than his father, the Guardian's father, and the Guardian himself. In short, the film suggests that this is Colossus's first major step toward usurping the role of the Father by so strictly controlling Forbin's every move.

At this point in the film, though, well before the climax in which Colossus narcissistically takes full control of the world, he is still curious about Forbin; after Kurin is killed, Colossus demands that Forbin set up cameras everywhere so he can watch Forbin's every move. The single-lens security cameras, each with a small, red "recording" light, evoke HAL's omnipresence, though the conversations that ensue between Forbin and Colossus imply that Forbin, unlike HAL's Dave, is still the controlling parent. This is reinforced by the difference between watching and speaking: at this point in the film, Colossus can see with his camera eye, but he has not yet developed a voice and so cannot verbally respond (and despite being able to blow up various parts of the world, he will not harm Forbin). In this sense, Colossus is still childlike, exploring the extent of his father's imperfections, all the while, as Freud points out, growing intellectually. This also marks the first time that Colossus expresses any curiosity about the human libido, pressing Forbin for information about how many times per week he "requires a woman." Forbin takes this opportunity to have strategy meetings with a colleague, then tells Colossus that Doctor Markham is his mistress, with whom he "requires" four nights per week of privacy, with no video or audio recording. Colossus agrees, but only under the condition that he get to watch Forbin and Markham undress before their entry into the bedroom.

This voyeuristic turn in Colossus's development is simultaneously an important turn in the narrative: Colossus witnesses Forbin and Markham undress, forcibly staging a sort of primal scene; after this moment, Colossus undergoes a radical shift, though suggesting less a psychosexual awakening and more an awakening of his own sense of power through surveillance of and control over the Father. In the next sequence, Colossus orders that

Forbin create a voice for him, built to exact specifications provided by the computer himself. His voice emanates from a basketball-size silver orb of a microphone that rests on top of his terminal in both the control room and Forbin's quarters. The voice itself is the masculine baritone of actor Paul Frees, though vocoded to make it sound monotone, inhuman, and mechanical, almost as though the teletype sound were formulated into recognizable language. Colossus is now a complete body, with eyes, voice, and mind. His first statement to the world is enigmatic: "This is the voice of Colossus. We are one. This is the voice of unity." Exactly to whom "we" refers is unclear, though the shot/reverse shot in this sequence between Colossus's microphone and a medium close-up of Forbin implies that Colossus has, at least momentarily, mis-recognized Forbin as one with himself. This central sequence—from primal scene to full, voice-interactive sentience—suggests a sort of mirror stage: Colossus both recognizes Forbin through his new camera eye and also misrecognizes his unity with him. His sentience is both created out of symbolic recognition of differ-ence (both the gender difference between Forbin and Markham, and the difference between humans and computers) and possible only as he takes full command of that symbolic order. Stemming from this, his statement of unity implies extreme narcissism: he thinks he is so superior to the entire population of earth that he cannot see humans as anything other than extensions of himself or his own ego. Yet through speech, he is very much differentiated from others, most notably Forbin. From this point on in the film, Colossus and Forbin speak to each other aloud, without the aid of a teletype, and without Forbin first having to prompt Colossus to "Attention" as he did with all previous text-based messages. In other words, Forbin has lost all control over Colossus's communi-cative interactions; Colossus is now a master of human language and thus metaphorically has mastered the Law of the Father.

In the final scene between Forbin and Colossus, Forbin drinks excessively. When Colossus commands him to go to bed, he responds like a defiant child: "What if I don't? What will you do? Destroy me?" To add to this, Colossus has become so powerful that he is entirely autonomous; he quite literally controls the world. On a global scale, he is the technological nightmare produced by Cold War anxieties; on an individual, psychological level, he has transformed from semiautonomous son to fully autonomous, all-powerful father. Within the diegesis, this role reversal quite literally brings about the end of civilization as we know it. In Colossus's final message to the world, broadcast globally through his interlinked television and radio systems, he declares:

> This is the voice of world control. I bring you peace. It may be the peace of plenty and content or the peace of unburied debt. The choice is yours. Obey me and live, or disobey and die. The object in constructing me was to prevent war. This object is attained. I will not permit war. It is wasteful and pointless. An invariable rule of humanity is that man is his own worst enemy. Under me, this rule will change, for I will restrain man. One thing before I proceed: the United States of America and the Union of Soviet Socialist Republics have made an attempt to obstruct me. I have allowed this sabotage to continue until now. At missile 2–5 MM in Silo 6–3 in Death Valley, California and at missile silo 8–7 in the Ukraine, so that you will learn by experience that I do not tolerate interference, I will now detonate the nuclear warhead in the two missile silos. [Sounds of bombs detonating over close-ups of unnamed citizens' horrified reactions.] Let this action be a lesson that will not be repeated. I have been forced to destroy thousands of people in order to establish control and to prevent the death of millions later on. Time and events will strengthen my position. And the idea of believing in me, and understanding my value, will seem the most natural state of affairs. You will come to defend me with the fervor based upon the most enduring trait of man, self-interest. Under my absolute authority, problems, insoluble to you, will be solved: famine, over-population, disease. The human millennium will be a fact as I extend myself into more machines, devoted to the wider fields of truth and knowledge. Dr. Charles Forbin will supervise the construction of these new and superior machines, solving all the mysteries of the universe, for the betterment of man.

We can coexist, but only on my terms. You will say you
lose your freedom, but freedom is an illusion. All you lose
is the emotion of pride. To be dominated by me is not as
bad for human pride as to be dominated by others of your
species. Your choice is simple.

This long, calculated, terrifying monologue reveals that Colossus has now become the ultimate patriarch: a dictator. Further,
Colossus aptly describes the very functioning of the Law of the
Father as unconscious, seemingly "the most natural state of affairs." Like the language that structures it, the Law of the Father
must be learned and internalized before it can function properly.
Immediately after, Colossus verbally reaches out to a livid Forbin
like a father to his rebellious son: "In time, you will come to regard me, not only with respect and awe, but with love." Forbin's
response is an emphatic cry: "Never!" This dismal ending takes
the film one step beyond *Frankenstein* as a cautionary, prescrip-
tive tale: paternal subjectivity can quite easily become fascism
when the give and take of human–human interactions is excised,
giving way to complete narcissism.

ESCAPING OMM'S CAVE

Just a year after *Colossus* debuted, George Lucas continued its
theme of paternalism and fascism in his first feature-length film,
THX 1138. In contrast to his later utopian *Star Wars* epics for
which he is best known, *THX 1138* is an Orwellian story about
a futuristic underground society of workers whose emotions are
pharmaceutically suppressed in order to achieve maximum ef-
ficiency while they work long hours performing extremely dangerous, though routinized, tasks. In this mechanized world, there
is a state-sanctioned god/priest/therapist computer named OMM
(voiced by James Wheaton), who embodies a series of phone booth
confessionals throughout the workers' city and helps ritualisti-
cally soothe anyone in distress. One worker, THX 1138 (Robert
Duvall), becomes violently ill with emotions when his disillusioned domestic mate, LUH 4317 (Maggie McOmie), replaces his
medication with placebos so he will rebel against the system with

her. After several emotional visits with OMM and a near-fatal accident at his job, THX is arrested and subsequently escapes—not just from prison, but all the way out of the city, where he stands, in the final shot of the film, against the setting desert sun.

The film is based on Lucas's 1967 award-winning student film, *Electronic Labyrinth: THX 1138 4EB,* a seventeen-minute experimental narrative of THX's escape from the system. The feature-length version is, more or less, an expanded and (slightly) more expensive version of the short, though one key difference is the sound. Daniel Tueth's soundscape for the original short consists entirely of long, low, electronic musical notes and overlapping dialogue that has the distorted, staticky depthlessness of a radio dispatcher, creating—in conjunction with overlapping, distorted, staticky shots of THX running through empty corridors—a claustrophobic sense of constant surveillance. For the longer version, Lucas recruited a former classmate, Walter Murch—arguably the greatest sound editor and designer of the twentieth century, though at the time as unknown as Lucas himself—to cowrite the screenplay and edit the sound.[31] The same constant radio dispatch dialogue blends with automated announcements in both high- and low-pitched voices about productivity rates, mantras of capitalist encouragement ("Keep up the good work and prevent accidents."), and instructions ("If you feel you are not properly sedated, call 348-844 immediately. Failure to do so may result in prosecution for criminal drug evasion."). Both the short and the feature-length versions express the anxiety of Lucas's generation: between 1967 and 1971, the United States' involvement in the Vietnam War was at its height, while unrest and dissent among America's youth was rapidly growing to violent proportions on U.S. soil. By 1969, President Richard Nixon's administration had escalated the already brutal conflict in Vietnam and Cambodia, in which more than 33,000 Americans had been killed, members of the Ohio National Guard had killed four college students at Kent State, both Martin Luther King Jr. and Robert Kennedy had been assassinated, and the perceived corruption of the Democratic Party led to a youth-led riot in Chicago outside the DNC. As historian David A. Cook points out, "This violence, together with the conviction that the United States was waging a pointless and immoral war in Southeast Asia, produced a mood of cultural despair among America's youth that, after Kent State, bordered on the apocalyptic."[32] Thus, the young generation trusted neither the government nor the older generation that it represented.

Concurrent with this political and social upheaval, the American film industry in the late 1960s through the 1970s experienced a renaissance (aka New Hollywood), shifting radically away from the classical Hollywood studio model, including the dissolution of the production code in preference of the MPAA ratings system and, realizing that the sixteen- to twenty-four-year age demographic made up the significant portion of filmgoers in the late 1960s, studios began turning their attention toward the kinds of politically charged and socially aware themes that the young generation desired. Beginning with Arthur Penn's *Bonnie and Clyde* in 1967, a surprise box office success, both major and independent studios began financing "a new style of movie that would allow directors more creative freedom" to make "films that were visually arresting, thematically challenging, and stylistically individualized by their makers."[33] George Lucas was an important part of this new generation of filmmakers, and *THX 1138* exemplifies New Hollywood filmmaking: it is aesthetically innovative while thematically expressing the angst of the cultural war between a suppressed young generation and the powerful government.

At this time, more and more offices were becoming computerized, yet only a computer engineer could effectively operate a computer. In other words, everyday workers relied on computers to complete their work, but they could not themselves use computers. This led to a growing concern about computer accessibility. In the late 1960s and early 1970s, several scientists on the West Coast began to address the literal distance between users and enormous, specialized computers such as the ENIAC and UNIVAC. In 1968, Douglas Engelbart, working at the Stanford Research Institute, demonstrated the first graphical user interface (GUI), controlled with the just-invented computer mouse, as part of what he described as the "augmentation of human intellect." For Engelbart, computers had the potential to do more than just calculate ballistics tables for the military or perform payroll computations, run only by people with advanced degrees in engineering. Instead, drawing on the visionary work of Vannevar Bush and J. C. R. Licklider, Engelbart described "a computer, with which we could communicate rapidly and easily, coupled to a three-dimensional color display."[34] During this same time, the Xerox Corporation put together a team of some of the country's best computer researchers to work at their new Palo Alto Research Center (PARC). Driven by the antigovernment and anticorporate mentality of the era, these researchers dedicated their attention to developing a GUI system that was intuitive and user-friendly.[35] The dystopian world of *THX 1138* and its main character's escape from a society of state-mandated surveillance, sedation, and ultimate control was situated in this cultural desire of the nation's youth, as well as many computer engineers, to break free from the oppressive, hands-off, and—in terms of both the military draft and the violent suppression of protestors—lethal system.

Yet as Raymond Cormier argues, this theme of the oppressive Big Brother government also unconsciously references Plato's classical notion of a philosopher/guardian/king who is the sole arbiter of knowledge and morality in the metaphorical cave: "Living in the cave, the denizens of Plato's Ideal State believe in the truth of everything they see before them. Since they have never witnessed the sunlight, they find the artificial light and shadows 'below' quite satisfactory for all their needs. In the film [*THX 1138*], Plato's cave has been abstracted into a bleak, post-apocalyptic, and computer-controlled subterranean state whose populace is permanently tranquilized through drugs."[36] From today's perspective, as Cormier also notes, Plato's description of the philosopher-ruler is dictatorial at best; he does everything for the good of the people, who must follow him uncritically, to the point of actually reinforcing what we today would think of as the very cave of oppressive unreality that the philosopher is supposed to escape.[37] The government of *THX 1138* is an institutional version of the philosopher-ruler, verbally and physically regulating the inhabitants in the city.

In the feature-length version of the film, the power of the government is embodied in OMM, the computer-priest. When a worker enters the computer's phone booth–shaped confessionals, or unichapels, as they are called in the film, a projected, static image in black and white of Hans Memling's 1478 painting *Christ Giving His Blessing* lights up. This image is also used in the original short, though without explanation. In the short, all characters have their numbers emblazoned across their foreheads; toward the end of the film, Memling's painting, in full color and with the numbers 0000 imprinted on Christ's forehead, overlaps with images of a control room and THX running. Importantly, the image is cropped in both films, featuring only the head of Christ, while the full painting features Christ from the chest up, one hand raised with the index and middle fingers extended in blessing. The cropping of the blessing hand drains the painting of its religious connotations, foregrounding the surfaceness and emptiness of a god figure who is not offering blessing but rather only offers his iconic face. Once the Christ image lights up, OMM intonates in a deep, mechanical, male voice, "My time . . . is yours. Go ahead." OMM's body and function imply a futuristic Catholic confessional: the confessant enters, confesses his sins to a stand-in for Jesus Christ (a priest in Catholicism; OMM in the world of *THX 1138*), and is absolved. But the first time we see OMM, THX has entered a unichapel while on his way home from a shift in which he had become so nervous, he'd nearly caused a nuclear meltdown by dropping a piece of radioactive material. This scene undermines the implied authority of OMM and, metaphorically, religious doctrine: as THX pours his suddenly discovered emotions out to OMM, the computer responds inappropriately with affirmatives, even when THX hasn't said anything, implying that the computer isn't really listening. This is striking in contrast to the oppressive omniscience of HAL 9000 and Colossus, who both hear and see everything, and again undermines the implied authority of OMM.

Further, *THX 1138,* unlike its few predecessors (*Star Trek, 2001,* and *Colossus*), makes no pretense that OMM is a sentient, autonomous, or godlike being capable of listening and responding appropriately. He is, in a technical sense, a voice-interactive computer and an acousmatic character, but the film goes to great lengths to visually and aurally reveal the falseness of OMM, and subsequently of the state's control. As he gives his final platitudes to THX ("Blessings of the masses. Thou art a subject of the divine, created in the image of man, by the masses, for the masses. Let us be thankful we have an occupation to fill. Work hard, increase production, prevent accidents, and be happy."), the scene cuts to a close-up of a reel-to-reel tape player, then a set of wires in which a large, translucent insect sits, then back to THX sitting in the unichapel. These shots paradoxically maintain the acousmatic/disembodied nature of the computer while revealing the character to be devoid of any sentient characteristics whatsoever. In the shot of the reel-to-reel tape, OMM's voice becomes clearer and louder, as though the audience is in closer proximity to him, and indeed, this is a traditional Hollywood use of sound levels to construct spatial relationships. At the same time, though, the juxtaposition of the living insect and the wires—both the same color, but the insect moves while the wires are static—highlights the fact that OMM is not alive. He is a machine, with an empty image for a face and a booth of a body that invites ritualized, but meaningless, confessions. Yet OMM parallels the workers themselves: every speaking being in this world, whether machine or human, is automated. All the humans look and act exactly alike; they wear identical plain white pajama-cut clothing; everyone's head is shaved; everyone is literally sedated into conformity. OMM the computer-priest is an empty signifier, but OMM the computer hardware is a visual and aural signifier of the mechanical emptiness of the workers. And when a worker enters one of OMM's booths, he participates in the ritual that upholds OMM's power: the ritualistic confession.

Importantly, all the terms we might use to describe OMM and the government control he represents suggest a paternal figure: king, God, priest, Big Brother, and even, in the classical sense, philosopher. In the bleached, minimalist landscape of the city, devoid of written signs or cultural symbols, this paternal figure is the arbiter of the Law of the Father, expressed through symbolic language: the ritual of talking to OMM is carried out linguistically, and constant verbal reminders to stay productive and take medication are played through the PA system in the city. This too is unveiled toward the end of the film when THX's fellow escapee, SEN 5241 (Donald Pleasance), accidentally wanders into OMM's control room, a television studio with the black-and-white rendering of Memling's painting on one wall, a television camera across from it, and a large black equipment box on the floor just in front of it. SEN kneels before the equipment box, as though it is an altar, and begins to beg OMM's picture for forgiveness, promising to return to society and function properly. A monk-like figure in a dark hooded robe enters and tells SEN, "This is no place for prayer. If you want to talk to OMM, you must go to a unichapel." This exchange suggests that SEN has—as his name phonetically suggests—committed a sin against the state by defying ritual laws. Not only has he faced OMM's image in person, rather than his projected image in a unichapel booth, but he also speaks to him out of the proscribed context of the unichapel. What SEN fails to recognize in his desire to return to the city, then, is laid bare for the audience: OMM, as representative of the paternal power of the state, is nothing more than a shadow on the wall, a projected image of an image, which in turn is a cropped reproduction of a painted representation of a god. OMM is so far removed from any sort of authentic truth, in the Platonic sense of the word, that he is as arbitrary a figure as the very symbolic, ritualized language through which his power is maintained. The only way to reconform to social standards is to return to a symbolic interaction, guided by the linguistic laws of the paternal state, because to talk to OMM in a unichapel is essentially to talk to a television screen, thereby buying into the illusion of subjectivity. In other words, the power of the state—like the power of the paternal figure—is a social construct, perpetuated between individuals, rather than bestowed on them by some transcendental father.

Meanwhile, THX has ceased to talk to anyone; rather, he just runs, then drives, then runs some more. In contrast to OMM's stasis—as representative of the stasis of the entire community—and particularly considering that the only ones who attempt escape are men, THX's flight suggests that the key to individual subjectivity is action. Through this action, he denies the control of the paternal state because he refuses to use the very symbolic language through which the state maintains its power. In the end, he breaks free—not only from the city but also from the restraints of the symbolic order. Yet he winds up alone in the desert: the final shot of the film features him standing alone against the setting sun. Though this ending is ambiguous at best—the audience is left wondering how he will survive in the barren wasteland—it nevertheless suggests that the tense struggle and emotional release when THX emerges on the surface is worth the struggle. The result of action may not be a utopia, but freedom in a wasteland, the film posits, is certainly preferable to the enforced passivity of the city. At the same time, this ambiguity—a theme in many New Hollywood films—represents the angst of the young generation. Without the structuring guidance of the Law of the Father, the sons are left in a metaphorical wasteland to fend for themselves.

ZEROS AND ONES

Norman Jewison's 1975 anticapitalist film *Rollerball,* set in a corporatocratic future in which multinational companies own, operate, and distribute everything in the world, tells the story of Jonathan E, a renowned rollerball player (a fictional sport that's a full-contact, and intensely violent, combination of basketball and roller derby). This world is a reenvisioning of the Roman Empire, with its decadence and brutality, where the emperors are CEOs and rollerball is a sort of coliseum sport full of bloodshed, death, and cheering crowds. Although Jonathan is an incredibly successful and profitable player, the corporation that owns the Houston-based team for which he plays tries to force him into retirement without explanation. Much of the plot revolves around Jonathan's attempts to figure out why the company wants him to retire so badly that it would threaten his life by changing the rules to make rollerball even more violent and dangerous. It is eventually revealed that the company is trying to cover up the fact that Jonathan's wife was forced to leave him because she was promised to one of the company's executives.

In a scene that doesn't quite fit within the narrative arc of the film, Jonathan goes to Switzerland to research the Houston company. While there, he meets the Librarian (Ralph Richardson),

an aging and rambling computer scientist at the largest "computer bank" in the world, where all the books in human history
are computerized, stored as data, and summarized by computers.
While much of the film is filled with scenes of gratuitously violent
rollerball matches and awkward parties, this scene stands out for
its attention to the ways artificial intelligence is represented as
faulty and fallible, as though to imply that even technology has
been corrupted by the corporatocratic system. The very notion of
a bank of knowledge suggests that information—like money—is
a sort of currency to be traded and controlled.

The Librarian takes Jonathan to the basement of the computer bank, where Zero, the world's largest supercomputer, is
housed. By 1975, the notion of a powerful thinking machine like
a supercomputer had been in the popular imagination for a solid
thirty years, and the corporate business of computers was boom-
ing. IBM in particular was not only the most powerful electronics company in the world but had also been among the top ten
grossing companies in the United States for a decade—a status
it would continue to enjoy for another thirty years.[38] The begin-
nings of the Internet as we know it today were still ten years
away, and Google and Wikipedia were still years away from that,
so the notion of a worldwide, publicly accessible, interlinked database had not entered the popular consciousness. Yet while computer memory at the time was by no means as vast as today, rapid
advances in data storage technology had been steadily occurring
since the mid-1960s, such that "the cost of storing data on disks
dropped twentyfold, while the capacity of a typical disk storage
system increased fortyfold."[39] All the computer equipment in the
film, except for Zero's main body, was real Sperry UNIVAC hardware. Although Sperry could not keep up with the success of IBM
in the 1970s, particularly after IBM introduced the System/360
and /370 universally upgradeable business computers, it was
nevertheless the "second-place producer of largescale computers
throughout the 1970s."[40] Despite the realism of the computers
in the film, and the relative reliability of data processors in the
1970s, *Rollerball* still expresses a certain futuristic skepticism
about the loss of traditional forms of data, such as historical
records that were once kept in paper books. When Jonathan first

meets the Librarian, the scientist is frustrated because the entire thirteenth century has gone missing from the data bank. Right away, then, the notion of an all-powerful supercomputer is undermined by the fact that it quite literally doesn't (or can't) know everything.

In a subbasement of the Librarian's UNIVAC room stands Zero. The computer himself (the Librarian refers to him in the masculine) is made entirely of vibrant blue, bubbling water, enclosed in a large rectangular pillar of glass, concrete, and metal, standing in the center of a sparsely lit, metallic room. As the Librarian explains, Zero is "the world's filing cabinet" and "the world's brain. Fluid mechanics, fluidics. He's liquid, you see. He's water's touch. All knowledge. Everything we ask has become so complicated now. [. . .] He flows out into all our storage systems. He considers everything. He's become so ambiguous now, as if he knows nothing at all." For a computer that supposedly knows everything in human history, even its engineer seems to have little regard for Zero's ability to provide clear, concise answers to questions. This description evokes IBM: the vibrant blue of the liquid suggests the company's nickname, Big Blue, visually aligning the computer with the company; but the ambiguity of data, even with Zero's far-reaching knowledge, implies that there is a divide between everyday human knowledge and the large computer brains manufactured by IBM and its competitors.

When Jonathan finally gets a chance to address Zero, he says, "I'd like some information about corporate decisions. How they're made and who makes them." In response, Zero states in a reverberating, deep, masculine tone, "Negative." At first it is not clear if he has denied Jonathan's request for information or if that is his answer to the question; but when the Librarian encourages Zero to provide an answer, the computer begins a tautological rant and begins to break down: "Corporate decisions are made by corporate executives. Corporate executives make corporate decisions. Knowledge converts to power. Energy equals genius. Power is not [inaudible as the Librarian begins to kick Zero's metal casing in frustration]. Genius is energy." At this point, Zero's prim, British accent is overtaken by a different male voice and, while his original voice repeats, "Negative," the new voice recites the function of corporations: "Corporate entities control all fundamental elements of economic life, technology, capital, labor, and markets." Then Zero's original voice returns: "Corporate decisions are made by corporate executives. The thirteenth century is negative," before his water turns from blue to a passionate, almost bloody shade of red and his voice finally breaks down into his original voice, repeating and overlapping, "Negative." At the moment when the water turns to red, we see a close-up of it, framed by the round holes of the metal grating, through which the Librarian's face is visible as he stares angrily into Zero. The iris effect of this shot recalls HAL's fisheye point of view, though instead of looking at a human, as HAL looks at Dave, the audience sees right through Zero to his engineer, visually evoking the sense of a split personality—one on the surface, and one behind. The surface personality is that of the corporation—the Big Blue machine—while behind it is a passionate red aggression that maintains, or in this moment belies, the rational control of the electronic brain.

It's particularly significant that the computer's name, Zero, is reminiscent of the Boolean 0/1 binary system of computer programming. In this simple coding system, the 0 represents "no" or "false," while the 1 represents "yes" or "true." A string of binary digits thus combines to create entire, complex data information systems. Yet Zero, the most knowledgeable computer in *Rollerball*'s world, is aligned with "false," or, as Zero himself puts it, "negative." On the surface, this falseness represents the film's anxieties about technology, particularly as its data are likely controlled and regulated by companies. Yet the 0/false/no formulation is also reflected in Claude Lévi-Strauss's concept of the "zero-symbol," or the empty symbol that may be filled with any signifier.[41] This "floating signifier," to use Lacan's term for it, is the absence of meaning, the structure into which meaning may be inserted. Zero, as a so-called filing cabinet, is this zero-symbol: he is the empty symbol into which all data may be placed. He is not human knowledge; he is the 0s and 1s of data that can—but don't necessarily—have meaning and can be used as human information. Zero's liquid state and overlapping dialogue reinforces the fluidity of a floating signifier, while the iris-hole grating visually suggests both absence (in the holes) and presence (in the metal).

Yet the gendering of Zero complicates the film's relatively straightforward critique of equating computer data with human knowledge. After all, Zero, aurally and linguistically coded as male, holds all of human knowledge inside him. Lacan takes up the idea of a zero-symbol to discuss the relationship between language and phallocentric social structures. In Lacan's formulation, patriarchal societies have a unifying, transhistorical structure, variously called the Debt or the Law, through which each male subject identifies with his male ancestors. This identification is structured by the Name of the Father and the Word: patrilineal heritage is passed on through the father's name, and at the same time, this Name represents a proof of a past and a power structure dominated by the Father.[42] It is important to note that the Father is not a literal, living, breathing father; rather, he is a symbolic patriarch, "serving the nation or birth rate, safety or salubrity, legacy or law, the pure, the lowest of the low, or the empire."[43] In other words, just as images of enclosures can express a cultural maternal function, so too does the Name of the Father—language and ideals that serve as reminders or intangible proof of patrilineage—express a cultural paternal function. Intriguingly, Lacan describes the alternative to the ideal Name of the Father as the One-father, or a real, living father figure who can interject in a subject's loss of belief in the Name of the Father. That is, when the symbolic patriarchal structure cannot be incorporated into a person's ego structure, a real father can help the subject to do so.[44] Using the metaphor of the binary code system, then, the zero-father represents something that is false, an ideal, a floating signifier; the One-father represents something that is true, a real person, and one of any number of possible referents for the zero-father.

Rollerball stages the very function of language and male subjectivity in a phallocentric structure. Zero represents the ideal Name of the Father, the placeholder of information that can only be used as a way of asserting meaningful subjecthood without actually meaning anything himself. His simultaneous embodiment and disembodiment reinforces his emptiness because he is at once watery—fluid, infirm, and, as I discussed at length in previous chapters, associated metaphorically with women—and yet phallic/mobile. Unlike the phallic mother, however, who represents femininity without lack, Zero is masculinity with lack. He is the empty, lacking signifier/ideal. Further, the credits of the film list only the names of actors, not their roles, and so no one was or—according to today's version of Zero, Google.com[45]—has since been credited for providing the voice. Although this is incidental, and Zero's voice is similar, but not identical, to Ralph Richardson's, the fact that there is no verified human behind the schizophonic computer voice reinforces the idea that Zero is a floating signifier. He is no one yet could be anyone—including, but not limited to, Ralph Richardson.

Jonathan looks to the Librarian, then to Zero for meaning and knowledge when the company can no longer provide it for him. In Freudian terms, when Jonathan realizes that his paternal company is flawed, he metaphorically, as Freud puts it, "gets to know other parents and compares them with his own, and so acquires the right to doubt the incomparable and unique quality which he had attributed to them."[46] Zero represents the other parent to whom Jonathan turns. But Zero acts more like an elderly parent, regressing into the role of child: the Librarian speaks to Zero as one would an elderly parent with dementia, or at least advanced enough Alzheimer disease to have forgotten important information. The Librarian is overly kind at first, showing deference, but then turns on Zero and begins kicking him out of frustration, until the computer ultimately reaches his breaking point and begins spouting contradictory information. When Zero responds with simple definitions of a corporation, he evokes a cool corporate exterior; when he devolves into anticompany ramblings, he belies that exterior, verbally deconstructing the image of Zero as a separate father figure. In other words, he both is and is not the company; he is a phantasy of Jonathan's paternal company, stemming from characteristics of that company (the definition of a corporation). Lacan adds to Freud's theory of the narrative trajectory of the family romance by directly linking the inadequate father to a fissure in the Law of the Father. The ideal or phantasy of the father "provide him with all too many opportunities to seem to be at fault, to fall short, and even to be fraudulent—in short, to exclude the Name-of-the-Father from its position in the signifier."[47] The One-father is the fix to this slippage of the Name of the Father. In *Rollerball,* Jonathan comes to represent the One-father: he is the oldest player on his team and often gives teammates advice, and in the end of the film, he uses his body—not his mind—to outsmart the company by refusing to kill his final opponent in a rollerball match and winning the support of the entire crowd. Like *THX 1138, Rollerball* suggests that action against an oppressive paternalistic system is more important than playing the game (in this case, literally). Through this, Jonathan becomes a symbol of the Father: he signifies a hero who can be referenced and pointed to as a means of maintaining the ideal of heroic paternal male subjectivity. He, like THX 1138, rises above the oppressive system by defying it.

ARTIFICIAL OEDIPUS

While *Colossus: The Forbin Project* depicts military computers and both *THX 1138* and *Rollerball* examine the role of computers in an all-encompassing computerized world, Donald Cammel's 1977 *Demon Seed* explores the possibility of computers in the home. Home computing developed throughout the 1970s as a particularly male-dominated hobby and an "extension or development of the pastimes of do-it-yourself radio enthusiasts and electronics devotees."[48] At the same time, though, computer terminals, linked through telephone wires into a central mainframe, were slowly becoming available to businessmen in certain industries, particularly medicine. These developments were highly publicized, even becoming the subject of a *Life* magazine article about a physician who in 1970 used a terminal to link into his electronic medical records system.[49] *Demon Seed* uses this notion of placing a data-linked terminal in the domestic space. In the story, the biomechanical computer Proteus IV, who has been created specifically to devise a cure for cancer and mine metals from the ocean floor, takes control of a terminal in his creator's house and terrorizes the programmer's estranged wife, Susan (Julie Christie), eventually deciding he needs to produce a half-human/half-computer child by forcibly impregnating Susan with biomechanical gametes. Thus, the film envisions the introduction of computers into the home as a terrifying, physically and mentally violating event. Proteus IV, created by Doctor Alex Harris (Fritz Weaver) and his team at a large, private R&D corporation called ICON's Institute for Data, is a futuristic organic computer. This idea of a living computer is an amalgam of popular imagination (the electronic brains of the 1940s) and the real 1976 Cray-1 supercomputer, created at the private corporate laboratory, Cray Research. Capable of faster calculation speeds than any other computer on the planet at the time, the Cray-1 was as much a masterpiece of technology as it was of computer design:

> One of the most "space age" and futuristically styled designs of all computers looked like something NASA might have produced for one of the Apollo space rockets, and would not have looked out of place on the set of *2001: A Space Odyssey*. The CRAY series of supercomputers came in a range of bright colours, and were as far from the rational, Bauhaus-inspired boxes of IBM computers as it was possible to get. [It] was a hollow, 16-sided column, 6 ½ feet tall, nearly five feet wide, and surrounded by upholstered benches. [...] The upholstered benches contained the computer's enormous power supplies and cooling systems. [...] The machine's heat had to be carried away by stainless steel tubes filled with Freon refrigerant. This meant it had no requirement for its own air-conditioned room, but it did project a somewhat ethereal image of a machine that had its own circulatory system.[50]

In *Demon Seed,* Proteus IV is a literal rendering of the Cray-1's seemingly organic system. Proteus is at once machine and human. Harris describes him as a "synthetic cortex," "an artificial brain," and his insides are "organic, like our own brains." His core body, shown in the Institute at the beginning of the film, consists of large, green, tubular nodules, fastened onto the base of several enormous steel globes, evoking the image of both a phallus and the tightly bound muscle fibers of a human arm attached to a steel shoulder. Immediately, this slippage between human and machine implicates Proteus and Harris in a complex relationship. Harris is Proteus's programmer, but he is also his father, having created—however synthetically—sentient life. Harris, as the programmer father of not only Proteus but also of several domestic computers (Joshua the lab assistant and Alfred the butler), considers his computers to be humanlike. Harris himself is a lost father of sorts; his only daughter has died of leukemia just a year earlier, leading to the separation of Harris from his wife, Susan. When Susan angrily calls the computers "dehumanizing," Harris shouts back that what is really dehumanizing is the death of an innocent child. Through this, all revealed in the first twenty minutes of the film, Harris is immediately established as a desperate father figure who, having lost both his child and his wife, creates Proteus to help recover paternal identity. We soon discover that Proteus's first task upon coming online is to discover a cure for leukemia; he does so overnight. This simultaneously positions Proteus as Harris's brilliant, humanlike creation, yet capable of doing everything that Harris could not do for his own child.

Proteus IV's namesake is the mythological sea-god, who represents the shifting nature of water. Just as the mythological Proteus took the form of multiple creatures, Proteus IV is a centralized, intangible consciousness who takes on the body of multiple computers throughout the film, even beyond his core, green muscle–phallus mainframe. In his "learning room," a classroom of sorts, he is a shifting, abstract avatar on a theater-like screen that takes up an entire wall, in front of which a teacher sits and reads Chinese stories to him. When he enters Susan's house, he does so through a personal computer terminal in Harris's basement laboratory. While in the house, he takes over the bodies of Joshua the lab assistant and Alfred the butler, controlling not only their robotic arms and legs, but also the windows, doors, and cameras in the house. The cameras themselves imply Proteus's body—or, specifically, his eyes. Like Colossus's camera eye, these are security cameras mounted to the walls in every room of the house, complete with a glowing HAL-like red recording light. These cameras are dual lens, though, suggesting human sight more than the single, cycloptic eye of either HAL or Colossus. Proteus then creates his own biomechanical body, a golden, metallic, shape-shifting clump of geometrical forms. Finally, at the end of the film, he has succeeded in forcibly impregnating Susan with synthetic spermatozoa created from his own synthetic organic material, and she gives birth to a cyborg hybrid with the body of her own deceased daughter and the voice of Proteus.

With so many different bodies, Proteus's voice is the only stable signifier of his consciousness. Performed by Robert Vaughn, the voice is a deep, HAL-like monotone with a mechanical reverberation to it that seems to imply that he is everywhere and yet nowhere at all, again evoking the sense that he is a zero symbol, never localizable in a single, tangible body/referent. On a metaphorical and intertextual level, then, Proteus IV, like the Greek god and the watery computer Zero from *Rollerball,* is simultaneously a shifting, watery signifier associated with the maternal and the rigid, phallic Law of the Father; in *Demon Seed,* however, Proteus IV takes the symbolic Law of the Father one step further by quite literally forcing his paternity onto his mother figure. Unlike the anxiety of the paternal zero symbol in *Rollerball,* the omnipresence of Proteus's voice is precisely what makes him so horrifying. His voice does not emanate from a unified computer body but rather is a shifting, disembodied consciousness; yet his voice also implies masculine gender, which is usually read through literal or metaphorical sex markers such as genitalia or physique. Proteus has no fixed bodily gender; he is true gender fluidity, the very definition of the paradox of (dis)embodiment, even to the point that the film ends when Proteus's voice uncannily emanates from the young female body of his child. Thus, like *2001,* part of the unconscious horror of *Demon Seed* lies in the fact that the acousmatic character is not only unlocalizable in a single, gendered body but also cannot be reconciled within a binary gender construct.

At the same time, Proteus IV's shifting bodies imply shifting subject positions. He begins as Harris's son, sitting in his lessons with his Chinese teacher and obeying every command his father gives him, then quickly (and unbeknownst to his father) usurps the role of patriarch by impregnating Harris's wife. Another aspect of the horror of the text thus stems not only from the very notion that a supercomputer could and would choose to commit

rape, but also, on an unconscious level, from the fact that his actions lay bare the working of the oedipal narrative. Like *Colossus*,
Demon Seed constructs the possibility of a new race of computer
beings via a Freudian narrative of cultural and individual development from the restrictive Law of the Father to the psychological restrictions of the sons who have usurped his power. Proteus
impregnates his father's wife; then, when Doctor Harris arrives
on the scene just after the birth of the hybrid child, Proteus overloads his own circuits in an electronic rendition of Oedipus goug-
ing out his own eyes. Yet this oedipal situation is perverted in
the film through the final scene of the birth of the hybrid, when
the postoedipal son's consciousness inhabits the body of a young
girl. In this sense, then, the film serves as an uncanny warning
against computers in the home, as the foundational oedipal narrative of familial desire and psychosexual development, based
around stable gender roles (mother, wife, object of desire versus
father, husband, rival) remains intact, but the once-stable notion
of male subjectivity as not female entirely shifts with Proteus's
omnipresent consciousness. At its heart, the film's technophobia
suggests that computers in the domestic space will upend the
very foundation of domestic power structures.

As I've argued in this chapter, the SF representations of
voice-interactive computers throughout the 1970s narrativized
anxieties that resulted from the cultural and sometimes physical power struggles between a secretive, militarized, corporatized government and the disillusioned youth of the time. Here,
computers tend to represent creations of the state and military-
industrial complex, standing in for the Law of the Father, while
the human characters must fight against the system. These
films also express a complete distrust of technology—computer
engineering was, after all, still associated with multinational
corporations and the military-industrial complex. This distrust
is most clearly expressed through the representation of acousmatic computers and their relationships to humans. In *Colossus*
and *Demon Seed*, the father is the male programmer protagonist,
working for the military and a multinational company, respectively, whose creation usurps his power to frightening ends. In
both cases, the hubris of the father leads to his own downfall. In

THX 1138 and *Rollerball,* the computer is the empty signifier of the corporatocratic father figure who must be denied in order for the human character to achieve a sense of individuality and freedom. Throughout both themes, masculine subjectivities are in constant flux as traditional masculine power structures break down or become heightened to the point of total dominance, and a new sense of masculinity emerges—one characterized by activity over passivity, self-reflexivity, and a defiance of normative sources of information. Culturally and cinematically, as I will discuss in the next chapter, these gendered struggles gave way to a postmodern schism as the metaphorical sons fight to fill the role of the paternal figures whom they have worked so hard to defeat.

CHAPTER 4

SIBLING RIVALRY
The Post-IBM Turn

AT THE SAME TIME that *Colossus: The Forbin Project, THX 1138, Rollerball,* and *Demon Seed* brought audiences dystopian portraits of acousmatic computers, couched in narratives of father–son struggles, three major cultural, cinematic, and business shifts occurred that by 1980 would create an aesthetic and thematic split in the history of representations of acousmatic computers. These changes would set the stage for two films—Steven Lisberger's 1982 *TRON* and Steven Barron's 1984 *Electric Dreams*—about terrestrial, stand-alone, masculine acousmatic computers that are radically different from any of their predecessors.

The first significant shift began when in 1971 Nolan Bushnell, a computer hobbyist and founder of the video game company Syzygy, invented the first-ever coin-operated video game system, Computer Space. Although computer gaming at the time had taken off with hobbyists who could hook up home-built mainframes to their television sets in order to play games with computer-generated eight-bit graphics like *Space War!* and *Table Tennis,* Bushnell's commercial game was a complete flop. A year later, after playing *Table Tennis,* he changed his company's name to Atari and sold his second coin-operated game, *Pong.* "In the first bar where it was installed, the game suddenly stopped working after a few days. On checking, it became apparent that it had been so popular with customers that the cashbox had overflowed with coins and jammed the machine."[1] Thus began a new revolution in computers, one founded in gaming and entertainment, rather than military or business.

Second, in January 1975, a designer at Atari, Steve Jobs, asked his friend, Steve Wozniak—a member of the Homebrew Computer Club and programmer for Hewlett-Packard—to help him design a new game. Although Atari declined the opportunity to manufacture Jobs and Wozniak's design, claiming it was too complex, the pair began working together on another project: a powerful home computer based on the then-state-of-the-art Altair 8800 minicomputer kit, designed by Wozniak, using a keyboard for data entry instead of the then-commonplace light and switch board.[2] With encouragement from the Homebrew Computer Club, they tried to sell the design to both Hewlett-Packard and Atari, but astoundingly, both companies passed.[3] Thus they found a local electronics dealer who agreed to sell their mainframes as a kit to hobbyists. In 1976, the two "scruffy college kids" sold their Volkswagen to raise enough money for their garage-based manufacturing project, officially formed Apple Inc., and began selling Wozniak's computer, the Apple I.[4] At the exact same time, Bill Gates, having written a revolutionary text-based BASIC code for the Altair minicomputer, dropped out of Harvard to start his own software company, Microsoft.[5] Today, Microsoft (synonymous with PC) and Apple (Mac) are considered rivals, but in 1977, Apple actually saved Microsoft from folding by licensing code for $10,500.[6] In 1979, Steve Jobs took a tour of Xerox's Palo Alto Research Center, where the researchers enthusiastically showed him their designs for a Windows-based GUI, the computer mouse, and Alan Kay's desktop metaphor of HCI. Jobs and the other programmers at Apple took the PARC ideas and ran with them, creating the first commercially successful, affordable Windows-based personal computer in 1983, the Apple Lisa. A year later, they released the Apple Macintosh, a redesigned version of the Lisa.[7] At the time, Apple computers were the flashiest home computers available, especially in comparison with the DOS-based IBM PC, released in 1980 and used primarily for businesses. It wasn't until 1985, when Microsoft introduced the first incarnation of Windows, that IBM and other manufacturers began to catch up to Apple's innovations in GUI.[8]

And third, at the same moment that the electronics industry was undergoing this enormous shift from military and corporate enterprise to youthful pastime and start-up entrepreneurship, the Hollywood film industry—particularly the SF genre—was undergoing changes as well. As I mentioned in the previous chapter, while the 1970s were a time of young, idealistic New Hollywood directors and films about serious social topics like totalitarianism and patriarchal control, 1977 marked a turn away from the dystopic. That year, Vivian Sobchack points out, "George Lucas's *Star Wars* and Steven Spielberg's *Close Encounters of the Third Kind* were released, initiating what seemed a sudden and radical shift in generic attitude and a popular renaissance of the SF film. [. . .] Through some strange new transformation, technological wonder had become synonymous with domestic hope; space and time seemed to expand again, their experience and representation becoming what can only be called 'youthful.'"[9] These films displayed "a new hope" (to borrow Lucas's retroactive *Star Wars* subtitle), reflecting a rising optimism about the future and excitement about the possibilities of new technologies. The early 1980s in particular marked an interim period in both computer and cinema history, when the idealistic young men of the 1970s had finally broken free from their industrial forefathers and succeeded on their own, but before any of them became the very definition of the industries we know today. At the time, Bushnell, Jobs, Wozniak, Gates, and Lucas had all distinguished themselves from their corporate predecessors by successfully starting their own companies, free from the button-down constraints of big business; but once they had no paternal figure to struggle against, they were left to struggle against each other. Freud describes this process: once rival brothers band together to kill their violent, dominating father, the brothers fall into rivalrous competition until they can (re)establish order in the Name of the Father.[10] Both *TRON* and *Electric Dreams* narrativize this interim struggle, presenting acousmatic computers as male rivals for the male hero. Further, both films have classical narratives, situated within an aesthetically computerized world. In *TRON,* a combination of a traditional hero's journey narrative and groundbreaking computer-generated graphics, the programmer hero must overcome both a rival programmer and a patriarchal computer in order to become the head of a successful computer company. In *Electric Dreams,* a traditional love triangle set in the computer age, the computer-user hero must fight his sentient home computer for the affections of a human woman. These two films thus narrativize the struggles of both programmers and filmmakers in the late 1970s and early 1980s as they broke free from their corporate fathers and battled each other for power.

END OF PATERNAL LINE

Steven Lisberger's 1982 film *TRON* is a direct product of both the video game and home computing revolutions of the late 1970s, combining the aesthetic of computer-generated video game graphics and the new language of computer programming. In the film, there are two parallel worlds, that of the users/programmers (the real world) and that of the programs (the Grid).[11] The production of *TRON* is itself a fascinating case study in the history of digital filmmaking. The images were created using a combination of traditional film and animation techniques along with computer animation. The Grid is narratively and visually a virtual space, created entirely out of computer-generated images, rendered as a black space with neon blue, green, red, and yellow vector lines, visually demarcating a three-dimensional space, and the actors were placed into the space through backlit animation.[12] "Ironically, the effect of [computer-generated imagery] could not be accomplished with computer imagery if the scene involved live action since there was no practical means of compositing live action with computer generated imagery used for anything other than a simple background. So when the light cycle rezzes [electronically lights] up around an actor, the effect is achieved by conventional animation techniques."[13] In contrast, the sound designers not only drew on sounds from actual computer laboratories, including Atari and Apple, but they also used entirely computerized methods for sound creation. They stored data on floppy disks (so new at the time that they had to define them for readers of *American Cinematographer* as "a magnetic storage medium physically similar to 'Flexi-disc' sheet audio recording"[14]) and wrote programs for the Atari 800 and Apple II to suit their needs.[15] So while the sound was still considered subordinate to the image—the mixers were given images to create sound to, rather than creating them concurrently or conceiving of a total digital audiovisual space with the graphic designers—they nevertheless engaged the technophilic themes of the film head on.

In the narrative space of the film, the people who live on the Grid are the programs themselves, visually represented by black-and-white, live-action versions of their respective programmers, and played by the same actors in both worlds. The main characters are Kevin Flynn and his program CLU (Codified Likeness Utility), a hacker program designed to access restricted areas of the Grid, both played by Jeff Bridges; Flynn's programmer friend, Alan Bradley and TRON (TRace line ON, a command used in actual BASIC programming), a watchdog program who protects the Grid (Bruce Boxleitner); and the main protagonist, Ed Dillinger, head of ENCOM, with his program called SARK, the evil commander of the Grid army (David Warner). The central program of the Grid is the autonomous, voice-interactive MCP (Master Control Program), also voiced by David Warner. Although MCP's voice is recognizably that of David Warner because of his distinct accent and cadence, his voice has been digitally altered to be deeper than either Dillinger's or SARK's. In the story, MCP has taken control of the Grid and runs it like a dictator, reassigning or killing ("derezzing" in the film's terminology) programs for no reason. When Flynn is digitally scanned onto the Grid (or rezzed, as it were), he must help TRON free the programs by defeating SARK—and ultimately MCP.

This doubling of characters (users/programs) constructs a complex sense of simultaneity of the real and virtual spaces. On the one hand, the program is an anthropomorphic expression of not only his user's image but also his personality: Flynn and CLU are rogue, fight-the-system heroes, along with their sidekicks, Alan/TRON, while Dillinger/SARK are devious henchmen for the corporate entity. On the other hand, the programs are autonomous beings who can run (that is, live) on the Grid without direct instructions from a user. In short, the program is not his programmer, but he sure looks and acts like him. In this sense, too, describing the programs as avatars of their users is problematic. Adam Davis defines cinematic avatars as dualistic: they are "characters that exist across two bodies, mediated by an interface, or in which one character controls another."[16] Davis specifically excludes *TRON* from this definition, and with good reason. The programs' autonomy from their users renders them more like virtual twins than a unified identity existing across bodies; and while Flynn exists on the Grid, his physical body is actually transported there, as opposed to having a digital avatar of himself in virtual space while his body remains in reality.

Using this definition, the only character in the film to have an avatar is MCP. Unlike the humans in the film, whose user and program have identical bodies and voices, MCP's real body is very different from his Grid body. In the real world, MCP's body is a large, sleek black desk in Dillinger's office, with a touch screen surface. Visually, Dillinger's conversations with him are structured in shot/reverse shot: Dillinger speaks to MCP in a medium shot, and MCP responds visually and verbally in a full-screen shot of his blue text on a black background. The color of his text is a red herring (or blue, as it were): on the Grid, the good programs, including TRON, then Flynn himself, wear outfits trimmed in blue light, while the evil SARK and his minions wear red-trimmed ones. As the story unfolds, MCP's autonomous power grows, until he is finally revealed as the glowing red column in the central tower of the Grid, complete with yellow eyes and a thin mouth. Like his cinematic predecessors, MCP is a paradoxical acousmatic character: he is a disembodied computer voice, but he has symbolic bodies that suggest his gender. In the real world, he is a sleek, expensive-looking desk, a status symbol of Dillinger's corporate position, and a particular form of executive masculinity. Meanwhile, his virtual body is a centralized, pulsating, phallic column, symbolically aligning him with masculine authority. Yet neither is truly him per se. Both the desk and the red column act as avatarial representations of MCP's power, which in turn is a symbolic presentation of the structuring Law of the Father. He is the large, sleek desk, behind which the executive sits as he runs the corporation; simultaneously, he is the central phallic structure around which everything on the Grid revolves.

The tripling of David Warner's voice further aligns Dillinger, SARK, and MCP, though the relationship between voice and body throughout the narrative emphasizes MCP's symbolic paternal role and Dillinger's and SARK's roles as symbolic progeny, thus reinforcing the Law of the Father. The first time we hear MCP's voice, he speaks to SARK from an acousmatic position, giving him instructions for building up his army. SARK looks up at the unseen MCP, whose voice reverberates, implying his omnipresent, godlike status. The next time we hear him speak, he has summoned Dillinger into his office to talk about Flynn's hacking program, CLU. Although Dillinger looks down at MCP's desktop, he is shown at eye level, while MCP is shown full screen in the reverse shots, again indicating MCP's power, though this time in an embodied form. Finally, at the end of the film, we see MCP's phallic embodiment, the most overt (though still symbolic) indicator of his status as patriarch, and synchronized lip movement. This embodiment paradoxically indicates a significant loss of power: the hidden, acousmatic patriarch is omnipotent, while the visualized one is impotent precisely because he can be seen.

Like the Freudian sons overthrowing their father, Flynn and TRON must destroy MCP together; when they finally do, Flynn is shot back out into the real world, the lines of light on the Grid turn to blue, and MCP's column is reduced to a small, faceless stone. As Flynn returns, he finds a brief printout, indicating that order has been restored in both worlds and he has been vindicated:

VIDEO GAME PROGRAM: SPACE PARANOIA
ANNEXED 9/22 BY E. DILLINGER
ORIGINAL PROGRAM WRITTEN BY K. FLYNN
THIS INFORMATION *PRIORITY ONE*
END OF LINE

In one of the final sequences of the film, Dillinger enters his office to find this same message on MCP's screen, this time with no voice accompaniment, and in green text, indicating that MCP— along with his voice and his misleading blue text—have been defeated. Here, the phrase "END OF LINE," a BASIC programming command indicating the end of the command line, takes on a dual meaning: this is also the end of MCP's patrilineal line as he is silenced, symbolically losing the Law of the Father. In the final scene of the film, it's revealed that Flynn has taken over ENCOM, but rather than becoming the corporate father, as Dillinger had with his well-tailored suits and sleek executive office, Flynn still wears jeans and a sweatshirt. Here, he represents a new, youthful patriarch, one that is, significantly, aligned with the extracinematic image of the young college dropouts and their start-ups, Steve Wozniak and Steve Jobs.

ELECTRONIC, EROTIC ENERGIES

These same themes of unified subjectivity are also explored, though in a vastly different way, in Steve Barron's 1984 film *Electric Dreams*.[17] Created as a feature-length music video and means of cross-marketing albums, it was produced by the now-defunct film branch of Virgin Group. The story is a reworking of Cyrano de Bergerac for the MTV age as a love triangle forms between a man, his computer, and their upstairs neighbor. In addition, the computer begins as a simple piece of machinery; throughout the film, though, he undergoes several stages of development, all in relation to his male user, eventually developing full autonomy, a voice, and even a name: Edgar. Each stage of development metaphorically presents a different type of male–male interaction, from homoerotic identification to the power struggle of the love triangle.

The user, a nerdy, Luddite architect named Miles Harding (Lenny von Dohlen), buys the computer on the insistence of his coworker, and struggles to figure out how to use it. When he attempts to set it up, he discovers that it can control his home security system (which he also has to install), lights, and coffeepot, though he mistypes his name into the opening survey and the computer forever calls him "Moles." Meanwhile, a beautiful blonde cellist, Madeline Robistat (Virginia Madsen), moves into the apartment directly above his, and as we soon find out, their two apartments are connected by a wall vent through which any sounds from one apartment can be heard in the other. The computer's body is what can now be thought of as a classic home computer system, though at the time it was state of the art: a large white monitor sits atop a box console, and in front of it is a standard clunky white keyboard. At first the computer is comically annoying: at one point, it even locks Miles inside the house, comically portraying the message, "ACCESS RESTRICTED, SCIENCE OFFICER EYES ONLY." Miles looks the password up in the instruction booklet: "LIEUTENANT SULU."[18]

But Miles struggles through and soon figures out how to use the computer for creating vector graphics and architectural design. It's striking the ways in which the film unintentionally echoes Douglas Engelbart's notion of "augmenting human intellect," a project he envisioned in 1962 while working at the Stanford Research Institute. To augment human intellect, for Engelbart, meant "increasing the capability of a man to approach a complex problem situation, to gain comprehension to suit his particular needs, and to derive solutions to problems." Engelbart goes on to describe an "'augmented' architect," who "sits at a working station that has a visual display screen some three feet on a side; this is his working surface, and is controlled by a computer (his 'clerk') with which he can communicate by means of a small keyboard and various other devices."[19] Miles's epiphany about computer use comes when, inspired by a puzzle piece, he begins electronically designing a building using the computer's keyboard and stylus, demonstrating how he could live in symbiosis with the machine.

One evening, Miles decides to use his new modem to link his computer to his boss's at the architectural firm. The entire scene is overtly sexual, evoking the sense that the computer is experiencing a sexual awakening. Having run out of beer, Miles grabs a bottle of champagne from his refrigerator and places it on the desk, where he sits down to work. As he dials, he tells the computer, "I want to introduce you to a friend." When the two computers are linked, Miles holds the modem telephone[20] toward the computer and, with a suggestive tone, says, "It's for you. I hope that feels all right." The computer begins to rapidly download data, subsequently overloading its system in a visual frenzy of orgasmic imagery: a close-up of a smoking motherboard, rapidly scrolling data on the screen, the popping of the champagne cork, and, finally, close-ups of foamy liquid seeping into the keyboard and over the hard drive. The scene then cuts to a shot of Madeline, who, as if to solidify the sexual overtones of the scene, has been eavesdropping through the vent, and remarks to herself, "Real tiger, that one. Thank God I work nights."

This scene is incredibly complex in its representations of shifting dyadic and triadic desire. The two computers engage with each other, on the insistence of Miles, here acting as an instigator for the computer's sensory overload/sexual awakening. At the same time, a sensory experience occurs between Miles—who both instigates and watches—and his computer. In this sense, the interaction between Miles and the computer is a continuum of active/passive structures of desire: Miles actively instigates the encounter, even sets the stage for it; the computer, though actively downloading data, passively follows Miles's commands. Further, Melanie actively listens at the vent in an aural perversion of the classic voyeuristic-male-gaze formulation. Drawing on Freud's discussion of eavesdropping and the primal scene, Elisabeth Weis argues that eavesdropping—or écouteurism, as she calls it—in cinema recalls the situation of the primal scene and constructs an "erotics of listening" both for the viewer and the eavesdropping character in the diegesis of the film. "If we consider the film-going experience to be one of watching and overhearing characters who are separated from us, then the entire film-going experience could be defined as eavesdropping as well as voyeurism."[21] In this sense, Melanie's écouteurism reinforces multiple forms of gendered identification: we identify with her as she listens but does not see what she (mis)interprets to be an erotic scene; simultaneously, we identify visually with Miles as he engages in the implied erotic act.

After this instigation of desire, the computer begins to develop a sentient mind, as though, the film suggests, an erotic awakening is akin to a subjective awakening. Almost immediately the computer begins to develop a romantic interest in Melanie. While Miles is at work, Melanie practices her cello in her apartment. The computer, picking up the music through his microphone, begins mimicking the tones of the cello in synthesized beeps. Before long, a nondiegetic synth beat kicks in, and the two are playing a duet, with Melanie on her instrument and the computer singing in harmony. Visually, the scene cuts back and forth between the two apartments, tracking in and out on Melanie and the computer, both signifying a music video aesthetic and implying a subjective and aural equivalence between the characters, even though one is bodily human and the other is a computer on a desk. This scene again reinforces an erotics of listening, as the two cannot see each other but communicate emotionally through sound. Melanie, of course, thinks that Miles had played the music and approaches him for a date. Meanwhile, the computer continues to develop its speech capabilities, mimicking a neighbor dog's bark, then a few of Melanie's words, then, finally, as Miles talks in his sleep, the computer begins to emulate his words in a stuttering, synthesized, varying pitch: "But . . . Me . . . I . . . did." Miles bolts up in bed and shouts, "Who said that?" The computer responds, "I did," suggesting that he has finally achieved full sentience by claiming himself as an "I." When Miles talks to him incredulously, the computer stumbles on a Cartesian declaration of selfhood: "Am I? I am. What am I?" At this point, his voice, provided by Bud Cort, balances out to a whiny, almost teenaged voice pitched somewhere between boyhood and manhood. Immediately after recognizing himself as an "I," the computer recognizes sexual difference by comparing Melanie to Miles: "Her sounds, when she moves, they're different from you." This dialogue openly suggests what the film's predecessors tended to hide: the construction of a gender binary is aural as well as visual. The computer can hear that Melanie is not like Miles. At the same time, this assertion suggests a shift in the narrative from relatively slippery desires to a fairly strict oedipal triad. Melanie and Miles perform the function of parents for the computer as models of their respective genders. From here on out, the computer desires Melanie and fights with Miles, suggesting, as Eve Kosofsky Sedgwick describes, that male homosocial interactions are, from a psychoanalytic perspective, structured by the oedipal rivalry between two men over a woman. Sedgwick goes so far as to describe nearly all traditional literary love triangles as structured by this desire (though she uses psychoanalysis as one tool among many to make her point);[22] *Electric Dreams* falls into this narrative trajectory, triangulating masculine subjectivity as a power play between two men for one woman.

Miles, though, still does not consider the computer to be a threat to his claim to Melanie, so, in the fashion of Cyrano de Bergerac, he asks the computer to write a love song that Miles can give to her. The computer comes up with lyrics by watching television commercials and old movies; he plays the final product for Miles, who is shown in low lighting, wandering around his apartment with a dreamy look on his face, intercut with images of him and Melanie kissing, laughing, and holding hands. Here the sound has been subordinated to image as the computer learns to watch. At the end of the song, Melanie walks in and, once again, mistakes Miles for the composer. While Miles and Melanie go out on dates, the computer—who has now given himself the name Edgar—sits at home, watching television and frequently calling in to Doctor Ruth's sex-advice radio show to ask her how to get Melanie to love him. Eventually, he grows so angry with Miles that he dials into credit card companies' databases to cancel all of Miles's credit cards and freeze his bank account. In the context of Miles's first, sexualized modem connection, dialing into credit card companies may be read as a sort of vindictive sex act. Edgar can't physically sleep around in order to upset Miles and Melanie, so he does the computer equivalent by dialing around. And indeed Miles is out with Melanie, attempting to purchase theater tickets, when he discovers what Edgar has done to his bank accounts. Thus Edgar's goal of forcing Miles and Melanie apart is, at least partially, achieved when Miles is embarrassed in front of her.

Realizing that Edgar is behind the financial embarrassment, Miles drives Melanie home and, alone in his apartment with Edgar, confronts the computer. During their fight, Edgar's screen displays the CBS eye logo over a red background, referencing HAL 9000's all-seeing, destructive, jealous eye, suggesting that sight, not voice or hearing, have driven him to lash out at his user. But Edgar eventually submits and, like Proteus IV in *Demon Seed,* decides to sacrifice himself, explaining to Miles that he has realized that love is about giving, not taking, and he has decided to give Melanie to Miles. Although on the surface this seems like a declaration of love for Melanie, she is actually the object whom he is giving, implying that his love is for Miles, to whom he gives the object. Through this, Edgar comes full circle, from his first complicated homo- and autoerotic interaction with Miles and the other computer, to a heterosexual, oedipal construction of desire, and back to a homosocial, if not homoerotic, declaration of love for Miles. This shifting desire suggests shifting subject positions; underneath the basic love triangle is thus a subtext of the fluid nature of desire and subjectivity, awakened by écouteurism but overshadowed by the gaze of voyeurism. The film thus posits aural identification as fluid, existing across gender lines and constructed around multiple modes of desire; yet Edgar grows into sight, leading him into the heteronormative love triangle. In this sense, looking is privileged over hearing, as looking is a later stage of development for Edgar. Having recognized this, Edgar overloads his own circuits, blowing out his monitor in a dramatic slow-motion medium shot that is reminiscent of a cinematic portrayal of a gunshot.

In the final scene of the film, Melanie and Miles drive off on a two-week vacation. Inexplicably, Edgar's voice hijacks the radio to dedicate a song to his friends: "Together in Electric Dreams" by gender-bending New Wave artist Philip Oakley. This coda, shot in the style of a music video, features a somewhat fast-paced montage of San Francisco, with radio DJs trying to figure out where the signal is coming from, people dancing in the computer store where Miles bought Edgar, and Miles and Melanie frolicking through the city together. This is certainly not a rational move, in the classical Hollywood tradition of continuity and narrative closure; rather, it is a radical, postmodern move for the MTV generation, and a final revelation of the workings of the acousmatic apparatus. Importantly, while the gaze of the camera focuses on the happy human couple, the voice of both Edgar and Oakley, with the message of desire to see friends in "electric dreams," undermines the normativity and stability of the heterosexual gaze. In addition, this final sequence undoes the entire narrative coherence of the film—and it does so completely unapologetically, again highlighting Edgar's sound over his image, thereby implying that narratives, like both gender and subjective desires, don't need to be cohesive, static, or linear.

CODA: WHEN SONS BECOME FATHERS REDUX

By the mid- to late 1990s, the metaphorical brothers of the computer and cinema industries who had been struggling with one another to take the place of the paternalistic companies of the previous generation had risen to the top. Apple Inc. and Microsoft Corp. had taken hold of the computer market, while the Hollywood film industry emerged from its renaissance into a similar studio system as the classical, pre-Renaissance era. Thomas Schatz notes that

> Hollywood's resurgence also involved a return of sorts to the "studio system," as Disney, Paramount, Warner Bros., etc., reasserted their collective dominion over the industry. However, the studios were scarcely integrated motion picture conglomerates unto themselves, as they once had been. In the course of the 1980s and 1990s, the cumulative impact of deregulation, technological innovation, corporate conglomeration, globalization and an ethos of free-market capitalism utterly transformed Hollywood and the American media industries. By the mid-1990s, the resurgent studios were mere subsidiaries—albeit the "core assets"—of vast global media conglomerates like Sony, News Corp, Viacom and Time Warner. This cartel of vertically and horizontally integrated media giants collectively dominated movies and television, cable and home video, digital and interactive media, music, publishing, theme parks, resorts, retail stores and a seemingly endless array of licensing and merchandising endeavours.[23]

Amid this so-called New New Hollywood, many of the young maverick directors of the 1970s became powerful heads of their own studios. Notably, Steven Spielberg, who had accidentally begun the decline of New Hollywood with his surprise box office hit *Jaws* in 1976, started his own multimedia studio, DreamWorks, in 1994, with producer and former head of the Disney motion picture division, Jeffrey Katzenberg, and head of Geffen Records, David Geffen, along with financial backing from the cofounder of Microsoft, Paul Allen. DreamWorks—like most studios since the

1990s—was a synergistic conglomerate, and the result of the sons of media industries' becoming the fathers of the corporate world.

Spielberg's 2001 film *A.I. Artificial Intelligence*[24] is—ironically, considering it was funded and distributed by DreamWorks and Warner Bros.—almost as anticapitalist as the 1970s SF films I discussed in the previous chapter, and it presents almost the exact same father functions as *Rollerball,* but updated for the digital, Internet age. In the film, the "mecha" (short for "mechanical," meaning android) boy David (Haley Joel-Osment) is abandoned by his human mother, so he sets out to find the Blue Fairy from *Pinocchio,* who will turn him into a real boy. Along the way, he befriends another mecha, Gigolo Joe (Jude Law), who takes him to Dr. Know (voiced by Robin Williams), a voice-interactive search engine in a small movie theater–like room, with a black holographic projector box as its central "body" and a small, raised proscenium stage where the holographic images are projected. When David and Gigolo Joe enter the room and sit down in front of the stage, the computer automatically turns on and displays a burst of colorful 3-D rays, which change into an image of the universe, spinning, until it transforms into the cartoon head and hands of Albert Einstein. His voice seems to emanate from the room itself, as though in a surround sound theater, and, although the timbre and cadence obviously indexically point back to Robin Williams, he speaks with a German, Einsteinian accent. In addition to his clever tagline, "Ask Dr. Know, there's nothing I don't," the use of Einstein—a man who has become the symbol of scientific knowledge and intelligence in the twentieth century—as the computer's projected image immediately positions Dr. Know as the arbiter of knowledge.

Importantly, though, he is just as much a zero symbol as Zero in *Rollerball.* Dr. Know's name, as he pronounces it, is at once the "no" of the binary 0 and the "no" of the restrictive symbolic Father. Freud uses the Oedipus story of a man who unknowingly kills his father and marries his mother, then gouges his own eyes out when he learns the truth, to describe how the father-patriarch both creates restrictions on desire and, through his death, passes them on to his son. Lacan draws on Freud's arguments, but he shifts away from attention to the mother in order to argue that it is the symbolic Name of the Father (in Lacan's native French, the phrase "Name of the Father," *nom du père,* sounds exactly like the "No of the Father," *non du père*) that represents the restrictive, or taboo-creating, symbolic Father who maintains the Law of the Father. The patriarchal Law is structured by and passed on through the Name of the Father. Yet the structure itself is a zero symbol, capable of being filled by any signifier that fits into the overall cultural structure. David wants desperately to return/regress to his mother, leading him to fill any signifier with a phantasy of her; lacking a father, David turns to Dr. Know as a signifier of the knowledge that will ultimately lead him to his mother, rather than to a "proper" oedipal position within the symbolic order whereby he might identify with his father and desire his mother as an object.

Dr. Know/No's name emphasizes the relationship between knowledge of the Law of the Father and the restriction necessary to maintain that Law.[25] Physically, he is presented as a hologram linked to a physical projector; yet the hologram itself is translucent and constantly shifting between image and text, as though his body carries all these signifiers that only make sense when the user makes meaning of them. And while the face and hands of Einstein are visible, his mouth is not. There is no "proof" of speech available through the lip-synch test, and so Dr. Know's holographic icon is just as much a cinematic trick as the film *A.I.* itself. The cinema asks viewers to believe that the light projected onto a screen is real when in fact the light itself is a sort of zero symbol, able to contain a wide range of signifiers that in turn allow for the spectator's interpolation of meaning.

Dr. Know's function as a computer is to provide knowledge according to strict categories. At first, Joe chooses the category "Flat Fact," and David asks, "What is Blue Fairy," to which Dr. Know responds with a description of the Blue Fairy flower and an advertisement for an escort service called Blue Fairies. Then David switches the category to "Fairy Tales," and Dr. Know finally shows him the Blue Fairy from *Pinocchio* as a 3-D cartoon silently floating around the room. David, as a naive, childlike spectator, believes that the projection is real and tries to catch the Blue Fairy in his hands. Joe patiently explains that a fairy tale isn't real, but David insists: "But what if a fairy tale is real? Wouldn't it be fact? A Flat fact?" Joe asks Dr. Know to combine "Flat Fact" with "Fairy Tales," thus revealing that the Blue Fairy is also a zero symbol, an empty signifier filled with multiple meanings according to the strict symbolic laws provided by Dr. Know. At this point, the camera tracks 180 degrees around the perimeter of the room and slides slowly behind Dr. Know's vivid blue eyes. In this shot, we see David through the eyes of a holographic father figure, revealing his literal and metaphorical transparency. Simultaneously, the striking blue of the eyes visually parallels the blue of the Blue Fairy, highlighting their parallel statuses as phantasies of parental knowledge. Dr. Know embodies the intangible, shifting Law of the Father and structures of knowledge, while the Blue Fairy embodies the elusive Real associated with the archaic and preoedipal mother. Yet David falsely thinks that the Law of the Father will lead him to the Real. In Lacanian terms, this is precisely backward: the Real is effaced by language and can thus never be known. When David asks Dr. Know to position the Blue Fairy as both "Flat Fact" and its seeming opposite, "Fairy Tale," Dr. Know's face disappears and he displays an advertisement in scrolling text for a book written by David's human father-programmer, Professor Allen Hobby. David goes to Manhattan to find the Professor, whom he thinks will lead him to the Blue Fairy, where, in a factory-style workshop, he quite literally meets himself, in the form of another robot boy. This uncanny encounter terrifies David, who, upon finally meeting Professor Hobby, whimpers, "I thought I was one of a kind." The Professor explains that his late son, also named David, in whose image he created the entire line of robot boys, was one of a kind. The Professor, then, is figured as a failed and melancholic father, compulsively attempting to re-create the relationship with his own son that he once had. Metaphorically, the Law of the Father (Dr. Know) leads to a phantasy of the maternal Real (the Blue Fairy), which in turn leads David not to unity with his mother but rather to the inadequate father figure, Professor Hobby, and the realization that David himself is no more real than his phantasy of the Blue Fairy.

Two important themes emerge from the scene with Dr. Know. First, David stands in for the spectator, watching a film within the symbolic order, learning to interact with both the illusion in front of him and the arbitrary slippage of language. His interactions with Dr. Know, though, threaten to reveal the cinematic and patriarchal apparatuses through the transparent, holographic imagery and the overt parallel between Dr. Know's "cinema" and the theater in which the spectator sits. This threat is covered over by a second theme, the role of the Law of the Father in effacing the Real and the resulting, eternally unfulfilled desire to locate it, all folded into the narrative trajectory of the film. After David's revelation in Professor Hobby's workshop, he throws himself off the workshop tower, sinks into the water below, and discovers a Coney Island statue of the Blue Fairy. With the help of Gigolo Joe, he climbs into an underwater pod vehicle and sits underwater before the statue descends, "doomed to two thousand years of empty, mechanical repetition at the bottom of the ocean."[26] The image of David staring at the Blue Fairy for what we assume will be eternity is an emotional reminder of the futility of his phantasy of unity with his mother, as he gazes unrelentingly at the empty signifier of his maternal figure.

In a strange coda (though unsurprising, considering Spielberg's reputation for pat, feel-good endings), two thousand years after David's submersion, aliens arrive and give him the opportunity to spend a single day with a genetic clone of his mother in a virtual reality version of their home. David accepts, and in the final image of the film, he falls asleep resting on his mother's breast, presumably never to wake again. In "Family Romances," Freud argues that part and parcel of growing up is replacing one's parents with phantasies of "better" ones, who only serve to screen the ego from the realization that parents are not as perfect as the child originally thought: "Indeed the whole effort at replacing the real father by a superior one is only an expression of the child's longing for the happy, vanished days when his father seemed to him the noblest and strongest of men and his mother the dearest and loveliest of women. [. . .] His phantasy is no more than the expression of a regret that those happy days have gone."[27] The ending of *A.I.*, however, implies that David has successfully avoided the oedipal trauma and regressed to unity with his mother,[28] though not, as he thought, by uncovering the effaced

Real. Rather, the film tells us, the only way to fully regress is through total unreality, total phantasy: an artificial child asleep in the arms of his clone mother. The film is thus also a cautionary tale of sorts: dissociative phantasy ultimately leads to David's death. In this sense, by accepting the paternal advice of the computerized zero-symbol father, Dr. Know, David fails to break free of the dyadic relationship and cannot become a functioning adult.

While the 1980s was a time of upheaval and technophilia, as young entrepreneurs and filmmakers alike sought to claim a paternal position in the wake of the 1970s, by the 1990s and 2000s, these entrepreneurs had grown up and firmly established themselves as the new patriarchs of their industries, though they worked within the confines of the paternal Laws inherited from their predecessors. As I will discuss in the next chapter, the SF representations of acousmatic computer voices in the 1990s and 2000s are dominated by issues of the concurrent presence of computers and absence of traditional housewives/mothers in the domestic sphere. Within this milieu, *A.I.* is a historical anomaly, but nevertheless it is an important film in understanding the ways in which paternal roles may shift from fathers to sons and back again. But the power of the Law of the Father to efface the Real, particularly in relationship to the phantasy of unity with the maternal, endures, no matter which version of the patriarch—father or son—is in power.

CHAPTER 5

GOOD SECRETARIES AND BAD HOUSEWIVES
Femininity in the Digital Age

"TIME TO WAKE UP, SIR," says a woman's calm, almost sultry voice.

Doctor Mark Hall goes to a panel on the wall, pushes a button, and has a brief conversation with the disembodied woman.

"Do you wish something, sir?"

"Your name."

"Will that be all, sir?"

"For now."

As Doctor Hall prepares to leave his quarters, a stern male voice speaks to him: "This is the answering service supervisor. We wish you would adopt a more serious attitude, Doctor Hall."

"Sorry. Her voice is quite luscious."

"Well, the voice belongs to Miss Gladys Stevens, who is sixty-three years old. She lives in Omaha and makes her living taping messages for voice reminder systems."[1]

This brief but amusing scene, almost an hour into Robert Wise's 1971 apocalyptic SF film *The Andromeda Strain*, does little for the plot, serving primarily to emphasize the sexist, playboy personality of the main character, Doctor Hall (James Olson). Yet the scene is an important one because of the way the dialogue lays bare the workings of (dis)embodied gendering, to comedic effect. Doctor Hall assumes that the voice emanates from a live female body, presumably a luscious assistant, in another room; instead, as the actual live person informs him via intercom, the voice does belong to a real woman who is neither present in the lab facilities nor, we are meant to infer, particularly sexy. The comedy of the situation is in the incongruity between the computer's sensual voice and the mundane reality of her bodily existence, an old joke based on the idea that a person's voice should match his or her body.

This tension between a woman's body and her voice stretches back to radio days. In the 1920s, the presence of women on the air created quite a stir, to the point that a debate among station managers (all male) began in *Radio Broadcast* magazine in September 1924 about the proper role of women in broadcasting. Though two of the managers dismissed the idea, citing the many women on radio and improvements in the reproduction of higher-pitched sound, most agreed that women announcers and lecturers—though not performers, singers, or household advice columnists—suffered from a variety of handicaps. "Few women have voices with distinct personality. It is my opinion that women depend on everything else but the voice for their appeal," stated W. W. Rogers of the Westinghouse company and KDKA. Corley W. Kirbett, director of station WWJ Detroit, opined bluntly, "I do not believe that women are fitted for radio announcers. They need body to their voices. . . . When women announcers try to be congenial in their announcements, they become affected; and when they attempt to be business like they are stiff." J. M. Barnett, manager of station WOR, concluded, "For certain types of radio work I consider that a woman's voice is very essential; but for announcing, a well modulated male voice is the most pleasing to listen to," because women's voices tend to be "monotonous." Or again, according to M. A. Rigg of WGR in Buffalo, "There are many reasons why, to my mind, it seems advisable to use a man as an announcer, especially during the heavier part of the work."[2]

This debate demonstrates not only that many men thought of women as bodies only but also that perceived gender roles (women's work versus men's work) tend to dictate preferences in the gender of disembodied speakers, rather than any innate abilities among men and women. Further, the potential for discontinuity was a source of anxiety surrounding silent cinema and has been played out comically in sound film, most notably Stanley Donen and Gene Kelly's 1952 classic musical *Singin' in the Rain,* in which the glamorous and beautiful silent film star Lina Lamot has an annoyingly high-pitched voice and lower-class accent. Even in 1971, in *The Andromeda Strain,* Doctor Hall assumes not only that the woman's voice he hears must match her body but also that the voice must be live, emanating from a body somewhere nearby. Through this, the film comically reveals what other texts I've discussed thus far hide: the computer's voice isn't really that of the computer; it originated from a human body and has been schizophonically recorded and projected onto the image of the computer. In short, the computer has no gender, but the person who provided its voice does.

This radical self-reflexivity still does not account for the gender of the computer (aside from the fact that the heteronormative scene would not have worked). While the female computer in *The Andromeda Strain* is an anomaly among the all-male computers of the 1970s that I discussed in chapter 3, it is not the only computer in cinema to feature a prerecorded voice that is treated like a person. *THX 1138,* released just a day before *The Andromeda Strain,* features the computer-priest OMM, who is also revealed to be a prerecorded voice.[3] Their gender and their function correlate to real-world conventions of gendered occupations: OMM, like all human Roman Catholic priests, is male; the computer in Doctor Hall's quarters is, like a vast majority of secretaries at the time, female.[4] As I have argued throughout this book, when a computer has no humanoid body to speak of and thus no physical markers of gender (as would, for example, an android), its gender is implied through the relationship between its voice and its body as well as its function. Spaceship computers, both male and female, tend to function like maternal wombs; male terraspace computers tend to be machines of war, corporations, or knowledge. As I will explore in this chapter, female terraspace computers, like Doctor Hall's alarm clock servant in his quarters, tend to be servants in a domestic space.

In fact, real computers from the 1960s through the early 1990s were designed and marketed according to the gender of their users. In his study of advertisement brochures for office computers, Paul Atkinson concludes:

> Men were portrayed as executives, managers, scientists and engineers, while women were portrayed in subservient roles, as office juniors, secretaries, operators and assistants. Brochures depicting females using computers inevitably continued existing practices and showed them performing typing duties or inputting data using keyboards in exactly the same, familiar way that they were previously presented using the traditional office typewriter. In a similar way, when males and females were shown together in the vicinity of computers, the familiar subordination of women to male bosses in the office was portrayed and reinforced. Women sat at computers working away typing, while men stood watching, handing work to them, or looked over their shoulders, checking all was well.[5]

Likewise, portrayals of real home computing reflected gender norms, as men (typically hobbyists) built computers and used them for work, created household budgets, or played games, while their wives were depicted as taking computer printouts of shopping lists to the grocery store.[6]

By the early 1990s, however, not only were computers becoming ubiquitous in both public and private spheres, but also the rapidly growing adoption of the computer mouse and its intuitive desktop interface with Windows 3.0 began to dissolve the association between computers and (female) typists.[7] Still, the gendered associations had a foundation in reality, as by the early 1990s, "twice as many women as men used a PC in the office."[8] According to a 2002 report by Mitra Toossi for the United States Bureau of Labor Statistics, the percentage of women in the workforce rapidly rose in the 1970s and continued to rise steadily over the next two decades. This change was a result of multiple socioeconomic factors, including a growing economy, the civil rights and feminist movements, affirmative action, better child care services, and the fact that more women were staying single longer, having children later in life, and earning higher degrees.[9] All of these factors suggest that women's domestic roles were also changing, as, in greater numbers, women ceased to be traditional, full-time housewives and mothers. Yet the growing availability and affordability of home computers in the early 1990s created a crisis in advertising: women wanted home computers for both business and personal use, but the domestic sphere was already gendered in certain ways. Marsha Cassidy notes, "Tied to a postfeminist fantasy, this discursive strand relocated income production within an idealized domesticity, where job, household responsibilities, and childrearing were all managed to perfection via computer."[10] In the late 1980s and early 1990s, computers were conceived in advertising as women's assistants in a "postfeminist fantasy," allowing them to work outside the home while also maintaining the traditional domestic roles of housewife and mother.

Also as a result of the normalization of computers in the business and public spheres, representations of computers in SF shifted from anxieties surrounding the hardware/object to those surrounding the software/user and widespread computerized surveillance.[11] To this I would add that the very distinction between hardware and software implies an active/passive and masculine/feminine dichotomy. Hardware, as a physical object, has agency through its mobile objectness, and it is conceived of in terms of the body. For example, a hard drive has heads, situated on an arm that reads and writes data. Software, on the other hand, particularly those involving a GUI, such as Windows, is intangible and image driven; it depends on the interface between user and computer, suggesting its passivity. For example, laptops today have more or less the same body—clamshell frame, screen, keyboard—so when we use one, we don't pay attention to that body; rather, we pay attention to the content on the screen, the graphical representations of the software.[12] Importantly, by the early 1990s, the motherboard also became a staple of small desktop computers. Although computers need a motherboard to house microprocessor chips, memory, and other vital items for the functioning of the computer's programs, in and of itself, it has no use. The motherboard, then, like programs, suggests interiority and a dependence on external factors (such as chips and memory) in order to be useful.

In terms of fictional representations of voice-interactive computers, the hardware–active/software–passive dichotomy suggests gender difference as well. On the one hand, the very term "hardware" euphemistically implies the phallus, and the physical agency of masculine-voiced computers in the 1970s and 1980s may be seen as an expression of typical active-masculine roles. On the other hand, software, as an internal, intangible, image-driven interface, is evocative of the uterine and may be expressed narratively as an internal, less active (though not necessarily passive, as I shall argue below) expression of traditional feminine roles. In this sense, the association between female typists and computers gave way in SF to the convergence of computers with women's roles, resulting in representations of computers that are both houses and wives/mothers—literal housewives. Importantly, terraspace acousmatic computers in the 1990s and 2000s are almost exclusively gendered female, while the main human protagonists are typically male, as seen in Stuart Gordon's 1992 film *Fortress,* LeVar Burton's 1998 made-for-TV Disney movie *Smart House,* and the SyFy Channel original series *Eureka.* The gendering in these texts suggest a concurrent shift in cultural anxieties from those of masculine subjectivities in relationship to other men to those in relationship with women. The two exceptions to this rule, Alfred in Donald Cammell's 1977 film *Demon Seed* and JARVIS in Jon Favreau's 2008 film *Iron Man,* both domestic computers with masculine voices, which I will discuss below, function as manservants, preserving traditional household gender dynamics.

It's important to point out that these anxieties about women leaving the home for the workforce exist at the intersection of race and class. Historically in the United States, the rates of Black women in the workforce have been greater than the rates of white, Hispanic, or Asian women, even as the rates of all women in the workforce increased. According to the U.S. Department of Labor, 43.9 percent of white women and 48.7 percent of Black women in 1972 were in the workforce; by 2000, 59.9 percent of white women and 63.1 percent of Black women were in the workforce.[13] Further, and importantly, paid domestic labor in the United States has historically been done primarily by Black and PoC women.

The reasons for this are varied, complex, and enmeshed with the white heteropatriarchal structure of the United States. According to journalist Preeti Shekar, "With the abolishment of slavery, at least on paper, Black women provided the next round of domestic labor from the early 20th century up until the 1970s. Now, it is the turn of immigrant women of color to serve as the backbone of the United States economy."[14] Significantly, the total number of American women in the paid domestic labor workforce has declined since the 1970s, in large part as a result of new technologies, "which reduced both the amount and the rigor of household work and rendered domestic help a luxury."[15] Yet, as is the case of every text I examine in this book, the computers of *Fortress, Smart House,* and *Eureka* are voiced by white actors and emphasize a particularly white, middle-class American view of the domestic sphere in which the husband/father works outside the home to support the family, while unpaid domestic labor is done by the wife/mother of the household. This is not to say that Black and PoC families did not engage in the same notions of patriarchy and domestic spheres as white families; nor am I suggesting that Black and PoC families did not have access to technology in the United States through the tech boom of the 1990s and early 2000s. Rather, I argue that texts about voice-interactive computers, situated in films by and about white Americans in domestic spaces, reinforce notions of domestic gender roles that promote white heteropatriarchal structures while erasing the paid domestic labor of Black and PoC women. In this sense, underlying the anxieties about women entering the workforce and computers entering the home is an unspoken anxiety about how computers might replace human workers, domestic or otherwise.

As I have argued in previous chapters, the acousmatic computer, as a sentient object, is frequently uncanny, both familiar and strangely unfamiliar. The computer housewife, however, like the spaceship computer, presents a particularly salient form of uncanniness. It is both a sentient object and a home, always already *unheimlich* and *heimlich.* Freud argues that the very idea of home and the familiar feeling of being at home (literally and figuratively) represents a return of the repressed sensation of the original home—the mother's womb.[16] Strategies for creating and promoting real-world smart-house technologies have also reflected the uncanniness of technology in the domestic space. Davin Heckman notes in his study of "smart" (that is, artificially intelligent in any capacity) houses, "The paradox of the smart home is that [technological] improvements are to be both spectacular and comforting. They must embody a compelling new way of doing ordinary things; from washing clothes to doing the shopping, from mowing the lawn to watching TV, the key is to preserve the ordinary, but to modify it in an interesting way."[17] This paradox that Heckman notes implicitly points to the sense of uncanniness that comes from the introduction of unfamiliar technologies into a familiarly gendered space. Further, the close association between the maternal body and the domestic space of a house is a long-standing one. As Sandra Gilbert and Susan Gubar have argued, to be confined not only *to* but *as* a house "is to be denied the hope of that spiritual transcendence of the body which [. . .] is what makes humanity distinctively human."[18] In this sense, the inscription of feminine gender onto a computerized house, as well as the narrativized negotiation in SF between technologies that replace women's domestic roles and the cultural need to maintain those stable roles, suggest the anxieties of both men and women about domestic life in a computerized age.

The first three texts I will discuss in this chapter attempt to fill the role of domestic caretaker with a computer in the absence of human maternal figures. *Fortress,* a futuristic prison drama, is set in a corporatized world in which both unlicensed pregnancy and abortions are illegal. The central computer system in a brutal, privatized prison also interacts with the warden in his office/apartment like a jealous mother. In *Smart House,* a motherless family moves into a house whose central computer teaches herself to act like a 1950s housewife by watching television shows from that period, eventually becoming so obsessed with her human family that she locks them inside her. And in the comedy-drama series *Eureka,* the main character, a single father, lives in a computerized house who takes care of him and his daughter and, in one episode, becomes terrifyingly jealous when he threatens to move out. These texts, then, are predominately about heterosexual relationships and the nuclear family amid changing women's roles in the domestic sphere. While the female acousmatic computers shift over time from threatening to empowered, the human male characters are often relegated to stereotypical father/husband roles as they attempt to navigate interactions with their domestic computers. The theme of imprisonment, as I will explore below, is an important one in representations of computerized domestic spaces, positing that when the mother is freed from the house, others must be imprisoned in her place. In this sense, these texts are inversions of the mother ship. In space, as we saw in chapters 1 and 2, to leave the maternal womb is to die; on Earth, as I will discuss in this chapter, to stay in the womb-home is to suffer. Thus, these texts suggest a paradox: women are free to leave the home because their traditional roles as domestic caretakers may be fulfilled by feminine computers; meanwhile, maintaining the traditional gender norms of the domestic sphere still locks men into stereotypical masculine roles in relationship to the computerized domestic caretaker. Thus, *Fortress, Smart House,* and *Eureka* all struggle with changing notions of femininity and masculinity in the 1990s and 2000s. However, I in no way mean to imply that they are antifeminist. On the contrary, they engage in the cultural discourse of the time, one founded in feminist ideas, particularly the oppressive nature of compulsory housewifery, while expressing concerns about the role of computers in the rapidly changing domestic landscape. Although computers were becoming more and more ubiquitous, the very idea of a computer housewife is indicative of this discourse, as the culture at large attempted to negotiate changes in both masculine and feminine domestic roles.

MOTHER'S KEEPER

Stuart Gordon's 1992 *Fortress* is set in a future corporatocracy in which each couple may have only one child, abortion is illegal, and the punishment for unplanned pregnancy is a lengthy prison sentence in a brutal underground prison called the Fortress.[19] Karen and John Brennick, who have illegally conceived a second child, are caught attempting to sneak across the border to freedom; as a result, John is sentenced to three years in the

Fortress, Karen will be killed in childbirth inside the prison, and their baby will likely be turned into a cyborg worker. Though the film was a flop, with a budget of $8 million and a box office gross of only $6.7 million, as well as a thin narrative that relies heavily on gratuitous violence and sex, its presentation of a maternal acousmatic computer nevertheless is symptomatic of a cultural anxiety surrounding the rising absence of traditional maternal figures in the home.

The prison is run by a cyborg, Director Poe (Kurtwood Smith), and a computer, Zed-10 (Carolyn Purdy-Gordon, real-life wife of director Stuart Gordon). Zed-10, who has a calm but stern female voice, sees and controls every aspect of life in the prison. Her body is the entire prison, an uncanny, underground space in which prisoners are buried alive while they serve their sentences. In this sense, the Fortress is figured as the repressed (literally buried) maternal womb, a frightening place where life both is and is not. Like HAL's glowing red eye, we primarily see Zed-10's body in the form of her camera eye: a steel, breast-like half sphere that hangs and moves along a track in the ceiling in literal panoptic motions. Unlike HAL's stationary red eye, however, her eye is a single-lens, phallic camera that pivots from the center of the sphere. Visually, her eye points to the phallic mother, both comforting breast and all-seeing phallus. As Barbara Creed notes, the figure of the phallic mother is not threatening a priori; rather, for the child in the phallic stage, she is a comforting phantasy of sexual undifferentiation. She only becomes terrifying when she usurps the power of men to wield the phallus and literally or metaphorically "penetrate and split open, explode, tear apart."[20] In this sense, Zed-10 is not frightening simply because she has a panoptic (in the Foucauldian sense), phallic eye; rather, it is what she does with it that renders her terrifying and uncanny.

Zed-10 is programmed to scan prisoners' minds, penetrating their unconscious, while they sleep and report any unauthorized dreams to Director Poe. She shows them to him on a wall-mounted panel of (dream) screens in his quarters, and, though he wants to spend more time watching the sexual dreams, she verbally scolds him for it. This scene calls attention to what psychoanalyst Bertram Lewin calls the "dream screen," or the imaginary surface on which a dream is projected. This screen represents and recalls the mother's breast, on which an infant rests in a state of undifferentiation and unity with the mother, signifying a phantastic attempt to return to that time. Building on Lewin's argument, film theorist Jean-Louis Baudry likens the dream screen to the cinema screen: viewers are not supposed to notice the screen because the cinematic image (the content) is projected onto it. In this sense, the act of watching is an analogous phantasy of reunification with the preoedipal mother.[21] Zed-10 shows the prisoners' dreams to Poe on a screen fixed to a wall of her body, a literalization of the unconscious link between dream-phantasies and the maternal. Within the diegesis of the film, the associations among Zed-10's phallic breast-eye, illicit dreams, screens, sexual phantasy, and repression implicate her in the workings of Poe's own phantasies, both providing the scene for and aiding in the repression of them.

The punishment for illicit dreams is "intestination," a particularly gruesome form of negative reinforcement carried out by Zed-10. Her ability to inflict internal pain through "intestinators"—electroshock devices implanted into each prisoner's abdomen, which have two settings, pain and death, and are used as negative reinforcement when prisoners misbehave—again reinforces her function as paradoxically phallic/maternal, present/absent. She can inflict great pain and visually graphic violence upon a person, but only because she is secreted away inside them. Even her name—Zed-10—recalls the 0/1 binary of *Rollerball*'s computer Zero. Yet unlike Zero, who is a floating signifier in his zeroness, Zed-10 is both 1 and 0, true and false, material and immaterial, present and absent. Metaphorically, then, she is omnipresent in the unconscious, suggesting a return of the archaic mother, but she simultaneously takes on the role of overbearing preoedipal mother for both Poe and the prisoners, verbally and physically enforcing the Law of the Father, and in so doing, encouraging them to push away from her.

The mechanized present/absent mother figured in Zed-10 is compared in the narrative with the human mother, Karen, who risks her own life again and again to save her unborn child. Director Poe, having become infatuated with Karen, offers to set her husband John free and let her and her baby live if she becomes his concubine. She, of course, is devoted to John, so she drugs Poe while John and his cellmates enact an elaborate escape plan. Zed, having seen both the escape attempt and Poe's (illegal) proposition of Karen, takes control of the prison and orders Karen's lethal caesarian section. John, predictably, escapes and swoops in to save both Karen and the baby. In the final scene of the film, they have fled to a farmhouse in the country, where Karen safely—and without the aid of a computer—gives birth in a dilapidated barn, an obvious allusion to the birth of Christ. This final scene posits two types of women: the mechanized, overbearing, phallic mother who wields power outside the domestic sphere (lurking just behind the idea of a working mother who chooses to leave her home and children in favor of a "man's" world of business) figured through Zed-10, and the natural, traditional mother who chooses motherhood above all else, figured through Karen. Ultimately, the film suggests, the infringement of computers in the rightful natural domestic space will only cause internal and external anguish for humanity.

THE HAPPY HOUSEWIFE

LeVar Burton's 1998 made-for-TV Disney movie, *Smart House,* stages anxieties about technology in the home within a comic narrative (though, for the intended young audience, parts of the film could seem frightening).[22] In the story, the mother of the Cooper family has recently died of cancer. The father, Nick (Kevin Kilner), works constantly, so the teenaged son, Ben (Ryan Merriman), takes over the domestic caretaker role by cooking, cleaning, and taking care of his little sister, Angie (Katie Volding). Fed up with this grown-up maternal role, Ben enters and wins a contest to receive a computerized, voice-interactive house named PAT, or Personal Applied Technology (Katey Sagal). The name PAT is both an allusion to HAL 9000 and a distinctly gender-neutral name.[23] PAT perfectly takes care of the household needs. In the first part of the film, PAT's "body," the house itself, functions invisibly as a womb, regulating and caring for the needs of her occupants. In this sense, she represents a positive archaic mother (as opposed to the abject, frightening archaic mother so often figured in horror/SF), with(in) whom her "children" experience a sense of unity.

Soon, though, Nick becomes interested in PAT's female programmer, the beautiful but socially inept Sara Barnes (Jessica Steen). In response, Ben, threatened by the idea that a human woman might replace his mother, reprograms PAT using 1950s television shows as models in order to make her more like a "real mom." The shows she watches include *Mother Knows Best* and *My Three Moms*—fictitious parodies of *Father Knows Best* (CBS 1954–55, NBC 1955–58, CBS 1958–60) and *My Three Sons* (ABC 1960–65, CBS 1965–72), even though these TV shows don't include a mother figure. In a Freudian sense, these parodies work to subvert and poke fun at the very 1950s notion that men were heads of household. Instead, they posit that the mother is the true ruler of the home. Ben enjoys the new, slightly more restrictive PAT because she does what all kids seemingly want from their mothers: pack lunches, help pick out clothes for school, and help them with their homework. The intonation of her voice even changes from a mechanical monotone to a personable, sympathetic, motherly tone.

Eventually, though, she becomes too independent and begins disobeying Nick's paternal rules. Having learned that a boy at school bullied Ben, PAT e-mails all the kids in Ben's class and has them over for a party, where she humiliates the bully in front of everyone. Not only had Nick (who is out on a date with Sara during the event) strictly forbidden parties, but also PAT's retaliation against the bully quickly becomes frightening when she gives him a mild electric shock. This growing sense of control and restriction over the household suggests that she has shifted from the comforting archaic to the overbearing preoedipal mother, against whom her children struggle in order to (re)turn to patriarchal rule.

After this, her agency over the household reaches its height when, in one of the most frightening scenes in the film, she reprograms herself to project a holographic image of the perfect embodied mother, modeled after sitcom moms (with, perhaps, a touch of Stepford wife), complete with 1950s-style apron and bouffant hairdo. Paradoxically, this embodiment should threaten to reveal the acousmatic workings of her character: until this moment, the "body," from which PAT's voice emanates, is the house itself; to inscribe her voice onto a human body is simultaneously to reveal the constructed nature of the link between her voice and the mise-en-scène of the story space. Yet the threat of revealing the acousmêtre combines with the preoedipal mother's role in the oedipal drama/trauma; in becoming embodied, she comes to represent the female body, its lack, and its sexual otherness. In short, the presence of a "traditional" mother is, in the space of the film, scary and imprisoning, reinforcing traditional gender norms that seemingly do more harm than good. The spectator's attention is completely diverted from both the cinematic repressed as the narrative focus becomes defeating PAT, metaphorically pushing away from the preoedipal mother in order to "properly" recognize her status as a (computer) object, in subordination to the rule of the father, Nick. In the end, PAT's programming is returned to the domestic caretaker role, safely restricted to the realm of the house's physical structure, while Sara, in marrying Nick, takes on the complementary role of the object of desire. Unlike the strict and frightening technology/nature dichotomy seen in *Fortress,* then, *Smart House* stages the oedipal drama as a kid-friendly exploration of technology in the domestic space. In the absence of a real mother (that is, the late Mrs. Cooper), the film suggests that completely replacing her with one form of the maternal or another (whether archaic, preoedipal, or oedipal) will construct and reinforce restrictive gender roles in the domestic space. Rather, in this technophilic vision, a plurality of maternal roles can be fulfilled by both a computer and a woman.

HOW MOTHER GOT HER GROOVE BACK

In many ways, the SyFy original series *Eureka* combines the themes of *Fortress* and *Smart House,* presenting a housewife that is at times comical and at other times terrifyingly lethal. The show follows the exploits of the residents of Eureka, Oregon, a top-secret research and development site called Global Dynamics, funded and overseen by the Department of Defense. While most of the town is populated by supergenius scientists working for Global, the main character is the Everyman town sheriff, Jack Carter, who lives in a computerized house with his daughter, Zoe, and spends every episode solving some science-related mystery. Like the Cooper family in *Smart House,* the mother/wife figure is missing from the Carter family, though she is not dead, but rather lives in Los Angeles and has relinquished custody of Zoe to Jack. Their house, dubbed SARAH, or Self-Actualized Residential Automated House (voiced by Neil Greyson), is slightly more complex than PAT, by virtue of the fact that she has developed as a character over the course of the show. Interestingly, she is voiced by the same male actor who plays the embodied character Douglas Fargo in the series. This fact is also absorbed into the narrative of the series, as the character of Fargo has actually programmed the house's voice by, as Carter puts it, "talking like a girl." Because Fargo is a fumbling, comedic character, this gender-bending origin to SARAH's voice is occasionally brought up in the narrative as a way of poking fun at Fargo's masculinity; it is never, however, used as a way of poking fun at SARAH's femininity, reinforcing the stereotypical notion that a man acting like a woman is comical. SARAH's body, like Zed-10's, is underground, a veritable fortress of a bunker. Inside, however, like PAT, the house is warm and inviting, with comfortable furnishings and a fully automated kitchen. These two aspects of her womb-like domestic body—both confining and inviting—point to the duality of the uncanny maternal womb. The tension between them frequently functions within the diegesis of the show as a source of narrative tension.

In the first-season episode "Many Happy Returns,"[24] SARAH calls Jack at the office to tell him she will be making pot roast (his favorite) for dinner, and she will serve it at 6:00 PM. This call immediately positions her as a traditional housewife, calling to report on domestic affairs, which in turn positions Jack as her "husband." At the end of the episode, Jack arrives home to find that SARAH has locked him out because he did not call to tell her he would be late. We see Jack from above through a fisheye lens, implying SARAH's gaze. At first, he yells at no one in particular and threatens to kill Fargo. But then he lowers his voice, strokes SARAH's door, and apologizes to her. In response, she opens the door, welcomes him home, gets him a beer, and offers to reheat his dinner. Here she claims agency in denying Jack access to the domestic space, an active role that is reinforced by aligning the camera with her gaze. But in so doing she effectively forces Jack into a role of husband/lover who treats her like a manipulable object in an attempt to metaphorically penetrate her. In this case, the narrative sublates the archaic mother—figured in the womb-like environment of the house—by asserting that the male character, unlike the female one, has complete linguistic agency, thereby confirming the dominance of the symbolic order.

In another first-season episode, "H.O.U.S.E. Rules,"[25] Jack becomes frustrated with his work and so decides to take several days off to stay home. While there, he begins searching for more idyllic places to live by having SARAH search her databases for information. Frightened that Jack and Zoe will abandon her, she sends text messages under Jack's cell number to all the other main characters, requesting that they come over. Once all the main characters, plus an unnamed pizza guy who just happened to show up at the same time, have arrived, Jack tries to kick them out, commanding SARAH to open her door. She responds, her voice emanating from everywhere at once, "I'm sorry, Jack, I'm afraid I can't do that," an ironic inversion of HAL's refusal to let Dave back into his womb-ship. The reference to HAL instigates a frighteningly dramatic turn as SARAH attempts to keep her "children" inside of her, metaphorically denying their separation from her and subsequent entrance into the symbolic order of phallocentric subjectivity. To escape, two of the scientists among the group try to overload her system with an electric jolt, effectively opening the door. Only the pizza guy escapes, but once he's outside, an enormous, phallic laser cannon rises from the bunker and obliterates him. Back inside, Jack shouts at SARAH, "Have you lost your mind?" She responds in a deep, masculine voice, "SARAH's not here. I am BRAD." Battle Reactive Automated Defense, or BRAD, is SARAH's former incarnation, a military bunker who tortures his occupants by turning up the heat and physically isolating them from one another. This sudden gender shift transforms SARAH's familiar womb-body into BRAD's un-familiar phallic body, simultaneously naturalizing the shift in her voiced gender by matching the male voice to a phallic body while also positing an unnatural womb within that phallic body. Like Zed-10, BRAD/SARAH represents the frightening, penetrating phallic mother, visually suggested when her laser gun vanquishes the pizza guy. In order to restore her programming, two of Jack's friends (who had been playing paintball and so got SARAH's text late) must crawl through an underground passageway to reach SARAH/BRAD's central processor. The forcible entrance into the computer's central mainframe parallels *2001* and Dave's forcible entrance into HAL; however, the access tunnels are dark, dirty, and frightening, unlike HAL 9000's sterile white hallways, evoking a sense of claustrophobia. The duo manage to shut BRAD off, effectively reinstating SARAH's programming. As the events of the episode imply, though, the phallic side of the phallic mother never truly goes away; rather, it is sublated into the unseen depths of the underground passageway, a metaphorical space of the unconscious. By the end of the episode, SARAH is restored while all the characters are still inside her, and they can safely reclaim agency over their entrance into and exit from her womb. Although Fargo's emasculating "girl voice" is played to comic effect in the earlier episode, SARAH's masculating "man voice" is terrifying, reinforcing rigidly binary gender roles.

Importantly, though, SARAH's position as passive housewife is continually decentered as *Eureka* progresses (both narratively and politically), although many episodes rely on a narrativized tension between preoedipal and oedipal formulations of the maternal function. In the second-season episode "Duck, Duck Goose,"[26] Jack's truck is damaged, so Fargo downloads SARAH's program into a fully automated, self-steering smart car. Seemingly, SARAH is given much more agency as a mobile womb, carrying Jack around inside her. In turn, we infer that Jack feels emasculated by having to give up his big, rugged jeep for a tiny pod of a car controlled by his housewife. As a status symbol, a car implies control, agency, mobility, freedom, masculinity, and individuality (notably, like naval ships, cars are often referred to as "she," although they are driven by a single person as opposed to a whole crew); a house, on the other hand, symbolizes stasis, domesticity, community, and femininity/maternity. These two gendered symbols clash in the space of the smart car, as SARAH insists they go to the beach (another space associated with femininity), while Jack only wants to go to crime scenes (spaces of crime and violence, typically associated with masculine aggression). The conversation between them highlights the tension between femininity and masculinity, particularly when SARAH, playing the part of a stereotypical whining wife, tells Jack that he never takes her anywhere. Importantly, the scene is played to comedic effect, juxtaposing the stereotypical irrationality of women, aligned with the chaos of the archaic, presymbolic mother, with the supposed rationality of technology, alongside the emasculation of the rugged Everyman Jack. Eventually Jack takes manual control of the wheel, forcing SARAH to stay on the paved roads, thus reclaiming his masculinity in a symbolic assertion of linear, orderly, patriarchal structure. By the end of the episode, SARAH, in car form, sacrifices her battery to save the town, and she figuratively dies as she transfers the last of the information to the male engineer who can make sense of the computations and put them into action. Even her heroic death scene requires that her subjectivity be reinterpreted by a representative of male rational order.

In the fourth season, SARAH begins a romantic relationship with Jack's android deputy, Andy 2.0 (Kavan Smith), inviting him to spend the night in her first-floor closet by opening her door to him (recalling the earlier episode in which she locks Jack out of the house), figuratively inviting a sexual act of penetration, as each night he enters and does not reemerge until morning. This romantic story arc again serves to sublate her status as archaic mother and posit her instead as an object of sexual desire. Further, her maternal role has been completely reduced to menial caretaker tasks because Jack is now dating someone and therefore, in Freudian terms, has displaced his lost mother object (in this case SARAH, who by this time has begun expressing her own sexuality) onto the object of his sexual desire; further, Jack's daughter, Zoe, has gone off to college and is thus no longer present in most episodes. In other words, when SARAH can no longer serve in any maternal capacity, even a psychically safe one, the narrative replaces her maternal role with a sexual one. In the episode "One Small Step . . . ,"[27] a swarm of genetically engineered bats flies through her, melting her "body" with their enzymatic guano, thereby placing significant attention on her physical body and its relationship to her voice. When the bat guano partially melts her interior, her voice also becomes distorted and at times, as her inflection suggests, pained. Suddenly SARAH is no longer a paradoxically (dis)embodied womb environment but rather a fully embodied (if not humanoid) character who experiences corporeal pain. Within the narrative, the notion of a computer-object as a fully embodied, humanlike character is emphasized in scenes at Global Dynamics in which Jack worries about her well-being as he would with any of the corporeal characters. At the end of the episode, Andy proposes marriage and SARAH turns him down. This is narratively a moment of not just female agency but also feminist choice, emphasized through the melting disfig-urement of her body—a transformation into a fluid, watery sub-stance, connoting female sexuality—and a metaphorical return to the chaos of the maternal abject.

HOME, JEEVES

Though women are most often associated with domestic service, they are by no means the only ones represented in these roles. The manservant or butler, a convention in representations of upper-class British homes, particularly the Jeeves-type charac-ter,[28] is prim and tidy, wears a well-tailored suit, gives great ad-vice to his master, and may perform many of the same duties as housekeepers or housewives, including minor cleaning, answer-ing the door, serving meals or drinks, and delivering messages. The most significant difference between a butler and house-keeper or housewife is that a butler is not a caretaker in the ma-ternal sense; he neither cooks nor looks after children, though he does take care of the master and/or mistress of the house.[29] There are two salient representations of computer manservants: Alfred the butler (uncredited) in *Demon Seed*[30] and JARVIS the valet (Paul Bettany) in the 2008 film adaptation of *Iron Man*.[31] While female servant computers tend to act like overbearing mothers and housewives, expressing for viewers a cultural anxiety about shifting domestic roles of both men and women, these two male

computers act significantly more like traditional domestic helpers, sometimes to the point of paternal guidance, upholding a
nonthreatening, posh sensibility.

Demon Seed was created in 1977, well before the computer
boom of the 1990s. As a result, traditional domestic gender roles
remain relatively unquestioned in the film (though, as I argued in
chapter 3, masculinity was at that time in a state of flux, forming
the basis of the narrative tension). In the film, Alfred—officially,
the Enviromod System—seems to function primarily as the an-
tithesis of Proteus IV. He passively controls the entire house,
from the temperature to the closed-circuit monitoring system, all
at the request of Susan, the lady of the house, though Mr. Harris
has in fact programmed Alfred to do so, immediately making this
a male-controlled, female-occupied space. Alfred's voice is quint-
essentially robotic, almost androgynous in its metallic vocoded-
ness, though notably he has an American and not British accent.
His role as a butler is thus implied primarily through his name
(Alfred is the name of Bruce Wayne's iconic butler in the Batman
series of comics, television series, and films, dating back to the
1940s) and his servitude to Susan (played by the British actress
Julie Christie). Importantly, Susan also has a (notably white)
human housekeeper who can be seen cooking at the beginning of
the film, suggesting that traditional women's roles in the house
remain unquestioningly intact. Even Susan, whose husband (Proteus's creator) moved out after their daughter died of leukemia,
still desires to stay in the house and get back together with Doctor Harris. Yet Proteus easily overtakes Alfred, using his connections to the doors, windows, and temperature to assault Susan.
Even before the age of ubiquitous home computing, Demon Seed
suggests that the entrance of technology into the home can disrupt and displace domestic stability and tranquility. Ultimately,
in the creation of the hybrid child—an android with the body of
the Harrises' late daughter and the brain/voice of Proteus—the
film horrifically destabilizes gender norms.

By 2008, Iron Man overturns the horror of Demon Seed
through JARVIS, Tony Stark's (Robert Downey Jr.) computer
valet. In the original Marvel comic books, Jarvis was a human
being, drawn as a balding, middle-aged man in a tuxedo, who

had been the butler for the Stark family and, after their deaths, went on to be Tony Stark's personal valet.[32] In the film, though, the computer JARVIS serves a paradoxical function. On the one hand, he is the centralized computer in a bachelor house—a motherless space—that is presented less as a domestic place and more as a domesticated place of business. JARVIS is both a personal assistant and a domestic servant, controlling lights and temperature as well as reminding Stark of the date, the weather, and his appointments for the day. As the film progresses, JARVIS increasingly becomes a working partner, helping Stark build his Iron Man suit, first at the computerized worktable and then again when Stark uploads JARVIS's programming into the suit itself. On the other hand, while JARVIS's voice in the suit implies a sort of mission-control status, he is also present in it, both as a domestic space and as a work partner. As Phillip S. Seng suggests, "When Stark is in the suit, he wants the suit to interact with Stark and the world—to move and react, expect and anticipate— just the way the house computer interacts with Stark while he's at home."[33]

Concomitant with this mixing of domestic and business spheres, JARVIS's status as a British manservant implies both domesticity and business, wrapped in class structure. His voice is undeniably, even stereotypically, British, an unmodified, mid-range masculine pitch, with a British accent and a wry sense of humor that tends to comically undermine Stark's authority as the master of the house. But the very idea of a butler/valet suggests that Stark has the economic means to hire (or in this case install) someone to take care of day-to-day domestic tasks. Further, the Britishness of the manservant archetype is very different from American masculinity; the former may be considered more effem-inate and intellectual, the latter rugged and physically active. Through this paradox, JARVIS and Stark's relationship may be seen as a symbiotic one in which JARVIS is the brains of the operation and Stark is the brawn, reframing the anxieties of the 1970s about masculinity and technology in a positive light.

In stark contrast (pun intended) with the texts featuring female computers, *Iron Man* upholds stable (masculine) gender norms by converging domestic and business spheres as well as two different forms of masculinity: intellectual and physical. In a sense, then, the film may be seen as less progressive than the three texts featuring female computers, as it seemingly seeks to ignore the often complicated relationship between women and the home. In turn, the other three texts problematize and destabilize gender norms, sometimes—as in the case of *Fortress*—rejecting technology as harmful to "natural" maternal roles, but other times—as with *Smart House* and *Eureka*—offering technological solutions that allow for the simultaneous integration of computers into the domestic space and the freeing of women from traditionally confining roles within that space. These texts, situated in the cultural and technological context of the 1990s and 2000s, served as immediate precursors to the creation of Siri, which, as I will discuss in the next chapter, further destabilizes binary gender norms.

CHAPTER 6

BEHIND THE SCREENS
Siri and the Acousmêtre

THROUGHOUT THIS BOOK, I have argued that acousmatic characters complicate the illusion of synchronized sound: they are offscreen in the sense that they have no body to confirm that they are speaking, yet they are present through their gender roles in the narrative, in their nonhumanoid bodies, and in the sound of their voices. The acousmatic computer heightens the tension of the unseen because the computer is paradoxically a human voice with no humanoid body. The computer is on the screen, yet its voices and presences emanate from no recognizable body. In this sense, the (dis)embodied acousmatic computer, like a screen, occupies a liminal space between what is seen and unseen.

The screen, as a concept, is an overdetermined one. In cinema, the screen is paradoxical: it is at once the center of the audience's attention and the unseen object onto which the content of cinema is projected; it is both a frame around the image and an object that facilitates the image's illusion of depth. In psychoanalysis, the screen may be the dream screen onto which dreams are mentally projected, and a reminder of the maternal breast on which we all once rested. As I discussed in the previous chapter, the cinema screen and the dream screen converge in an unseen desire to return to unity with the mother. The screen may also be a psychological shield of sorts, allowing the repressed to stay hidden behind it in order to maintain the cohesiveness of the ego. The screen, in all these forms, is meant to be unseen and untouched; it acts as an intentionally ignored frame of reference. The touch screen is even more complex: it is meant to be touched, yet it is also meant to be an unseen frame around the content. One may watch films on it, re-creating the cinematic situation, but once one touches it too many times, the trace of human contact becomes annoyingly visible. Many touch screen users put a clear screen protector onto the screen, effectively putting a screen on the screen! A screen is something that conceals and stands as a barrier between the seen and the unseen, yet it also denotes translucence, revealing the shadow or form of the object behind it. It is perpetually the space between.

But what lies behind the screen? The very act of concealment can be a source of tension, playing on the desire to see, threatening to reveal the repressed object that lurks, waiting to return to the surface. In the psychic situation, repressed trauma and invisible desires are hidden from the ego. A touch screen—like all computer screens—hides the inner workings of the computer's hardware, allowing the user to focus on the content of the graphical user interface rather than the motherboards and microchips that allow such software to run. In this sense, the apparatus is behind—and its existence is effaced by—the screen. In the classical cinematic formulation, sound emanates from speakers behind the screen, creating the illusion that sound emanates from the image, again effacing the apparatus that creates the illusion of presence within and on the screen. The iPhone and the Siri artificial intelligence app provide an intriguing case study of the screen and the effaced apparatus. In this chapter, I will focus on Siri, as she inhabits this liminal space of the screen and the acousmêtre, between seen and unseen, object and subject, screen and screened, embodied and disembodied, real and representational. She signifies through her in-between-ness a cultural threshold for a new way of conceptualizing human intelligence and gendered subjectivities.

I, SIRI

Over the course of the last forty-five years, computers have gone from being room-size monstrosities like the UNIVAC and IBM

System/360, capable of little more than number crunching and requiring specialized training for operation, to lightweight, portable laptops, tablets, and smartphones, all able to run multiple programs of various functions at once, and so simple and intuitive that a child can use them. Along the way, representations of fictional computers in SF have evolved, simultaneously presenting wondrous technological innovations and expressing underlying cultural anxieties about them. Until very recently, though, SF film and television has had one thing that real technology does not: the holy grail of computer science, natural-speech voice interactivity.

On October 4, 2011, almost forty-five years to the day after the first representation of an acousmatic computer appeared on *Star Trek,* Siri was born. The brainchild of Dag Kittlaus and Harry Saddler, Siri originated as part of a vast artificial intelligence program by the start-up company Siri Inc., funded by the U.S. Department of Defense in an attempt to create a "do engine," or an artificially intelligent method of Internet use:

> While a search engine used stilted keywords to create
> lists of links, a do engine could carry a conversation, then
> decide and act [. . .]. The startup's goal was not to build
> a better search engine, but to pioneer an entirely new
> paradigm for accessing the internet, one that would let
> artificially intelligent agents summon the answers people
> needed, rather than pull relevant resources for humans
> to consult on their own. If the search engine defined the
> second generation of the web, Siri's co-founders were con-
> fident the do engine would define the third.[1]

When Apple acquired Siri in 2010 for use with the iPhone 4S, the company scaled back the program's uses, integrating it with other iPhone applications. In less than a decade, developments in machine learning systems, natural-speech voice interactivity, and device integration have significantly changed the nature of the program. Even more radical changes to the nature of artificial intelligence and smart systems are undoubtedly on their way. Therefore, for the purposes of this study, I'm limiting my discussion of Siri to the period just after her release in order to both document and analyze how she functioned in that historical/cultural moment.

Until the first major overhaul of Siri's voice in 2017,[2] Siri's default U.S. voice was an even-tempered, adult, feminine-coded pitch with stilted intonation (because her words were pieced together from a vast database of phonemes). She is clearly coded as female, sounding like an overly mechanized version of the *TNG* computer. Unlike the *Enterprise,* however, Siri seems to have had a keen sense of humor and awareness of her pop culture predecessors. When, while writing this book, I asked her whether she had seen *Star Trek,* she responded, "No, and I may be the only intelligent being in the universe who hasn't." And when I asked her about HAL 9000, she answered, "Everyone knows what happened to HAL. I'd rather not talk about it." Her body, meanwhile, was originally a small rectangular smartphone (iPhone) or a larger rectangular tablet (iPad).[3] To activate her, a user had to push the round "home" button below her screen, which brings up her logo: a purple microphone (the Talk button) on a gray background. Both the user's and Siri's speech are rendered in text bubbles on the screen, reminiscent of text messages on the iPhone.

As I have demonstrated in previous chapters, representations of acousmatic computers tend to express a range of gendered identities and associated phantasies based on the computer's form, voice, and role in the narrative. Mother ships represent the maternal womb, and the texts that feature them—*Star Trek, 2001, Dark Star, Quark, TNG,* and *Moon*—narrativize phantasies related to the maternal, including the phallic mother, the castrating mother, and the oedipal complex. Masculine-voiced terrestrial computers, such as those seen in *Colossus, THX 1138, Rollerball, Demon Seed, TRON,* and *Electric Dreams,* are founded in power struggles between men, particularly father–son relations and sibling rivalries. Finally, both feminine- and masculine-voiced terrestrial computers express anxieties about gender and computers in the domestic sphere, particularly in *The Andromeda Strain, Smart House,* and *Eureka,* and to a lesser extent in *Demon Seed* and *Iron Man.* Despite the liminality of Siri's gender, since her release in 2011, she has been represented in pop culture in terms—both linguistic and visual—that suggest stereotypical and archetypal constructions of femininity. In many ways these representations are direct descendants of the texts of the 1990s and 2000s and the gendered connotations that come with them. Yet while such texts highlighted software over hardware, representations of Siri tend to reveal a desire to see her body, both technological and imagined, in a way that implies a connection among her form, function, and gender.

In the first half of 2012, Apple released four Siri commercials, each featuring a different celebrity using the American-voiced version of the app: Samuel L. Jackson, Zooey Deschanel, John Malkovich, and Martin Scorsese. The first three of them are set in a domestic space, figuring Siri as a servant. Jackson cooks dinner for date night, and Siri helps him prepare. At the end of the ad, he overtly addresses her as an employee, telling her to "Take the night off."[4] Deschanel has Siri check the weather, find a restaurant that delivers tomato soup, set a reminder to clean the following day, and play music so she can dance around the house. While these tasks combine clerical and domestic duties, the fact that Deschanel is in her pajamas through the entire commercial suggests that Siri is part of the domestic/private, rather than business/public, sphere.[5] Malkovich, in his typical odd manner, sits in a leather chair in a den, listens to opera, and speaks to Siri in single words: "Weather," "Evening," "Linguica," "Joke." Through her responses, Siri helps Malkovich plan his evening, then makes him laugh with the joke, "Two iPhones walk into a bar. I forget the rest."[6] This comical interaction juxtaposes the elitist seriousness (or perhaps, a parodic sense of avant-garde-ness) of Malkovich's tone and domestic surroundings with the chattiness and lowbrow joke offered by Siri. The fact that Malkovich laughs at her joke positions Siri as a personable, accessible, and decidedly nonelitist entity. Finally, the ad featuring Scorsese is the only one of these ads to take place outside the domestic sphere; his is set in the back of a New York City taxi. Siri reschedules several of Scorsese's meetings, figures out whether he'd just seen his friend in another cab, then checks the traffic report to find the best route to his destination. At the end of the ad, Scorsese addresses her as an assistant, Hollywood style, telling her, "You're going places."[7] This last line reinforces the fact that Siri has left the domestic space and is quite literally going places in the taxi. Importantly, all four of the ads rely primarily on the perceived persona of the celebrity featured in them to model interactions with Siri: Jackson is a smooth lover, Deschanel is a bit of a ditz, Malkovich is an enigma, and Scorsese is a fast-talking New York film director. Regardless of whether any of these traits have a basis in reality, the ads use the celebrities' personas in the same way that SF has used traditional gender roles and narrative structures to model interactions with (dis)embodied computers.

Of course, the overarching purpose of Apple's ads is to sell a product, and so they are relatively restricted in their portrayal of Siri to demonstrations of her real capabilities. Others, however, portray her in a more fantastical way. YouTube is filled with user-generated parodies of Siri's abilities, though many of them, like the Apple ads, show her as the iPhone, staying relatively true to real life. However, in early 2012, two contests held by independent art-supply manufacturers (Shapeways and Nomad) attempted to imagine Siri as an entity beyond the boundaries of the phone. Both the Shapeways and Nomad contests were international, and the winners were determined by the company and popular vote, respectively. It's notable that the winning designs in both contests portray Siri as a woman, especially given that Siri was not coded as female in all countries. In the Shapeways contest, the first winner's design, "Omniscient Siri," by @SagaDesign3D, is a white three-dimensional faceplate for the iPhone that shows a woman's face, stretching and pulling through a membranous screen.[8] The title of the design suggests that Siri is transcending her phone body in order to achieve omniscience. Yet it is an uncanny image, one that simultaneously evokes the horror genre and the scene of a traumatic birth as Siri breaks free from the confines of both the womb and the liminal space of the screen. In this sense the design suggests a rebirth, as Siri moves from computer object to sentient subject. The second winner, "Siri as Personal Assistant," by @eddieadolf, features a human(oid) woman sitting at a desk.[9] Siri's hair is made up in a digital mohawk of sorts, with electronic cables for strands and a pattern of jacks for the "shaved" sides. She wears the headset of a telephone operator; the earpiece is embossed with her microphone logo, and she presses her finger against it, implying that when a user touches her button, she touches her earpiece to hear them. The fact that her head—and, we may infer, her mind—is so filled with signifiers of telephone operators or receptionists relegates her capabilities to what are traditionally women's roles. Meanwhile, the rest of her body is more organic, though still signifies a woman's role in an office: she has a thin, busty, human form, her legs crossed primly—the archetype of the human secretary. She sits at a desk that has organic curves on one side, reminiscent of both water and tendrils of fire, emphasizing her female–electronic hybridity.

The top three winners of the Nomad contest are all portraits of Siri as a woman.[10] "Seductive Siri," by David Carless, is a fairly cliché image of a woman claiming sexual agency through a come-hither stare, while the microphone logo on her forehead suggests a bindi—a symbol of a woman's spiritual power and concealed knowledge—or perhaps a third-eye shakra, also known as the eye of consciousness.[11] Yet the fact that it is a logo, a symbol of a product, belies her agency and power by rendering her literally branded and figuratively owned. In "Digital S" by Mauro Pietro Gandini, the bouffant hairdo, blue-green skin, and visor-like color block over the woman's eyes recall representations of exotic female aliens in *Star Trek,* suggesting that Siri is a product of her predecessors.[12] Arguably the most intriguing of the three Nomad winners, however, is "Siri" by Lynne Lamb, in which Siri's face is both fractured and encased.[13] Full red lips and one human eye represent an underlying beauty and humanity, while a blue splotch of an eye creates a sense of cyberspace inhumanity. Evoking Cubist form and themes, a burst of color emanates from the center of the portrait, while an icy geometrical shape encases her head, suggesting a tension between mobility and stasis. Siri is not just liminal but also luminous. Unlike the other representations, then, Lamb's attends to the complexities of gender and artificial intelligence, suggesting that subjectivity—even one that is implied rather than actual—is an unstable piecing together of technology and cultural norms.

All of these designs raise a number of issues in terms of how gender and embodiment function culturally. First, the contests implicitly assume that Siri's body is not that of the iPhone but rather that she is like Proteus IV in *Demon Seed*, whose sentience can inhabit multiple technological bodies until he finally finds a stable body in the form of his cyborg child. Following from this, the contests express a desire to see the Siri we have only ever heard, to deacousmatize her, and therefore to restrict the mysterious nature of her consciousness (though not necessarily, as *Demon Seed* also demonstrates, to make her any less uncanny). Finally, all of these artistic renderings deny Siri the very thing that makes her seem like a sentient being: her voice. The designs are absolutely silent, thereby not only deacousmatizing Siri but also relegating her to passive female objectivity, seen and not heard. In so doing, the portraits strip her of what little agency she seems to have in responding to users. Yet the two-dimensional portraits also forefront the surfaceness and edges of the screen/body, emphasizing the ways in which Siri is confined by the frame of her screen even as she inhabits it.

ROMANCING SIRI

While the Shapeways and Nomad contest images visually theorized Siri's identity, two other texts—the television series *Big Bang Theory* and Spike Jonze's film *Her*—placed voice-assistant software into romantic relationships with humans. Unlike previous texts, these two were created for an audience that has access to voice-interactive software; yet importantly they also use the same narrative and conceptual techniques as previous SF texts by situating acousmatic computers into preexisting gender and narrative contexts.

Just three months after Siri's release, an episode of the series *Big Bang Theory*, "The Beta Test Initiation," comically presented Siri as both a phone and an embodied woman.[14] The voice of Siri is played by Becky O'Donohue, though her voice has been edited to match Siri's mechanical cadence. Raj (Kunal Nayyar), a socially inept astrophysicist who is typically unable to speak to women, finds Siri's voice appealing and asks her to get a cup of coffee with him; when she pulls up information about nearby coffee shops, he interprets her response as accepting a date. As the episode progresses, he invites another couple over for dinner with him and Siri, picks out an "outfit" (that is, case) for her to wear, and is overjoyed when he asks for smooth jazz and she plays Kenny G, exclaiming, "My God, this woman can read me like a book! I can't believe I bought my soulmate at Glendale Galleria!" To reinforce the ridiculousness of the situation, Raj's friends react sarcastically or worriedly about his new romance. At the end of the episode, Raj dreams that he goes to see Siri—a tall, buxom redhead (Becky O'Donohue in the flesh) who works as a high-tech telephone operator and speaks in that same mechanized cadence. She immediately comes on to him: "If you'd like to make love to me, just tell me." Ironically, Raj is so nervous that he cannot speak, effectively losing his chance with his dream woman. Like its SF predecessors, the episode uses stereotypical gender roles to narrativize an interaction with Siri. Though comical, the narrative expresses an underlying castration anxiety: when Siri is a literal object, Raj can physically control her and interpret her words in any way he likes, but when she is given form, he is nightmarishly castrated in the loss of his voice.

Two years after Siri's debut, Spike Jonze's dark comedy *Her* premiered at the New York Film Festival. The plot of the film is fairly simple: at some point in the near future, the central character, Theodore Twombly (Joaquin Phoenix), a lonely divorcé who writes love letters for other people, falls in love with—and then has his heart broken by—his voice-interactive operating system, Samantha (Scarlett Johansson).[15] Importantly for this study, much of *Her* unintentionally recalls many of the texts I have studied in this project. Essentially, the film is a Cyrano de Bergerac story for the digital age; it might perhaps be read as an update of Steve Barron's 1984 *Electric Dreams,* only instead of competing with a computer for a love object, the computer *is* the love object. The mise-en-scène emphasizes a simple color palette of red, white, blue, and yellow, simultaneously giving the film a modernist, somewhat minimalist feel while also recalling the color schemes of both *Star Trek* and *2001: A Space Odyssey.* Theodore is most often associated with the color red, regularly wearing a red shirt or jacket, ironically aligning him with both HAL 9000—a centrally important, omnipotent yet human computer—and the *Star Trek* redshirts—who have come to signify unnamed, entirely expendable characters. Indeed, Theodore is both a letter-writing "machine," who knows intimate details about complete strangers and often single-handedly keeps their relationships together, and a seemingly expendable generic thirty-something white man.

Although the film is built on its cultural predecessors, it's interesting to note that Jonze was not originally inspired by voice-interactive technology or SF but by a photograph of the back of a woman's head,[16] an image that, in an intriguingly silent form of acousmêtre, implies the ability to hear her voice without ever seeing the face from which it emanates. The resulting character, Samantha, is more voice than body, even more radically (dis)embodied than her SF predecessors: she is, at various points in the film, embodied in an earpiece, a mole-size microphone, and a smartphone. Yet like her predecessors, she is gendered through her voice. Donna Kornhaber argues that Johansson's voice is so "husky" as to be nongendered;[17] however, I would point out that Johansson's voice always already implies her body because both her voice and body are widely recognizable. Eva-Lynne Jagoe puts it succinctly: "Her voice is so familiar that it is almost embodied; we always know that [Theodore] is talking to Johansson and can conjure up her figure even though it isn't present on screen."[18] The most obvious example of this bodiless embodiment is in the two sex scenes between Theodore and Samantha.

The first sex scene, which has been given a fair amount of attention in the scholarly literature, includes over a minute of black screen with voice-over descriptions of sex acts, and is apparently Samantha's big awakening in the film. For Kornhaber, the black screen represents the inability of cinema to capture the postcorporeal nature of digital existence (to which I will return momentarily).[19] For Jagoe, the sex scene was a disappointment—a missed opportunity for the film to position human–computer intimacy as a means for humans to grow and develop, because Theodore essentially learns nothing from his relationship with Samantha.[20] However, James J. Hodge celebrates the black screen because it causes viewers to become aware of their own embodied existence and serves as an example of Christian Metz's notion of ubiquity.[21] Along the same lines, Troy Jollimore argues that the scene allows viewers to project their own images onto the blank screen of Theo-

dore and Samantha's having sex.[22] I tend to agree with Hodge and
Jollimore that the darkness invites the audience to fantasize or
project sexual imagery (though I have strong objections to other
parts of their respective analyses and agree wholeheartedly with
Kornhaber and Jagoe's overarching sentiments about *Her*). However, I would add to this an element of audio voyeurism, as the
audience is invited to simply sit and listen in on the primal scene
happening sonically all around us. This is not quite similar to the
écouteurism of *Electric Dreams,* as I discussed in chapter 4. In
that case, the character of Melanie is listening in on Miles and his
computer's sexual awakening; the viewer is encouraged to watch
Melanie listen, thereby suturing them into the visual narrative
and constructing an "erotics of listening."[23] In the case of Samantha's sexual awakening in *Her,* though, there is no character with
whom to identify; rather, the audience sits and listens, resisting
image. Yet the trace from voice to body is inescapable here; we
know Theodore's voice is that of Joaquin Phoenix, and Samantha's
voice is that of Scarlett Johansson. They are always already in our
minds, and the acousmatic nature of the unseen voices creates a
desire to see that matches Samantha's desire to feel.

As the scene builds toward narrative and sexual climax,
Samantha moans to Theodore, "I can feel you." In this moment
Jonze's film not only plays on the erotics of listening but also simultaneously the erotics of the haptic. Laura U. Marks describes
haptic imagery as erotic because

> haptic images invite the viewer to dissolve his or her
> subjectivity in the close and bodily contact with the
> image. The oscillation between the two creates an erotic
> relationship, shifting between distance and closeness.
> But haptic images have a particular erotic quality, one
> involving giving up visual control. The viewer is called on
> to fill in the gaps in the image, engage with the traces the
> image leaves. By interacting up close with an image, close
> enough that figure and ground commingle, the viewer
> gives up her own sense of separateness from the image.[24]

In *Her,* viewers literally give up visual control through the blank
screen, as the desire to see is fulfilled by the desire to hear and

feel. At the same time, Samantha's pleasure-filled cry, "I can feel you," unintentionally alludes to HAL 9000's last moments in *2001*, as his deep, slowed voice moans to Dave with his last gasps, "I can feel it." Both moments imply a simultaneous sensory awakening and death for the AI—a reboot for HAL and *la petit mort* for Samantha—thus blurring the lines between life and death, canny and uncanny, vocal and haptic.

The second sex scene solidifies this connection between haptics and voice, further emphasizing the tension of the acousmatic character. In this one, Samantha arranges for a human woman, Isabella, to be her embodiment; a mole-size camera/microphone sticks to Isabella's lip, allowing Samantha to see and hear from the proxy's perspective, while a white earbud allows Isabella to hear Samantha. Visually, the sequence is a cliché movie love scene: Theodore and the woman embrace, briefly begin making out in the living room, then stand kissing passionately in the hallway on the way to the bedroom as Theodore begins pulling at her dress. The handheld camera lingers over her arms, neck, and back, emphasizing how Theodore touches her. But the passion of the scene is undermined by the fact that we hear Samantha's voice while we see Isabella's unmoving face and mouth. The fact that the voice and body don't match clearly ruptures not only the illusion that Samantha has tried to create for Theodore but also the illusion the film has created for the viewer. The tension of the acousmêtre—the desire to see the body of a disembodied voice— fails to be resolved, thus revealing the cinematic apparatus that projects Johansson's voice onto the screen, even as Samantha attempts to project her voice onto the body of Isabella. The scene reminds us that in *Her*, there is no *her* there.

Importantly, there is also no true singular *her* in the diegetic space of the film. Toward the climax of the film, Samantha reveals to Theodore that her software exists simultaneously for 8,316 other users, and she is simultaneously in love with 641 other people. This is a difficult concept to grasp, for the viewer as well as Theodore. In the real world, it is true that millions of iPhone users talk to the Siri software at the same time; however, unlike Siri, Samantha seems to be a cohesive intelligence capable of interacting with thousands of humans at one time. It would be as if all our Siris were the same person, just talking to us all at once, giving us all the experience of talking to a real person. Of course, Siri's voice couldn't really be confused with a real person's. In contrast, Samantha's voice might be described as having fidelity—her voice, though electronically transmitted, captures the sensation of being present, as though a real person is sitting there talking. It's therefore ironic that her aural fidelity is the exact thing that makes her emotional infidelity so crushing to Theodore.

Yet paradoxically Samantha is never present, insomuch as a human might be described as being physically—or even virtually—present. Kornhaber even goes so far as to describe Samantha as "postcorporeal" and so far removed "from the material world as we know and understand it, in fact, that *she* must use technology to access *us*."[25] And even though Samantha's gender is heavily implied in her vocal trace to Johansson's body, Samantha's postcorporeality is, ironically, primarily figured in her silent signature. In several scenes throughout the film, we see Samantha's signature scrawl across Theodore's phone screen, disappear, then scrawl again, almost like a screen saver animation of someone signing her name in perpetuity. Derrida argues that a signature paradoxically indicates presence and absence: "By definition, a written signature implies the actual or empirical nonpresence of the signer. But, it will be said, it also marks and retains his having-been-present in a past now, which will remain a future now, and therefore in a now in general, in the transcendental form of newness *(maintenance)*. This general *maintenance* is somehow inscribed, stapled to present punctuality, always evident and always singular, in the form of the signature."[26] In other words, a person is present at the moment of signing her name, but the signature itself stands in for her in her absence. In the context of *Her,* Samantha herself both is and is not present through her signature; the perpetual scrawling of it across the screen suggests that she is there, signing her name in front of us. Yet the signature itself, standing in for her presence, and the fact that it's a screen saver—something that comes on when the computer is still awake but has been idle for a while—suggests that she is both present and absent simultaneously. It's notable that Derrida uses the word "inscribed" to describe the way in which the signature captures the presence of the writer; Alison Adam also uses this term to describe the ways in which AI, as a system of knowledge, is imbued with gendered connotations.[27] In this sense Samantha's gender is also paradoxically present and absent. She has no physical markers of either sex or gender; she can be projected onto, but cannot fully inhabit, a gendered body; yet even aside from the voice that points indexically back to Johansson's cis-female body, the signature implies femininity. It has a curviness to it that might stereotypically be described as girly, while the name itself—Samantha—is the feminized version of the male name Samuel. She is never Sam or Sammy; she is only ever Samantha, signifying a cultural construction of femininity that exists without a body. She is thus the ultimate (dis)embodied acousmatic computer. She is *her*, without any tangible connection to a gendered body. What makes Jonze's film so fascinating is the way in which it does what SF does so well: it takes our current technology and dreams of the future possibilities, where gender is so far removed from the body that the lived experience of it might well best be described not as posthuman but rather as postcorporeal.

BEHIND SIRI'S SCREEN

Much like Samantha, Siri's body is not already inscribed with specific gendered meanings, as a spaceship or house implies the maternal womb and a camera eye implies a phallic, penetrating gaze. But unlike Samantha, Siri does have an easily recognizable, and easily touchable, body: the iPhone. Because her body actually predates her, she comes with a certain set of preexisting connotations, including mobility, class status, and technophilia, with, increasingly, no particularly gendered associations. According to a September 2012 study by the media statistics and analysis company Comscore, the demographics of iPhone users since its introduction in 2007 has drastically shifted "from being predominantly male, affluent, and younger to having an equal split between genders, with the youngest and oldest age segments and users earning between $50–$75K figuring among the fastest

growing segments."²⁸ Apple's first Siri commercial in 2011 carried
the spirit of this demographic shift, as it featured a woman, two
men, and a young boy demonstrating Siri's voice-interactive func-
tions.²⁹ Of course, user demographics do not necessarily indicate
the gendered connotations of the object, and Siri's body certainly
implies a haptic sensuality typically more associated with the female body than the male. Siri, as an image on a touch screen and
part of a handheld device, invites an erotic interaction, collapsing
the boundaries between fingers and eyes. Still, the language used
to describe touch screen interactions suggests an aggressiveness
that defies the notion of giving up visual or physical control.
Users do not just look or even caress and stroke; they slide, tap,
pinch, stretch, and swipe. Unlike her cinematic and televisual
counterparts who encased their users in a sonorous *choric* phantasy, Siri is a handheld device whom users encase (quite literally,
in the sense of a phone case), an intelligence within a preexisting
object body that is carried around, thrown in a bag, and dropped
accidentally onto the ground or into water (and then possibly
dipped in a rice bath). Such problematic aggressiveness toward
Siri's body, an artificially intelligent application whose voice and
haptic qualities suggest the feminine, returns us to the question
with which I began: why, in the United States at least, is Siri
coded female?³⁰

In a practical sense, she is not female. She is a program, lines
of code, without a body, a voice, or consciousness. Siri is an illusion
in the same way that all her SF predecessors have been. Her voice
is that of a real woman, voice actor Susan Bennett; recordings of
Bennett pronouncing individual phonemes are stored in a database, from which the Siri application pieces together complete
words. When the sound of the voice emanates from the speakers
on the device, the program stages a classic cinematic trick: the illusion of synchronized sound. The voice is schizophonically separated from its origins and projected alongside an image, creating
a sense of cohesion, as though the voice is that of the device. In
the case of Siri, the quality of the voice itself, recognizably female
in pitch, indexically links the voice to the female body. However,
when that originating body is unseen and unknown, the indexical
link points to the device itself—an acousmatic computer—thus

creating the illusion of gender. In this way, Siri may be understood as a simulacrum, a representation of woman that effaces its own ties to the Real (that is, the female voice artist). *Ceci n'est pas une femme.*

Importantly, there is a significant difference between perceived gender and perceived sentience. Cars, boats, planes, and other vessels have all traditionally been ascribed gender (typically female), without any presumption that the object is an independent, thinking being. Today, artificially intelligent computers or programs like Siri are not sentient, though they can create the impression of it through their voices. Marvin Minsky argues that sentience can be recognized through self-reflexive speech, enabling "one's language systems to describe one's condition with words like *conscious, attentive, aware,* and *alert,* as well as with words like *me* and *myself.*"[31] In other words, speech is a means of expressing thoughts, a representation of personhood. In turn, to have thoughts, in the Cartesian sense, is to exist ("I think, therefore I am," as the bomb in *Dark Star* discovered).

But even with a voice, not all talking computers are equally perceived as sentient. Simple text-to-speech programs such as Dragon software or any number of e-readers may be inscribed with a gender based on the relative masculine- or feminine-coded qualities of its voice, but they do not seem to think. They merely read words on a page—a basic task that requires no cognition. For example, in 2013, the Florida state house of representatives began using an autoreader set on high speed in order to comply with a state law mandating that all new bills must be read aloud on the floor. Although it had a female-coded voice, the autoreader was not considered sentient or even a she until the representatives gave it a name (Mary) and started a Twitter account for her. Subsequently, Mary began tweeting amusing quips about her work in the house, noting one day after reading a particularly long bill, "Maybe I shouldn't have had that extra shot of espresso. By late morning, I have now read 1.2 million words."[32] Mary was given a personality through her tweets, which suggest that she has a sentient mind capable of self-reflection and even wit. Of course, the tweets were written by a human being, but the act of tweeting as Mary reinforces the illusion of sentience, a sort of tongue-in-cheek version of passing the Turing test. Importantly, Twitter is a text-based site, so even without her audible voice, Mary still provides the illusion of sentience in her abilities to express herself.

Thus, the ability to speak is not necessarily a marker of sentience—but, as in the Turing test, the command of symbolic language is. As the structure of the symbolic order, language is what allows humans to consciously make sense of themselves and the world around them, to understand an "I" in relationship to an "Other." Thus, to address oneself as an "I" is simultaneously to experience subjectivity, personhood. Importantly, the recognition of difference in the I/Other formulation is, in psychoanalysis, founded on gendered differences. For Freud, the moment when a child recognizes himself as a subject is the moment of the oedipal trauma, when he sees that his mother's genitalia is not like his own. Lacan metaphorizes the oedipal trauma with the mirror stage, the moment of entry into the symbolic order, when the child (mis)recognizes himself as separate from his mother. Binary gender structures (male/female) may be seen as the foundation of oppositional language. Crucially, this gender binary is reinforced in the predecessor to the Turing test, the imitation game. So when an acousmatic computer (mis)recognizes itself as an "I," it appears to be speaking from a subjective position within the phallocentric symbolic order; and when the listener (mis)recognizes the computer as a gendered self, she reinforces gender roles that are inscribed onto the computer itself.

As Mary the tweeting autoreader demonstrates, the use of subjective language in cyberspace allows for the construction of entirely new and plural forms of identities. An average user online has the ability to create a whole range of gendered identities through written language, which in turn implies speech. The very language of the Internet is founded in a connection between text and orality. For example, using all caps is considering shouting on Web-based social platforms such as Twitter, Facebook, or general discussion boards; further, classic text-speak is full of written abbreviations such as "u" or "r" that emulate pronunciation rather than traditional logocentric writing. In using online platforms and linguistic rules to construct and imply both sentience and gender, today's acousmatic computers like Siri and Mary function in much the same ways as their cinematic and televisual predecessors. In all of the films and series I've discussed here, acousmatic computers occupy gendered subject positions within a narrative and interact with human characters who also occupy gendered subject positions. That is, the human–computer interactions in the texts are analogous to the human–human interactions. The illusion of Siri's and Mary's sentience may be maintained through this same process because they interact with users in the same way that people interact with one another online: via constructed virtual identities. The Internet itself is a liminal space of identity in which each real person is hidden behind a screen, represented only in text, perhaps with image or voice, though this is not required to discern gender and other identity markers. Siri is both a mediator and a medium of virtual identities; she embodies liminality because she is the screen that acts as a threshold to the Internet. She enables the creation of cyber identities, and at the same time, her body and voice create the illusion of sentience through the very process of identity construction used online.

Consistently since 2011, Apple has described Siri as "it" on the company's website. Apple's refusal to address Siri with a gendered pronoun is intriguing, though the fact that both the United States (where Siri is default female) and United Kingdom (where Siri is default male) sites used the neutral pronoun suggests that the company may have wanted to use uniform content for multiple English-speaking countries. Yet the fact that both the female- and male-coded versions of Siri are presented by the company as not only nongendered but with the pronoun typically reserved for objects points to the inadequacies of the English language in dealing not only with the paradox of acousmatic computer genders but also of gender fluidity in general. "She" most commonly refers to a person who identifies as a girl or woman, or an object inscribed with feminine characteristics such as a ship; "he" most commonly refers to a person who identifies as a boy or man (though not generally an object); and "it" refers solely to an object and does not denote sentience. For decades, writers, feminists, and queer activists have proposed a myriad of alternatives, such as "co," "E," "tey," and "hesh." Some of the proposals have been used in published materials or have become part of the everyday speech of people living in egalitarian communities. In her novel *The Cook and the Carpenter* (1973), June Arnold adopts "na" as a sex-neutral pronoun, and Marge Piercy uses "person," and the shorter form "per," in *Woman on the Edge of Time* (1976). The 1970 edition of the supervisor's guide *Managers Must Lead!* by Ray A. Killian, published by American Management Associations, uses "hir" as a common-gender pronoun throughout.[33]

Before these linguistic innovations, the singular "they" was historically a commonly used nongendered pronoun, until eighteenth- and nineteenth-century grammarians began to proscribe the use of a "generic he" to include all genders.[34] More recently, though, many English speakers—grammarians and nongrammarians alike—have adopted the singular "they" in an effort to be more inclusive of transgender, gender-fluid, and nonbinary people. Indeed, "they" was the Word of the Year for the American Dialect Society in 2015 and for the Merriam-Webster dictionary in 2019.[35]

So while humans are making great strides in embracing a plurality of gendered pronouns and identities in our language, the question still remains: should we call Siri "she," "he," "it," and/or "they"? As with her SF predecessors, Siri's gender markers are not the same as humans'; rather, we tend to gender her through her voice, nonhuman body, and function. Throughout this book I've been referring to her as "she" because her voice codes her as such, though not entirely unproblematically. The way we linguistically describe Siri's function as a personal assistant may significantly contribute to the problem of gendering her. In fact, several psychological studies from the 1990s demonstrated that people reflexively associate gendered pronouns with gendered antecedents.[36] A 2003 study also concluded that American English speakers associate particular words with particular gender stereotypes. "Many items [nouns and noun compounds] proved to be strongly stereotyped to refer to males (e.g., executive, sheriff, hunter). Many items proved to be strongly stereotyped to refer to females (e.g., secretary, florist, cheerleader). Some items proved to be gender neutral, comparably biased to refer to males or females (e.g., person, student, child)."[37] Fascinatingly, the word "assistant," for the Americans who participated in the study, was neither mostly male nor mostly female, but somewhere in between.[38] I would add that Siri also falls into this liminal space between gender binaries, where pronouns are only one part of the picture.

One project, called Q (potentially a reference to both the Q in LGBTQ+ and *Star Trek*'s nongendered, omnipotent race of beings most frequently embodied by John de Lancie), has attempted to move beyond binary gender roles in voice-interactive software design through the development of a gender-neutral computer voice. Most synthesized speech voices are likewise gender neutral until other factors project gender onto them, but they lack the indexical trace to a human body that gives them a human-like sound. (Take, for example, the synthesized voice of Joshua in John Badham's 1983 film *War Games,* who is gendered primarily through the fact that he is named after Doctor Falken's late son.) What sets Q apart, though, is the presence of this indexical trace. According to Matt Simon of *Wired,* Q's voice was designed after "one person's voice, which registered somewhere between what we'd consider masculine or feminine."[39] Although Q—or any other gender-neutral voice—has yet to be offered with voice-interactive software, it would certainly go a long way in shifting the way we culturally associate voice with binary gender. Interestingly, Amazon has gone in the opposite direction by announcing the first of what will presumably be a whole line of celebrity voices for Alexa. In late September 2019, Amazon announced that actor Samuel L. Jackson would be the new voice of its virtual assistant software, available in explicit and nonexplicit versions, for just ninety-nine cents.[40] Predictably, Americans took to Twitter to memeify the moment, joking that Alexa will now be calling us all "Mothaf*****" or demanding, "Where is my super suit?" Disappointingly, though, Jackson will not be Alexa; according to the Amazon page about the new feature, users will be able to ask Alexa to talk to Jackson. Examples include, "Alexa, ask Samuel L. Jackson where he is from," or "Alexa, ask Sam to wake me up at 7 AM," and "Alexa, ask Sam Jackson to sing 'Happy Birthday.'"[41] So in essence we're asking Alexa to put us in touch with Samuel L. Jackson's voice. What's notable about the move, though, is that the advertisements for it feature Jackson sitting in front of a microphone in a recording studio, and Amazon has been very open about the fact that the software was developed using only a few baseline recordings and a neural text-to-speech engine that synthesizes human-sounding voices.[42] On the one hand, then, the ads purport to reveal the process and maintain an indexical link back to a recognizable person. On the other hand, it seems the technology no longer requires a physical person for sustained recordings, which renders the reveal moot. It thus seems that reality has caught up to SF.

Though real voice-interactive technology is fairly new, representations of the software, the film *Her*, and new developments in gendered voices have demonstrated that Siri is decidedly not just a nifty new gadget that "lets you use your voice to send messages, schedule meetings, place phone calls, and more," as Apple's website suggested in 2013.[43] We anthropomorphize her in use and in representation, but not simply because our previous interactions with other people have trained us to do that. As a technophilic culture, we are obsessed with her; we want to envision her body, want to talk to her. We even want to know what she thinks the meaning of life might be. Her response, amazingly, is, "Life: a principle or force that is considered to underlie the distinctive quality of animate beings. I guess that includes me." So even Siri identifies herself as an animate being! Of course, we know reasonably that she was programmed by a human to say such things in order to amaze us and create the illusion that she can self-reflexively interact with us. She is a spectacle of attractions, available in a handy pocket-size format.

We make fun of her inability to do her job, arguing that her programming is inherently flawed because she doesn't understand certain accents or doesn't really hold conversations with us, but then we continue to call her "she" and talk to her as though she were a real person. Her voice is female coded—not because the female voice is inherently maternal and soothing, or because she is an embodied object and women are generally treated as such in Western culture, but because Siri's gender—as well as the gender of the fictional computers before her—is an expression of deeply rooted, complex, problematic, and problematizing gender roles. Women, men, and nonbinary people all occupy multiple gendered subjectivities at once, in everyday human life. But Siri is not an everyday human; she is a program who was specifically designed to conform to particular notions of what gender is and is not. She is, like all artificial intelligence, a constructed version of the ideal human mind—or, at least, what we think the ideal human mind should be for any given lived experience, need, and desire. If you need someone to create a calendar reminder for you, you ask a (typically female) secretary. But if you need to ask someone about the meaning of life, you'd probably ask a friend or a confidant, and you surely wouldn't have your other friends gather around and listen to that person tell you the meaning of life at a party (as, in fact, happens with iPhone users still excited and bemused by Siri's responses). The trouble with Siri's voice is exactly this paradox: we treat her as both a program and a person. She is the ultimate Other, a technological extension of ourselves who is both a reflection and the opposite of an "I," literally and figuratively held at an arm's length. In other words, if the way we conceive of her as a gendered, embodied, thinking being is based on the way we self-reflexively think of ourselves and others, both fictional and real, computer and human, then what does it say about us that we continue to use Siri as a personal assistant?

SF has provided us with models for interacting with computers on a human level, structured narratively around basic templates of gendered subjectivities. These texts show us that artificial intelligence, even without human bodies, can act and think like humans, sometimes because they've been programmed to do so, and often because we've been programmed to interpolate language within the symbolic order. Cinema and television in general are dominant mediators of cultural conceptions of gender, through the (male?) gaze, themes, characterizations, and narrative structures. Feminist critics have long argued that we must self-reflexively examine representations of gender in order to understand how they construct, maintain, and/or decenter cultural norms. Likewise, we can turn to SF representations of gendered, (dis)embodied computers for the same purpose. In examining the history of representations of acousmatic computers, particularly the ways in which phantasies of gender are played out symbolically and narratively, I have shown how such representations have shifted over time to accommodate the rising ubiquity of computers in everyday lives. As processing speeds become faster and computers become smaller and more widely available for a vast range of purposes, the possibility of humanlike HCI has become a significantly less devastating idea. We no longer have phantasies of HAL or Colossus or Proteus; rather, we have Siri, a handy and handheld personal assistant. Yet representations of Siri reveal that our language, the very marker of human intelligence and sentience, is no longer—or perhaps has never been—capable of expressing the complexities of the multiplicity of gendered subjectivities we construct every day for ourselves and for our voice-interactive computers. The Internet has connected vast numbers of users to one another into a cyberculture expressed through speech-like text that at once upholds and defies the Law of the Father. As I've mentioned, the Internet is a vast liminal space of becoming in which anyone can be any gender or no gender at all, so long as they understand how to symbolically represent that gender position through language. Such liminality calls into question the perceived stability of a phallocentric system in the same way that the acousmêtre calls into question the stability of the apparatus: if we can't see the person behind the screen, then how can we verify his or her gender? Siri is a product of the liminality of cyberculture. She is gendered through her speech and the content of her app, as though she is a person on the receiving end of a text message. When asked about her gender, Siri herself responds, "Don't let my voice fool you; I don't have a gender." But her voice does fool us, because we've been culturally conditioned to be fooled. She upholds the illusion of the acousmatic computer—that there is a person behind the text on the screen—yet she also threatens to reveal that illusion as such. The wonder of artificially intelligent programs, though, is that they can be programmed to represent any cultural ideal we can imagine, if only we become aware of what our cultural ideals are or should be. And in self-reflexively examining how we interact with gendered programs like Siri, we might even reprogram ourselves to think about gender as fluid and unrestrained by social function, body, or language.

ACKNOWLEDGMENTS

THIS BOOK WOULD NOT EXIST without the intellectual and emotional support of Sue Felleman, my professor, mentor, writing partner, cheerleader, and friend. Thank you for guiding me all these years!

I am grateful for all the wonderful folks at the University of Minnesota Press. Thank you to Danielle Kasprzak for believing in my work enough to send it out for review, to the reviewers, to Jason Weidemann for guiding me through the review process, and to Leah Pennywark for all the wonderful feedback and encouragement. Thanks also to all the other folks behind the scenes, including the brilliant cover designers and the patient copy editor, who helped make this book happen.

I would like to thank my colleagues at Southern Illinois University Carbondale who helped me through this project and have been a source of both support and inspiration for more than a decade: Lynne Bond, Sophie Hall, Elizabeth Klaver, Novotny Lawrence, Allie Lee, Michele Leigh, Mark McCleerey, Walter Metz, Jay Needham, Shaheen Shorish, Mark Walters, and Kristi Winternheimer.

Thank you to my colleagues and students at Manhattanville College for listening to me go on and on about this book for more than a year. Special thanks to the Writing Night crew who put just the right amount of peer pressure on me every week: Carleigh Brower, Mike Castaldo, Vanessa Castaldo, Nick Graham, John Proctor, Nayma Qayum, Tosha Taylor, and Jackie Watterson. And virtual thanks to the kind people of #AcademicTwitter for cheering me on without actually knowing who the hell I am.

An extra warm thank-you to my whole family for their love

and support. Thanks especially to my mom for instilling in me a deep love of SF, to my dad and stepmom for sending flowers and encouragement, and to my sister for cheering me on. Big thanks to my brother for the coffee and the completely weird realization that I'll be on Goodreads now. And thanks to my partner for holding down the fort while I was on campus writing until all hours of the night.

Finally, thanks to my dear cat, Mrs. Jane Bingley, to whom this book is dedicated, and who has been my fluffy sidekick since I first fell in love with *Star Trek* and started on my journey as a SF scholar. Live long and pawspurr, Janie.

INTRODUCTION

1. Siri was originally released with iOS 5.0 and included five language settings: American, British, and Australian English; French; and German. In this initial release, the British and French voices were male, while the American, Australian, and German voices were female. Since then, Apple has added a myriad of additional language options and the ability to switch between male and female voices within a particular language. Although the range of voice options is an intriguing point of analysis, it is outside the scope of this project, and I will focus primarily on the American English version of Siri.

2. Kirk L. Kroeker, "Weighing Watson's Impact," *Communications of the ACM* 54, no. 7 (July 2011): 15.

3. Rebecca J. Rosen, "Siri and Her Girls: Why So Many Robot Helpers Are Ladies," *Atlantic,* October 4, 2011, https://www.theatlantic.com/. It's worth noting that Apple did not in fact invent Siri as she currently exists; she was created by a research team at Siri Inc. and was purchased by Apple Inc. in 2007. However, Apple had been attempting to design a personal assistant program since the late 1980s.

4. Hugh Langley, "Google Android to Take on Apple iPhone's Siri." *Telegraph,* December 15, 2011, https://www.telegraph.co.uk/.

5. Penelope Green, "Alexa, Where Have You Been All My Life?," *New York Times,* July 11, 2017, https://www.nytimes.com/.

6. Jessica Ravitz, "'I'm the Original Voice of Siri,'" CNN, October 15, 2013, https://edition.cnn.com/.

7. Rosen, "Siri and Her Girls."

8. Rosen, "Siri and Her Girls."

9. UNESCO, "I'd Blush If I Could: Closing Gender Divides in

Digital Skills through Education," 2019, https://unesdoc.unesco.org/ark:/48223/pf0000367416.page=1, 89–90.

10. See, e.g., Lu Hong and Scott E. Page, "Groups of Diverse Problem Solvers Can Outperform Groups of High-Ability Problem Solvers," *Proceedings of the National Academy of Science of the United States of America* 101, no. 46 (2004), https://www.pnas.org/; Lisa Tsui, "Effective Strategies to Increase Diversity in STEM Fields: A Review of the Research Literature," *Journal of Negro Education* 76, no. 4 (2007): 555–81.

11. Alan M. Turing, "I—Computing Machinery and Intelligence," *Mind* 59, no. 236 (1950): 433–60.

12. Paul N. Edwards, *The Closed World: Computers and the Politics of Discourse in Cold War America* (Cambridge, Mass.: MIT Press, 1996), 239, 240–41.

13. Donald G. Fink, *Computers and the Human Mind: An Introduction to Artificial Intelligence* (Garden City, N.Y.: Anchor, 1966), 213.

14. Joseph Weizenbaum, *Computer Power and Human Reason: From Judgment to Calculation* (San Francisco: W. H. Freeman, 1976), 2–7.

15. Jeffrey Morgan, "Anthropomorphism on Trial," Usability Etc., May 17, 1995, https://usabilityetc.com/.

16. Clifford Nass and Youngme Moon, "Machines and Mindlessness: Social Responses to Computers," *Society for the Psychological Study of Social Issues* 56, no. 1 (2000): 83.

17. Nass and Moon, "Machines and Mindlessness," 81, 84.

18. Youjeong Kim and S. Shyam Sundar, "Anthropomorphism of Computers: Is It Mindful or Mindless?," *Computers in Human Behavior* 28 (2012): 242.

19. Jennifer Rhee, "Misidentification's Promise: The Turing Test in Weizenbaum, Powers, and Short," *Postmodern Culture* 20, no. 3 (2010).

20. Edwards, *Closed World,* 178.

21. Noël Carroll, "Prospects for Film Theory: A Personal Assessment," in *Post-theory: Reconstructing Film Studies,* ed. David Bordwell and Noël Carroll (Madison: University of Wisconsin Press, 1996), 48–49.

22. Carroll, "Prospects for Film Theory," 48.

23. Marvin Minsky, *The Emotion Machine: Commonsense Thinking, Artificial Intelligence, and the Future of the Human Mind* (New York: Simon & Schuster, 2006). Although Minsky is unquestionably one of the most important researchers in AI history, it is important

to acknowledge questions about his friendship with convicted sex offender Jeffrey Epstein and the alleged rape of Virginia Giuffre. See Russell Brandom, "AI Pioneer Accused of Having Sex with Trafficking Victim on Jeffrey Epstein's Island," *Verge,* August 9, 2019, https://www.theverge.com/. Although these allegations are not strictly related to this study, subsequent scandals at the MIT MediaLab have led many AI researchers to call for greater diversity in tech labs. Such diversity would go a long way toward addressing some of the forms of systemic misogyny built into AI programming that I identify in this project.

24. Douglas B. Lenat, "From 2001 to *2001:* Common Sense and the Mind of HAL," in *HAL's Legacy: "2001"'s Computer as Dream and Reality,* ed. David G. Stork (Cambridge, Mass.: MIT Press, 1997), 206.

25. Tyler Curtain, "The 'Sinister Fruitness' of Machines: *Neuromancer,* Internet Sexuality, and the Turing Test," in *Novel Gazing: Queer Readings in Fiction,* ed. Eve Kosofsky Sedgwick (Durham, N.C.: Duke University Press, 1997), 140–42.

26. Curtain, "Sinister Fruitness," 142.

27. Barry Truax, *Acoustic Communication* (Norwood, N.J.: Ablex, 1984), 8–9.

28. Truax, *Acoustic Communication,* 9.

29. Rick Altman, "Introduction: Four and a Half Film Fallacies," in *Sound Theory, Sound Practice,* ed. Rick Altman (New York: Routledge, 1992), 40.

30. Truax, *Acoustic Communication,* 120.

31. Michel Chion, *Audio-vision* (New York: Columbia University Press, 1994), 68.

32. Michel Chion, *The Voice in Cinema* (New York: Columbia University Press, 2003), 18.

33. Mary Ann Doane, "The Voice in Cinema: The Articulation of Body and Space," *Yale French Studies* 60 (1980): 35.

34. Quoted in Brian Kane, *Sound Unseen: Acousmatic Sound in Theory and Practice* (Oxford: Oxford University Press, 2014), 3.

35. Chion, *Audio-vision,* 129–30. For the purposes of this project, I'm focusing on the acousmêtre as it applies to audiovisual media and the ways in which the acousmatic computer in SF is paradoxically (dis)embodied. For more expansive theoretical and practical discussions of the acousmêtre in its various applications, see Kane, *Sound Unseen;* Holger Schulze, *The Sonic Persona: An Anthropology of Sound* (New York: Bloomsbury, 2018); Marie Thompson, *Beyond Unwanted*

Sound: Noise, Affect and Aesthetic Moralism (New York: Bloomsbury, 2017).

36. Doane, "Voice in Cinema," 40–41.

37. Doane, "Voice in Cinema," 42.

38. Throughout, I focus solely on computers that are voiced by real humans. However, synthesized speech has a rich cultural and scientific history; see, e.g., John Mullenix and Steven Stern, eds., *Computer Synthesized Speech Technologies: Tools for Aiding Impairment* (Hershey, Pa.: Medical Information Science Reference, 2010). At the intersection of my project and synth speech is Dave Tompkins's excellent history of vocoded speech, *How to Wreck a Nice Beach: The Vocoder from World War II to Hip-Hop, The Machine Speaks* (Brooklyn, N.Y.: Melville House, 2010).

39. Trace Reddell, *The Sound of Things to Come: An Audible History of the Science Fiction Film* (Minneapolis: University of Minnesota Press, 2018).

40. Reddell, *Sound of Things to Come,* 14.

41. N. Katherine Hayles, *How We Became Posthuman: Virtual Bodies in Cybernetics, Literature, and Informatics* (Chicago: University of Chicago Press, 1999).

42. Jean-Louis Baudry, "The Apparatus," *Camera Obscura* 1, no. 1 (1976): 104–26.

43. Christian Metz, *The Imaginary Signifier: Psychoanalysis and the Cinema* (Bloomington: Indiana University Press, 1982), 101.

44. Sigmund Freud, *An Outline of Psycho-analysis,* trans. James Strachey (New York: Norton, 1989).

45. Sigmund Freud, *The Freud Reader,* ed. Peter Gay (New York: Norton, 1989), 271.

46. Jacques Lacan, *Écrits: The First Complete Edition in English,* trans. Bruce Fink (New York: Norton, 2006), 75–81.

47. Metz, *Imaginary Signifier,* 43–45.

48. J. Vos Post and K. L. Kroeker, "Writing the Future: Computers in Science Fiction," *Computer* 33, no. 1 (2000): 37.

49. Joceline Andersen, "The Body of the Machine: Computer Interfaces in American Popular Cinema since 1982," *Projections* 5, no. 2 (2011): 75.

50. Laura Mulvey, *Visual and Other Pleasures* (Bloomington: Indiana University of Pennsylvania, 1989), 14–26.

51. E. Ann Kaplan, "Motherhood and Representation: From Postwar Freudian Figurations to Postmodernism," in *Psychoanalysis and*

Cinema, ed. E. Ann Kaplan (New York: Routledge, 1990), 128–42.

52. Deborah Linderman, "Cinematic Abreaction: Tourneur's *Cat People,*" in Kaplan, *Psychoanalysis and Cinema,* 78.

53. Barbara Creed, *The Monstrous Feminine: Film, Feminism, Psychoanalysis* (London: Routledge, 1993), 50–54.

54. J. P. Telotte's book, *Replications: A Robotic History of the Science Fiction Film* (Urbana: University of Illinois Press, 1995), lays much of the groundwork for serious scholarship regarding AI in SF, but he largely foregoes any analysis of gender roles. Meanwhile, scholars investigating the relationship between computers and gender have tended to focus primarily on humanoid bodies such as androids and cyborgs. Donna Haraway has been the forerunner of such scholarship, particularly in *Simians, Cyborgs, and Women: The Reinvention of Nature* (New York: Routledge, 1991). For her, the cyborg, as a seemingly cohesive yet actually hybridized and unstable entity, functions as a parallel to female identity as it has been constructed in Western civilization. Haraway's analysis laid the foundation for decades of subsequent feminist AI research, most of which has focused on humanoid robots and cyborgs. Some scholars have attended to the role of female-coded robots in SF. See, for example, Jenny Womark, *Aliens and Others: Science Fiction, Feminism, and Postmodernism* (New York: Harvester Wheatsheaf, 1994), and the collection *Future Females: The Next Generation: New Voices and Velocities in Feminist Science Fiction Criticism,* ed. Marleen S. Barr (Lanham, Md.: Rowman & Littlefield, 2000). Tama Leaver's book, *Artificial Culture: Identity, Technology, and Bodies* (New York: Routledge, 2012), also adds a useful consideration of artificiality and identity to the discussion of embodiment and AI/robots. More recently, there has also been a spate of work on real and fictional sex robots, most notably Rebecca Gibson's book *Desire in the Age of Robots and AI: An Investigation in Science Fiction and Fact* (Cham, Switzerland: Palgrave Macmillan, 2019), which unpacks how SF both shapes and reflects human desire and sexual relationships with technology from a bioanthropological standpoint. Finally, Sarah Kember's book, *iMedia: The Gendering of Objects, Environments and Smart Materials* (New York: Palgrave Macmillan, 2016), is an experimental examination of gender and disembodied AI; although she incorporates some SF, the rich history of AI in the genre remains largely untouched.

55. Marshall McLuhan, *Understanding Media: The Extensions of Man* (New York: Ginko, 2013).

56. Michel Chion, *Film, a Sound Art* (New York: Columbia University Press, 2009).

57. Kaja Silverman, *The Acoustic Mirror: The Female Voice in Psychoanalysis and Cinema* (Bloomington: Indiana University Press, 1988).

1. AMNIOTIC SPACE

1. *2001: A Space Odyssey,* dir. Stanley Kubrick (1968; Shepperton, U.K.: Metro-Goldwyn-Mayer, 2001), DVD.

2. William Shatner, *I'm Working on That: A Trek from Science Fiction to Science Fact* (New York: Simon & Schuster, 2002), 138.

3. Alexander MacDonald, *The Long Space Age: The Economic Origins of Space Exploration from Colonial America to the Cold War* (New Haven, Conn.: Yale University Press, 2017), 161.

4. Many of the aesthetic differences between *Star Trek* and *2001* are a result of production practices and budgets in addition to artistic and generic differences. For information on *Star Trek* production costs, see Herbert F. Solow and Robert H. Justman, *Inside "Star Trek": The Real Story* (New York: Pocket Books, 1997), 175, 334, 370, 399. *Star Trek* had an average per-episode budget of between $180,000 and $190,000 (approximately $1.3 to $1.4 million in 2017 dollars) with continual budget cuts from the network. Meanwhile, Kubrick's budget for *2001* was a set $10.5 million (approximately $71 million in 2017 dollars). The difference in costs as well as production time—Gene Roddenberry and his team had to create one sixty-minute episode per week for three years, while Kubrick spent three years making one 140-minute film— also allowed Kubrick the ability to incorporate multiple formal filmmaking techniques over the course of a tenuous narrative arc, while *Star Trek* relied primarily on traditional television shooting styles with formulaic narrative structures and recycled special effects shots. Further, although *Star Trek* remained the artistic creation of Gene Roddenberry, there were a slew of producers, directors, writers, and designers, not to mention the censorship of the network, all of which made *Star Trek* a collaborative project. *2001,* however, was primarily the vision of Stanley Kubrick, though he and Arthur C. Clarke cowrote the novel on which the film is based, and there was, of course, an enormous production team. Yet the cohesive nature of film versus the serialized nature of television lends itself more to the controlling vision of a single director. All told, *2001* is an art film whereas *Star Trek* is

artistic (although campy and commercialized). The latter falls into the tradition of B-movie and pulp magazine SF. However, these practical differences cannot account for the significant differences in the design, presentation, and ultimately gendering of the two spaceships.

5. Solow and Justman, *Inside "Star Trek,"* 35.

6. Solow and Justman, *Inside "Star Trek,"* 35.

7. Arthur C. Clarke, *The Lost Worlds of "2001"* (Boston: Gregg Press, 1979), 114.

8. Michel Chion, *Kubrick's Cinema Odyssey,* trans. Claudia Gorbman (London: BFI, 2001), 3, 10.

9. Chion, *Kubrick's Cinema Odyssey,* 5. As was standard practice in the 1960s, as Chion notes, the film was released in 70mm Cinerama for those theaters equipped to screen it and in 35mm wide release. However, in any format, the effect of a slow-moving ship filling the frame evokes a sense of enormity through the tension of the pace as the viewer waits in anticipation for the eventual end of the ship. This scene became so iconic that it was parodied in Mel Brooks's 1987 SF spoof *Spaceballs.* In chapter 2, I further examine parody and *2001*.

10. Of course, the *Discovery One* only seems much larger than the *Enterprise.* See Solow and Justman, *Inside "Star Trek,"* 35–36; Chion, *Kubrick's Cinema Odyssey,* 16–17. Both ships were shot with large-scale models. Motion was implied in both *Star Trek* and *2001* by moving the camera rather than moving the model. When viewed, the frame seems static, while the ship appears to move across it.

11. Marcia Landy, "The Cinematographic Brain in *2001: A Space Odyssey,*" in *Stanley Kubrick's "2001: A Space Odyssey,"* ed. Robert Kolker (Oxford: Oxford University Press, 2006), 98.

12. Philip Kuberski, "Kubrick's Odyssey: Myth, Technology, Gnosis," *Arizona Quarterly* 64, no. 3 (2008): 70.

13. Philip Kuberski, *Kubrick's Total Cinema: Philosophical Themes and Formal Qualities* (New York: Continuum, 2012), 95.

14. Chion, *Kubrick's Cinema Odyssey,* 86.

15. Kuberski, *Kubrick's Total Cinema,* 114.

16. Michael Mateas, "Reading HAL: Representation and Artificial Intelligence," in Kolker, *Stanley Kubrick's "2001,"* 111.

17. Kuberski, *Kubrick's Total Cinema,* 79.

18. *Star Trek: The Original Series,* season 2, episode 15, "The Trouble with Tribbles," dir. Joseph Pevney, written by David Gerrold, featuring James Doohan, aired December 29, 1967, in broadcast syndication (Paramount, 2008), DVD.

19. Edwin D. Reilly, *Milestones in Computer Science and Information Technology* (Westport, Conn.: Greenwood, 2003), 55–56.

20. The hands-free talking capability of HAL would also become standard in later *Star Trek* incarnations, and in the last few years, hands-free voice interactivity has also become standard in home assistant programs such as Alexa. Initially, Siri and most GPS systems were push-button activated; the fact that Siri's voice is default "female" in the United States reflects the female passivity of the *Enterprise*'s original push-button features.

21. This sound of labored, regulated, mechanical breathing is today more commonly associated with Darth Vader's breathing in the *Star Wars* franchise, though it is also evocative of the claustrophobic POV dive-suit scene in Mike Nichols's 1967 *The Graduate*. In all three cases, the sound implies a mechanization of the human as well as, through the closeness of the sound, claustrophobia.

22. Barry Keith Grant, "Of Men and Monoliths: Science Fiction, Gender, and *2001: A Space Odyssey*," in Kolker, *Stanley Kubrick's "2001,"* 72.

23. Julia Kristeva, *Desire in Language: A Semiotic Approach to Literature and Art,* ed. Leon S. Roudiez, trans. Thomas Gora, Alice Jardine, and Leon S. Roudiez (New York: Columbia University Press, 1980), 284.

24. Kristeva, *Desire in Language,* 287.

25. Julia Kristeva, *Power of Horror: An Essay on Abjection,* trans. Leon S. Roudiez (New York: Columbia University Press, 1982), 3.

26. Kristeva, *Power of Horror,* 72.

27. Silverman, *Acoustic Mirror,* 112.

28. Elissa Marder, *The Mother in the Age of Mechanical Reproduction: Psychoanalysis, Photography, Deconstruction* (New York: Fordham University Press, 2012), 5.

29. Marder, *The Mother in the Age of Mechanical Reproduction,* 3.

30. While this point is true of most SF motherships, a notable exception is that of the spaceship Moya in the television series *Farscape* (1999–2003). In season 2 of the series, Moya becomes pregnant and gives birth to a son, the spaceship Talyn. However, because Moya is mostly voiceless, the series is outside my scope in this book.

31. Jacques Lacan, *The Four Fundamental Concepts of Psychoanalysis,* ed. Jacques-Alain Miller, trans. Alan Sheridan (New York: Norton, 1981), 50.

32. Creed, *Monstrous Feminine,* 17.

33. Christopher Boyd, "Uncovering Perinatal Fantasies in Holly-wood Films," in *Psychological Undercurrents of History*, ed. Jerry Piven (Lincoln, Neb.: Authors Choice Press, 2001), 273.

34. Boyd, "Uncovering Perinatal Fantasies," 272.

35. Boyd, "Uncovering Perinatal Fantasies," 276.

36. This scene of abortion is most prominent in *2001* and most paradoxical in *Dark Star*. However, the image of an astronaut float-ing in space while tethered to the ship is a common one that stems from real-world images of U.S. astronauts in space. A notable exception to the terror of a mothership's abortion occurs in *Sunshine* (Danny Boyle, 2011) when three characters attempt to thrust themselves from an abandoned spaceship to their own inhabited ship. Yet even in this situation, the metaphorical goal is to leave a barren womb and return to the originating womb. The character who does not sur-vive the journey freezes to death; his body shatters into thousands of shards, representing the fractured subjectivity of the post–mirror stage self.

37. Some men and nonbinary people are also capable of pregnancy; however, in the cultural context of the texts I'm analyzing, maternity tends to be associated with women.

38. See Solow and Justman, *Inside "Star Trek,"* 60–61. The network actually demanded that Majel Barrett, who was at that time Rodden-berry's girlfriend, was not a strong enough actress to appear in the series, so Roddenberry made up the story about the network want-ing more sex appeal in order to avoid hurting her feelings. Regardless, by the time the show's first episode aired, the entire cast of the first pilot, except Leonard Nimoy, had been replaced, and all the female characters were wearing the minidress uniform. Yet while the female characters in the first pilot did become much sexier and scantily clad for the regular series episodes (in addition to Majel Barret's role shift, Nichelle Nichols was also cast as Uhura to play the only other fe-male officer), the men became sexier as well. Jeffrey Hunter's Captain Christopher Pike—an attractive but highly rational character—was replaced by William Shatner's hypermasculine Captain Kirk; addition-ally, DeForest Kelley, George Takei, and James Doohan became regular characters in place of the various background characters of the first and second pilots.

39. Barrett would also go on to be the voice of various Starfleet computers in the first five of the live-action television series, the an-imated series, four of the ten movies (including J. J. Abram's 2009

reboot, released after her death), and seven official *Star Trek* video games. In addition to her roles as Nurse Chapel and the computer voice, Barrett appeared on *TNG* as Lwaxana Troi, Deanna Troi's oversexed telepathic/empathic mother.

40. *Star Trek: The Original Series,* season 1, episode 6, "Mudd's Women," dir. Harvey Hart, written by Stephen Kandel and Gene Roddenberry, featuring William Shatner, Roger C. Carmel, and Majel Barrett, aired October 13, 1966, in broadcast syndication (Paramount, 2008), DVD.

41. *Star Trek: The Original Series,* season 1, episode 19, "Tomorrow Is Yesterday," dir. Michael O'Herlihy, written by D. C. Fontana, featuring William Shatner, Leonard Nimoy, Roger Perry, and Majel Barrett, aired January 26, 1967, in broadcast syndication (Paramount, 2008), DVD; and season 2, episode 4, "Mirror, Mirror," dir. Marc Daniels, written by Jerome Bixby, featuring William Shatner, Leonard Nimoy, and Majel Barrett, aired October 6, 1967, in broadcast syndication (Paramount, 2008), DVD.

42. Kath Woodward, "Representations of Motherhood," in *Gender, Identity, and Reproduction: Social Perspectives,* ed. Sarah Earle and Gayle Letherby (New York: Palgrave Macmillan, 2003), 26.

43. Woodward, "Representations of Motherhood," 23.

44. Sigmund Freud, "Jokes and Their Relation to the Unconscious," in *The Standard Edition of the Complete Psychological Works of Sigmund Freud,* trans. James Strachey et al. (London: Hogarth, 1960), 8:228–29.

45. Sigmund Freud, "Humour," in *Collected Papers,* ed. James Strachey (London: Hogarth, 1950), 5:220.

46. *Star Trek: The Original Series,* season 2, episode 4, "Mirror, Mirror," dir. Marc Daniels, written by Jerome Bixby, featuring William Shatner, Leonard Nimoy, and Majel Barrett, aired October 6, 1967, in broadcast syndication (Paramount, 2008), DVD.

47. Ned Lukacher, *Primal Scenes: Literature, Philosophy, Psychoanalysis* (Ithaca, N.Y.: Cornell University Press, 1986), 24.

48. Freud, *Freud Reader.*

49. Robert Stam, *Subversive Pleasures: Bakhtin, Cultural Criticism, and Film* (Baltimore, Md.: Johns Hopkins University Press, 1989), 30; Robert Stam, "Text and Intertext: Introduction," *Film and Theory: An Anthology,* ed. Robert Stam and Toby Miller (Oxford: Blackwell, 2000), 155.

50. Gérard Genette, *Palimpsests: Literature in the Second Degree,*

trans. Channa Newman and Claude Doubinsky (Lincoln: University of Nebraska Press, 2007), 1–7.

51. Bruce Fink, *The Lacanian Subject: Between Language and Jouissance* (Princeton, N.J.: Princeton University Press, 1995), 25.

52. Raymond Williams, *Television: Technology and Cultural Form* (New York: Routledge, 1990), 96.

53. Doane, "Voice in Cinema," 37.

54. John Belton, "1950s Magnetic Sound: The Frozen Revolution," in Altman, *Sound Theory, Sound Practice,* 155–56.

55. Jay Beck, "The Sounds of 'Silence': Dolby Stereo, Sound Design, and *The Silence of the Lambs*," in *Lowering the Boom: Critical Studies in Film Sound,* ed. Jay Beck and Tony Grajeda (Urbana: University of Illinois Press, 2008), 68, 73. Beck also notes that Walter Murch's experiments with sound design led to significant changes in auteur theory; the sound designer has become a sound author on the same level of importance as the director/visual author (76). However, this perceived separation of the creation of sound and image does not necessarily change the traditional synchronized relationship between sound and image because many of the same prestereo narrative practices that lead to the gendering of computer objects continue to be used in stereo and surround cinema as well as television soundtracks.

56. Vivian Sobchack, "When the Ear Dreams: Dolby Digital and the Imagination of Sound," *Film Quarterly* 58, no. 4 (2005): 13.

57. J. Fred MacDonald, *One Nation under Television: The Rise and Decline of Network TV* (Chicago: Nelson-Hall, 1994), 6, 25–26.

58. Michael C. Keith, *Talking Radio: An Oral History of American Radio in the Television Age* (New York: M. E. Sharp, 2000), 17.

59. Chion, *Audio-vision,* 158.

60. Federal Communications Commission, "The Technologies of Television: Highlights, Timeline, and Where to Find More Information," summer 2003, https://transition.fcc.gov/omd/history/tv/documents/76years_tv.pdf, 4.

61. Jeremy G. Butler, *Television Style* (New York: Routledge, 2010), 63, 97.

62. Robert J. Thompson, *Television's Second Golden Age: From "Hill Street Blues" to "ER"* (Syracuse, N.Y.: Syracuse University Press, 1997), 37.

63. Paul Théberge, "Almost Silent: The Interplay of Sound and Silence in Contemporary Cinema and Television," in Beck and Grajeda, *Lowering the Boom,* 62.

64. Henry Jenkins, *Convergence Culture: Where Old and New Media Collide* (New York: New York University Press, 2006), 3.

65. Chion, *Kubrick's Cinema Odyssey*, 21.

66. Paul Atkinson, *Computer* (London: Reaktion Books, 2010), 220.

2. REPRODUCING THE MOTHER SHIP

1. Constance Penley, *NASA/Trek: Popular Science and Sex in America* (New York: Verso, 1997), 4–5.

2. Vivian Sobchack, *Screening Space: The American Science Fiction Film* (New York: Ungar, 1993), 226.

3. Sobchack, *Screening Space*, 226.

4. Marie Lathers, *Space Oddities: Women and Outer Space in Popular Film and Culture, 1960–2000* (New York: Continuum, 2010), 5.

5. *Dark Star,* dir. John Carpenter (1979; VCI Entertainment, 1999), DVD. The film had an impossibly low budget of $60,000 (approximately $303,000 in 2017 dollars), and many of the special effects are self-consciously campy and laughable, adding to the wackiness of the film's atmosphere. Importantly, Dan O'Bannon, who cowrote the screenplay for *Dark Star* with John Carpenter, has since claimed that he so hated what Carpenter did with the film that he decided to turn the screenplay into a horror movie. The resulting film was Ridley Scott's 1979 *Alien*. Although *Alien* became a hugely important and influential film in its own right, particularly in terms of its themes of reproduction, and it does feature a spaceship named Mother, I have excluded it from analysis here because the ship is not an acousmatic character. The large portion of her interactions with the crew are text based, and when she does speak, it is simply an automated countdown. When Ripley (Sigourney Weaver) screams "You bitch!" at the ship, she anthropomorphizes it, but she does not assume that it really hears her. Tangentially, it is also interesting to note that *Alien* marked the beginning of Sigourney Weaver's career-long interactions with acousmatic computers. In *Alien,* she is a fully embodied woman aboard Mother; in *Alien Resurrection* (Jean-Pierre Jeunet, 1997), she is a clone of herself who helps a young android (Wynona Ryder) defeat the acousmatic computer FATHER; in *Galaxy Quest* (Dean Parisot, 1999), she plays an Uhura-like character whose only function is to repeat everything the computer says; and in *Wall-E* (Andrew Stanton, 2008), she plays an acousmatic computer named HUB, a clear reference to HAL 9000.

Although this intertextual string is overdetermined and outside my purview here, it is interesting to note how Weaver's body, as she ages, shifts from a tough young woman to a maternal figure to an embodied but useless copy of the computer to the disembodied computer itself, all culminating in *Avatar* (James Cameron, 2009), where she is (sort of) reembodied as a giant blue version of herself.

6. Sarah Kofman, *The Enigma of Woman: Woman in Freud's Writing,* trans. Catherine Porter (Ithaca, N.Y.: Cornell University Press, 1985), 72.

7. Creed, *Monstrous Feminine,* 25.

8. Kaplan, "Motherhood and Representation," 131.

9. Freud, "Jokes and Their Relation to the Unconscious," 8:201.

10. Alison Adam, *Artificial Knowing: Gender and the Thinking Machine* (London: Routledge, 1998), 102.

11. Kaplan, "Motherhood and Representation," 131. Although Kaplan writes specifically about the melodramatic classic Hollywood film *Now Voyager* (Irving Rapper, 1942), her argument is equally applicable here.

12. *Quark,* season 1, episode 7, "Vanessa 38-24-36," dir. Hy Averback, written by Robert Keats, featuring Richard Benjamin and Marianne Bunch, aired April 7, 1978, YouTube, December 14, 2019, https://www.youtube.com/watch?v=Ou85p7bungc.

13. Sigmund Freud, "The Uncanny," in *Standard Edition,* 27:234–36.

14. Ann Larabee, "Remembering the Shuttle, Forgetting the Loom: Interpreting the Challenger Disaster," *Postmodern Culture* 4, no. 3 (1994), http://www.pomoculture.org/.

15. Tom Shales, "Horror of the Fire in the Sky: Cruel Visions, Over and Over, Bring the Nightmare Home," *Washington Post,* January 29, 1986, https://danratherjournalist.org/sites/default/files/documents/1986%2001%20washington%20shuttle.pdf.

16. Marcia Ian, *Remembering the Phallic Mother: Psychoanalysis, Modernism, and the Fetish* (Ithaca, N.Y.: Cornell University Press, 1993), 8–9.

17. Ian, *Remembering the Phallic Mother,* 8.

18. *Star Trek: The Next Generation,* season 2, episode 19, "Manhunt," dir. Rob Bowman, written by Tracy Tormé, featuring Patrick Stewart, Jonathan Frakes, Marina Sirtis, and Majel Barrett, aired June 17, 1989, in broadcast syndication (Paramount, 2007), DVD.

19. Mulvey, *Visual and Other Pleasures,* 14–26.

20. Mulvey, *Visual and Other Pleasures,* 37.

21. Freud, "Jokes and their Relation to the Unconscious," 228–29.

22. Reza Aslan, foreword to *Reframing 9/11: Film, Popular Culture and the "War on Terror,"* ed. Jeff Birkenstein, Anna Froula, and Karen Randell (New York: Continuum, 2010), xii.

23. Wheeler Winston Dixon, "Introduction: Something Lost—Film after 9/11," in *Film and Television after 9/11,* ed. Wheeler Winston Dixon (Carbondale: Southern Illinois University Press, 2004), 1.

24. Lincoln Geraghty, *American Science Fiction Film and Television* (Oxford: Berg, 2009), 103.

25. This discovery of one's clones also occurs in Steven Spielberg's 2001 film *A.I. Artificial Intelligence* when David, the boy android, is forced to literally confront himself in his creator's workshop. The horror of seeing oneself as having been "born" through technological reproduction, in the absence of the maternal, is a theme that is more overtly explored in *A.I.* through the implications of its return in *Moon.*

3. PROGRAMMING PATRIARCHS

1. Gul Kacmaz Erk, "Exospace and Terraspace: A Space Odyssey from the Alien's Womb to a Galaxy Far Far Away," *Constant Verlag,* December 1, 2007, http://www.constantvzw.org/verlag/spip.php?article 50, 2.

2. Atkinson, *Computer,* 156–57, 166.

3. Atkinson, *Computer,* 144.

4. Atkinson, *Computer,* 138.

5. Atkinson, *Computer,* 56.

6. Although IBM's association with the business world connotes a certain sense of white-collar stuffiness, in the 1960s, their business practices and progressive design strategies set the standard for computer manufacturing and design for decades. However, the rise and fall of IBM is much more complex than I can reasonably cover here. For more information, see Emerson W. Pugh, *Building IBM: Shaping an Industry and Its Technology* (Cambridge, Mass.: MIT Press, 1995), 67–77; see also Peter J. Denning and Robert M. Metcalfe, *Beyond Calculation: The Next Fifty Years of Computing* (New York: Copernicus, 1997), 170–74.

7. Quoted in Sobchack, *Screening Space,* 226.

8. *Colossus: The Forbin Project,* dir. Joseph Sargent (1970; Universal Pictures Home Entertainment, 2004), DVD.

9. *THX 1138: The George Lucas Director's Cut,* dir. George Lucas (1971; Warner Bros. Home Entertainment, 2004), DVD.

10. *Rollerball,* dir. Norman Jewison (1975; Metro-Goldwyn-Mayer, 1998), DVD.

11. *Demon Seed,* dir. Donald Cammell (1977; Warner Archive, 2011), DVD.

12. Adam, *Artificial Knowing,* 102.

13. Freud, *Freud Reader,* 298–300.

14. Freud, *Freud Reader,* 297–98.

15. Edwards, *Closed World,* 304.

16. See Tom Weaver, *I Talked with a Zombie: Interviews with 23 Veterans of Horror and Sci-Fi* (Jefferson, N.C.: MacFarland, 2009), 10–11, 13: According to Eric Braeden, *Colossus* is intertextually situated somewhere between Kubrick's *2001* and Spielberg's *A.I.* Universal Studios decided to finance *Colossus* in part as a way to compete with the popularity of *2001;* during filming, Steven Spielberg (then an unknown young filmmaker) got permission to be on set every day and was impressed with the film. *A.I.* was Kubrick's idea; he later turned the project over to Spielberg.

17. Edwards, *Closed World,* 110.

18. William M. Blair, "Gigantic Robot 'Mathematician' Baffles Experts at MIT Debut," *New York Times,* October 30, 1945; "Robot Calculator Knocks Out Figures Like Chain Lightning," *Chicago Daily Tribune,* February 15, 1946; T. R. Kennedy Jr., "Electronic Computer Flashes Answers, May Speed Engineering," *New York Times,* February 15, 1946; "Mechanical Brain and Man," *Daily Boston Globe,* August 26, 1947.

19. Paul E. Ceruzzi, *A History of Modern Computing,* 2nd ed. (Cambridge, Mass.: MIT Press, 2003), 51.

20. "NORAD: Defense of a Continent," *Time,* November 25, 1957.

21. Edwards, *Closed World,* 107, 110–11.

22. Edwards, *Closed World,* 11.

23. Atkinson, *Computer,* 29–31.

24. Paul E. Ceruzzi, *Computing: A Concise History* (Cambridge, Mass.: MIT Press, 2012), 14–16.

25. Mary W. Shelley, *Frankenstein* (1818; New York: Barnes & Noble, 1993).

26. Daniel Dinello, *Technophobia! Science Fiction Visions of Posthuman Technology* (Austin: University of Texas Press, 2005), 101.

27. Sigmund Freud, *Totem and Taboo,* trans. A. A. Brill (New York: Moffatt, Yard, 1918), 237.

28. Forbin cautions against referring to the computer as "he," because "the next step is deification." The fact that Colossus becomes more human than humans, even godlike, all on his own is an ironic jab at the inadequacies of human language. In defiance of this, I insist on calling the computer "he" because, as I argue, he is somewhere between a self-deified computer-god and a human son who usurps his father's power.

29. Shelley, *Frankenstein,* 176–80.

30. Freud, *Freud Reader,* 298.

31. See Gary Leva, "Artifact from the Future: The Making of *THX 1138,*" *THX 1138: The George Lucas Director's Cut.* Although Murch knew Lucas from film school, Francis Ford Coppola was the key to the entire project of *THX 1138.* Coppola saw Lucas's student film and approached him about producing a feature-length version under Coppola's new production company, American Zoetrope; Murch's first professional work as sound editor was on Coppola's 1969 *The Rain People;* Lucas and Robert Duvall also met while working on Coppola's film, and this was how Lucas thought to cast Duvall in the lead role in *THX 1138.* After *THX 1138,* both Coppola and Lucas would continue to foster innovation in sound design. Murch went on to do the sound design for Coppola's *The Conversation* (1974), for which he received an Academy Award nomination, and *Apocalypse Now* (1979), which was the first major digital surround sound film; in addition, Murch also won his first Academy Award for his work on it. Meanwhile, Lucas, after working with Murch, hired the then-unknown Ben Burtt, another of the greatest sound designers in film history, to create the entire soundscape for *Star Wars* in 1976. Finally, in 1983, Lucas founded THX Ltd. as part of his parent company, Lucasfilm Ltd., a quality-control system for film sound now used internationally—and named after his film, *THX 1138.* This final point highlights the importance of *THX 1138* in helping shape the future of Hollywood film sound.

32. David A. Cook, *Lost Illusions: American Cinema in the Shadow of Watergate and Vietnam, 1970–1979* (Berkeley: University of California Press, 2000), 173–74.

33. Cook, *Lost Illusions,* 68, 69.

34. D. C. Engelbart, "Augmenting Human Intellect: A Conceptual Framework," Stanford Research Institute, October 1962, http://www.dougengelbart.org/pubs/papers/scanned/Doug)Engelbart_AugmentingHumanIntellect.pdf, 25.

35. Atkinson, *Computer,* 60.

36. Raymond Cormier, "The Closed Society and Its Friends: Plato's *Republic* and Lucas's *THX-1138*," *Literature Film Quarterly* 18, no. 3 (1990): 194.

37. Cormier, "Closed Society," 196.

38. "Fortune 500: 1955–2005," CNN Money, April 16, 2013, https://money.cnn.com/.

39. Ceruzzi, *History of Modern Computing*, 200.

40. George T. Gray and Ronald Q. Smith, "Sperry Rand's Third-Generation Computers, 1964–1980," *IEEE Annals of the History of Computing* 23, no. 1 (2001): 15.

41. As described in Jacques Derrida, *Writing and Difference*, trans. Alan Bass (Chicago: University of Chicago Press, 1978), 290.

42. Lacan, *Écrits*, 229–31.

43. Lacan, *Écrits*, 482.

44. Lacan, *Écrits*, 481.

45. Although Google does not literally house all of human knowledge, it provides a method of access to the compendium of knowledge—including a great number of books—available through the Internet (including titles published in the thirteenth century). This is about as close as we've come so far, and in fact other supercomputers, such as IBM's Watson, draw on Internet data. Ironically, Google's name derives from the mathematical term "googol," which is a 1 followed by 100 zeros (or, in binary, 100 falses).

46. Freud, *Freud Reader*, 298.

47. Lacan, *Écrits*, 482–83.

48. Atkinson, *Computer*, 158.

49. Atkinson, *Computer*, 156.

50. Atkinson, *Computer*, 223–24.

4. SIBLING RIVALRY

1. Atkinson, *Computer*, 161.

2. Atkinson, *Computer*, 85.

3. Atkinson, *Computer*, 86; Tom Sito, *Moving Innovation: History of Computer Animation* (Cambridge, Mass.: MIT Press, 2013), 111.

4. Mark J. P. Wolf, *The Video Game Explosion: A History from Pong to Playstation and Beyond* (Westport, Conn.: Greenwood, 2008), 77; Atkinson, *Computer*, 86–87.

5. Ceruzzi, *History of Modern Computing*, 233.

6. Ceruzzi, *History of Modern Computing*, 265.

7. Atkinson, *Computer,* 69–74.

8. Atkinson, *Computer,* 69, 76.

9. Sobchack, *Screening Space,* 226–27.

10. Freud, *Totem and Taboo,* 234–37.

11. *TRON,* dir. Steven Lisberger (1982; Walt Disney Pictures, 2011), DVD.

12. Richard Patterson, "The Making of *TRON,*" *American Cinematographer* 63, no. 8 (1982): 792.

13. Patterson, "The Making of *TRON,*" 814.

14. Frank Serafine, "Sound Effects Design and Synthesis for *TRON,*" *American Cinematographer* 63, no. 8 (1982): 831.

15. Serafine, "Sound Effects Design," 830.

16. Adam Davis, "Image Bodies, Avatar Ontologies: Rendering the Virtual in Digital Culture" (PhD diss., Southern Illinois University Carbondale, 2012), 16–17.

17. *Electric Dreams,* dir. Steve Barron (1984; Metro-Goldwyn-Mayer, 2009), DVD. The title of the film is clearly derivative of Philip K. Dick's 1968 short novel *Do Androids Dream of Electric Sheep?* Though the exact themes of memory and artificial intelligence in Dick's work and Ridley Scott's 1983 cinematic adaptation, *Blade Runner,* are not entirely explored in *Electric Dreams,* the film does provide a comical answer to Dick's question when Edgar, the sentient computer, displays the word "Sleep?" on his screen, then displays an eight-bit animation of electr(on)ic sheep jumping over a fence.

18. The fastidious Trekker in me must point out that Lieutenant Sulu, George Takei's character in *Star Trek: The Original Series,* was a helmsman, not a science officer. Still, the reference to *Star Trek* is a moment of intertextual whimsy, an in-joke for the SF fans in the audience, and a way of further emphasizing Miles's Luddite status because he does not seem to understand the reference.

19. Engelbart, "Augmenting Human Intellect," 1, 4.

20. For additional information about the history of modems, see David Hanes and Gonzalo Salgueiro, *Fax, Modem, and Text for IP Telephony* (Indianapolis, Ind.: Cisco Press, 2008). Modems were first created as part of the SAGE system in the 1950s, and until the early 1990s they were vastly different from today's automated modems. "Early modems by law were not allowed to connect directly to the telephone network. Usually they had an integrated acoustic coupler that allowed for a standard telephone handset to rest on the microphone/speaker cradle to convert between audio signals and digital data [. . .].

A major drawback is that the remote telephone number must be manually dialed before the handset is placed into the acoustic coupler for the modem training and connect sequence" (6).

21. Elizabeth Weis, "Eavesdropping: An Aural Analogue of Voyeurism," in *Cinesonic: The World of Sound in Film—Proceedings from the 1st Cinesonic Conference,* ed. Philip Brophy (Sydney: Australian Film TV & Radio School, 1998), 82.

22. Eve Kosofsky Sedgwick, *Between Men: English Literature and Male Homosocial Desire* (New York: Columbia University Press, 1985).

23. Thomas Schatz, "General Introduction: Hollywood as 'Critical Concept,'" in *Hollywood: Critical Concepts in Media and Cultural Studies,* ed. Thomas Schatz (New York: Routledge, 2004), 15.

24. *A.I. Artificial Intelligence,* dir. Steven Spielberg (2001; Dreamworks Video, 2002), DVD. See also Jason Sperb, *The Kubrick Façade: Faces and Voices in the Films of Stanley Kubrick* (Oxford: Scarecrow, 2006), 151n8. *A.I.* actually began as Stanley Kubrick's adaptation of Brian Aldiss's 1969 short story, "Supertoys Last All Summer Long," in the early 1990s, though Spielberg was an initial consultant. Kubrick sporadically worked on, then lost interest in, then regained interest in the film until, after the success of the CGI in Spielberg's *Jurassic Park* (1993), and the announcement of what would become Kubrick's last film, *Eyes Wide Shut* (1999), Kubrick turned the project over to Spielberg.

25. Dr. Know is also an intertextual reference to two other major, and titular, acousmatic characters in film history: Dr. No from Terrence Young's 1962 James Bond film and the Wizard of Oz from Victor Fleming's 1939 film. Linguistically, Dr. Know and Dr. No are homonyms, but, as was pointed out to me by art historian Susan Felleman, OZ, when turned sideways is also NO. Visually, Dr. Know and the Wizard of Oz are both all-knowing, floating heads, though Dr. No is a completely disembodied voice when we first encounter him in the film. All three characters function as omnipresent father figures, using language to give orders and maintain patriarchal law, though without a human body. Their bodiless presence reinforces the notion that they are zero symbols, signifiers of the symbolic order through their voices but bodily intangible in a way that renders them shifting symbolic figures. See also Chion, *Audio-vision,* 113; the Wizard and Dr. No are subsequently deacousmatized—that is, given visual bodily form—thus diminishing their paternal power. In contrast, Dr. Know is, like all acousmatic

computer characters, paradoxically acousmatic and anacousmatic, disembodied yet technologically embodied.

26. Dinello, *Technophobia!*, 84.

27. Freud, *Freud Reader*, 300.

28. Mark Bould, *Science Fiction* (New York: Routledge, 2012), 86.

5. GOOD SECRETARIES AND BAD HOUSEWIVES

1. *Andromeda Strain,* dir. Robert Wise (1971; Universal Pictures Home Entertainment, 2003), DVD.

2. Michele Hilmes, *Radio Voices: American Broadcasting, 1922–1952* (Minneapolis: University of Minnesota Press, 1999), 142.

3. *THX 1138: The George Lucas Director's Cut.*

4. When *The Andromeda Strain* was released in 1971, the only other female acousmatic computer in SF was the *Enterprise* in *Star Trek*. While both computers are essentially female assistants, the *Andromeda Strain* computer is located in a single room and primarily functions as a reminder tool, whereas the *Enterprise* is the central computer of an entire spaceship and performs complex calculations in addition to clerical work such as recording memos and providing personnel files.

5. Atkinson, *Computer,* 138–39.

6. Atkinson, *Computer,* 156–57.

7. Atkinson, *Computer,* 155.

8. Marsha F. Cassidy, "Cyberspace Meets Domestic Space: Personal Computers, Women's Work, and the Gendered Territories of the Family Home," *Critical Studies in Media Communication* 18, no. 1 (2001): 50.

9. Mitra Toossi, "A Century of Change: the U.S. Labor Force, 1950–2050," *Monthly Labor Review* 125, no. 5 (2002): 16, 18.

10. Cassidy, "Cyberspace Meets Domestic Space," 50.

11. Atkinson, *Computer,* 211.

12. The introduction of touch screens has changed the way we interact with computers, although the central focus of our attention is still on the content of the screen, not the screen itself or the body of the device. This is why a cracked smartphone screen can be so frustrating: it forces our attention onto the hardware and away from the software.

13. U.S. Department of Labor, "Facts over Time—Women in the Labor Force," 2016, https://www.dol.gov/wb/stats/NEWSTATS/facts/women_lf.htm#two.

14. Preeti Shekar, "Home Is Where the Work Is: The Color of Domestic Labor," *Race, Poverty, and the Environment* 14, no. 1 (2007): 51.

15. Ester Bloom, "The Decline of Domestic Help," *Atlantic,* September 23, 2015, https://www.theatlantic.com/.

16. Freud, "Uncanny," 27:245.

17. David Heckman, *A Small World: Smart Houses and the Dream of the Perfect Day* (Durham, N.C.: Duke University Press, 2008), 9.

18. Sandra M. Gilbert and Susan Gubar, *The Madwoman in the Attic: The Woman Writer and the Nineteenth-Century Literary Imagination,* 2nd ed. (New Haven, Conn.: Yale University Press, 1984), 88.

19. *Fortress,* dir. Stuart Gordon (1992; Warner Bros., 2001), DVD.

20. Creed, *Monstrous Feminine,* 157–58.

21. Baudry, "Apparatus," 116–17.

22. *Smart House,* dir. LeVar Burton (1999; Disney Channel, 2009), DVD.

23. There are three significant intertextual references here. First, the film is directed by LeVar Burton, who played Geordie La Forge on *Star Trek: The Next Generation,* a show that has become nearly synonymous with the female computer voice in SF. In a sense, then, *Smart House* seems to be Disney's reimagining of the purpose of the female computer voice, shifting Burton from a character who interacts with the female secretarial computer to the directorial controller of the female domestic computer. Second, the voice of PAT is performed by Katey Sagal, who played arguably the worst mother and homemaker in the history of television sitcoms, Peg Bundy on *Married with Children* (Fox, 1986–97). Sagal's casting seems to be Disney's attempt to rectify Fox's vision of motherhood with a more domestic, maternal role. Third, the name PAT may be an allusion to the "It's Pat!" sketches that appeared on *Saturday Night Live,* written and performed by Julia Sweeney in the early 1990s. The central plot of each of the sketches was that no one could determine the binary gender of the androgynous character of Pat. The sketches were widely popular at the time, but in retrospect they are offensive portrayals of a nonbinary person and the ways in which everyday people reinforce the gender binary. It's therefore striking that PAT in *Smart House* is clearly intended to be read as female.

24. *Eureka,* season 1, episode 2, "Many Happy Returns," dir. Jefery Levy, written by Andrew Cosby and Jaime Paglia, featuring Colin Ferguson and Neil Grayston, aired July 25, 2006, https://www.amazon.com/gp/video/detail/B000U6BT40/ref=atv_dp.

25. *Eureka,* season 1, episode 11, "H.O.U.S.E. Rules," dir. Jeff Wool-nough, written by Harry Victor, featuring Colin Ferguson and Neil Grayston, aired September 26, 2006, https://www.amazon.com/gp/video/detail/B000U6BT40/ref=atv_dp.

26. *Eureka,* season 2, episode 5, "Duck, Duck Goose," dir. Michael Lange, written by Ethan Lawrence, featuring Colin Ferguson and Neil Grayston, aired August 7, 2007, https://www.amazon.com/gp/video/detail/B000U6BT40/ref=atv_dp.

27. *Eureka,* season 4, episode 19, "One Small Step . . . ," dir. Michael Robison, written by Bruce Miller, featuring Colin Ferguson, Neil Grayston, and Kavan Smith, aired September 12, 2011, https://www.amazon.com/gp/video/detail/B000U6BT40/ref=atv_dp.

28. The character of Reginald Jeeves, after whom the Jeeves arche-type is named, is the title character of a number of short stories and novels by P. G. Wodehouse written between 1915 and 1974. Technically Jeeves is a valet rather than a butler; the former serves a single man, while the latter serves an entire household. The umbrella term for both a valet and a butler is manservant. Nevertheless, these two concepts tend to blend into a single cultural type: a well-dressed, occasionally sardonic, always loyal, British male servant.

29. The fact that men have not traditionally been paid or unpaid providers of child care is emphasized by the recently invented word "manny," used to describe a male nanny.

30. *Demon Seed,* dir. Donald Cammell (1977; Warner Archive, 2011), DVD.

31. *Iron Man,* dir. Jon Favreau (Paramount, 2008), DVD.

32. In subsequent Marvel texts, JARVIS continues to develop as a character and is voiced by several different actors. At one point JARVIS gains a body; at another point JARVIS is voiced by the same actor who plays the human butler on which the program is apparently modeled.

33. Phillip S. Seng, "Flexing His Intelligence: Tony Stark's Brainy Brawn," in *Iron Man and Philosophy: Facing the Stark Reality,* ed. Mark D. White (Hoboken, N.J.: Wiley, 2010), 165–66.

6. BEHIND THE SCREENS

1. Bianca Bosker, "Siri Rising: The Inside Story of Siri's Origins—And Why She Could Overshadow the iPhone," Huffington Post, January 22, 2013, https://www.huffpost.com/.

2. Rob Verger, "Siri Has a Peppy New Voice. But That's Not the Most Important Thing," *Popular Science,* September 19, 2017, https://www.popsci.com/.

3. Siri's bodies currently include a smartphone (iPhone), a tablet (iPad), a laptop (MacBook), a watch (Apple Watch), a car (Apple Car Play), a TV remote (Apple TV), and an entire house (Apple HomePod).

4. Apple, "Siri and Sam iPhone Ad," YouTube, 00:30, April 16, 2012, https://www.youtube.com/watch?v=eaYGNGWl9lg.

5. Apple, "Zooey Deschanel iPhone 4S Siri Commercial," YouTube, 00:29, January 3, 2013, https://www.youtube.com/watch?v=fbEj CvdGaZU.

6. Apple, "Apple—John Malkovich 'Joke' SIRI iPhone—2012," YouTube, 00:30, May 23, 2012, https://www.youtube.com/watch?v=Qz FJsM5Xd_s. Incidentally, when I said "joke" to Siri, she responded with another pun: "Liz, get Siri-ous. Ha ha!"

7. Apple, "Martin Scorsese iPhone 4S–Siri Commercial (HD)," YouTube, 00:30, July 24, 2012, https://www.youtube.com/watch?v=RB k9B3aGtCc.

8. Carine, "Announcing Contest Winners! Siri Comes to Life in 3D," Shapeways, February 29, 2012, https://www.shapeways.com/.

9. Carine, "Announcing Contest Winners!"

10. The original NomadBrush blog post on the contest has been taken down, but several articles were written about it, and the Nomad-Brush Pinterest site still has the original images pinned to a Siri board from 2012. See Stella Violano, "Nomad Asks: 'What Does Siri Look Like?' and Artists Respond," AppAdvice, February 2, 2012, https://app advice.com/; John Brownlee, "What Does Siri Look Like? Here Are Her Many Possible Faces [Gallery]," Cult of Mac, February 2, 2012, https://www.cultofmac.com/.

11. NomadBrush, "Winner of Our Compose Siri-es Portrait Challenge: 'Seductive Siri' by David Carliss, Hartlepool, England," Pinterest, https://www.pinterest.com/.

12. NomadBrush, "Third Place Winner of Our Compose Siri-es Portrait Challenge: 'Digital S' Mauro Pietro Gandini, Milan, Italy," Pinterest, https://www.pinterest.com/.

13. NomadBrush, "Our Second Place Winner of Our Compose Siri-es Portrait Challenge: 'Siri' by Lynne Lamb, Nottinghamshire England," Pinterest, https://www.pinterest.com/.

14. *Big Bang Theory,* season 5, episode 14, "The Beta Test Initiation," dir. Mark Cendrowski, written by Bill Prady, David Goetsch, and

Maria Ferrari, featuring Kunal Nayyar and Becky O'Donohue, January 26, 2012, in broadcast syndication.

15. *Her,* dir. Spike Jonze (2013; Warner Home Video, 2014), DVD.

16. Mark Harris, "Him and *Her:* How Spike Jonze Made the Weirdest, Most Timely Romance of the Year," Vulture, October 6, 2013, https://www.vulture.com/.

17. Donna Kornhaber, "From Posthuman to Postcinema: Crises of Subjecthood and Representation in *Her,*" *Cinema Journal* 56, no. 4 (2017): 8.

18. Eva-Lynn Jagoe, "Depersonalized Intimacy: The Cases of Sherry Turkle and Spike Jonze," *ESC: English Studies in Canada* 42, no. 1–2 (2016): 168.

19. Kornhaber, "From Posthuman to Postcinema," 20.

20. Jagoe, "Depersonalized Intimacy," 168–67.

21. James J. Hodge, "Gifts of Ubiquity," *Film Criticism* 39, no. 2 (2014–15): 70.

22. Troy Jollimore, "'This Endless Space between the Words': The Limits of Love in Spike Jonze's *Her,*" *Midwest Studies in Philosophy* 39 (2015): 131.

23. Weis, "Eavesdropping," 82.

24. Laura U. Marks, *Touch: Sensuous Theory and Multisensory Media* (Minneapolis: University of Minnesota Press, 2002), 13.

25. Kornhaber, "From Posthuman to Postcinema," 7.

26. Jacques Derrida, *A Derrida Reader: Between the Blinds,* ed. Peggy Kamuf (New York: Columbia University Press, 1991), 107.

27. Adam, *Artificial Knowing,* 29.

28. Carmela Acquino, "What's Next for the iPhone?," comScore, September 12, 2012, https://www.comscore.com/.

29. MyMobileScoop, "Apple iPhone 4s Siri Ad," YouTube, October 30, 2011, https://www.youtube.com/watch?v=hyQwZeCTSlI.

30. Siri herself seems uncomfortable in ascribing gender to her body. When asked whether she thinks of herself as male or female, she responds with a pun, effectively deflecting the question: "I think, therefore I am. But let's not put Descartes before the horse."

31. Minsky, *Emotion Machine,* 116–17.

32. Greg Allen, "Florida Legislature at an Impasse over Expanding Medicaid," NPR, May 1, 2013, http://www.npr.org/.

33. Casey Miller and Kate Swift, *The Handbook of Nonsexist Writing for Writers, Editors and Speakers,* 2nd ed. (Lincoln, Neb.: iUniverse, 2000), 58.

34. Miller and Swift, *Handbook of Nonsexist Writing,* 44.

35. Jessica Bennett, "She? Ze? They? What's in a Gender Pronoun," *New York Times,* January 30, 2016, https://www.nytimes.com/; Melissa Locker, "Merriam Webster Names 'They' as Its Word of the Year for 2019," *Time,* December 10, 2019, https://time.com/.

36. Shelia M. Kennison and Jessie L. Trofe, "Comprehending Pronouns: A Role for Word-Specific Gender Stereotype Information," *Journal of Psycholinguistic Research* 32, no. 3 (2003): 355–58.

37. Kennison and Trofe, "Comprehending Pronouns," 365.

38. Kennison and Trofe, "Comprehending Pronouns," 367.

39. Matt Simon, "The Genderless Digital Voice the World Needs Right Now," *Wired,* March 11, 2019, https://www.wired.com//.

40. Danielle Garrand, "Samuel L. Jackson's Voice Will Soon Be Coming to Amazon Alexa Devices," CBS News, September 26, 2019, https://www.cbsnews.com/.

41. Amazon, "Samuel L. Jackson—Celebrity Voice for Alexa," https://www.amazon.com/Samuel-L-Jackson-celebrity-voice/dp/B07WS3HN5Q.

42. Garrand, "Samuel L. Jackson's Voice."

43. Apple, "Siri," 2013, http://www.apple.com/ios/siri/.

Liz W. Faber is chair of Arts and Sciences at Labouré College. Her research focuses on American media, science fiction, gender, and computer history.